Mark and Luke
in Poststructuralist
Perspectives

stephen d. moore

Mark and Luke

in Poststructuralist

Perspectives

Jesus Begins to Write

Yale University Press

New Haven and London

Designed by Jill Breitbarth.
Set in Perpetua and Gill Sans by
Keystone Typesetting, Inc., Orwigsburg, Pennsylvania.
Printed in the United States of America by
Thomson-Shore, Dexter, Michigan.

Library of Congress Cataloging-in-Publication Data
Moore, Stephen D., 1954–
Mark and Luke in poststructuralist perspectives : Jesus begins to write /
Stephen D. Moore
p.   cm.
Includes bibliographical references and index.
ISBN 0-300-05197-2 (alk. paper)
1. Bible. N.T. Mark—Criticism, interpretation, etc.   2. Bible. N.T. Luke—
Criticism, interpretation, etc.   3. Structuralism (Literary analysis)   I. Title.
BS2585.2.M66   1992
226.3'06—dc20   91-30523
                                                                                    CIP

The paper in this book meets the guidelines for permanence and durability of
the Committee on Production Guidelines for Book Longevity of the Council
on Library Resources.

1   3   5   7   9   10   8   6   4   2

Jesus appeared; he put on that book; . . . he
published the edict of the Father on the cross.
—*The Gospel of Truth* 20,24–25

[He] . . . wrote over every square inch of the only
foolscap available, his own body.
—James Joyce, *Finnegans Wake*

Contents

Acknowledgments

Francis Watson, Dale Martin, and George Aichele passed my first draft through their sieve nets. Their acumen, wit, and erudition have enriched almost every page. Earlier still, Pat Anderson, Temma Berg, Bob Fowler, Sean Freyne, Susan Graham, and Kirk Hughes sifted chapter drafts and demanded more of me. Mikeal Parsons and the Literary Aspects of the Gospels and Acts Group chastised me, while Gary Phillips, Joy Lawrence, and the Biblical Exegesis in the Postmodern Context Seminar encouraged me. Janice Anderson said a crucial thing at a critical time, although without letting me off the hook. My wife, Jane Hurwitz, said much that I can't repeat, but without her this book might not have been written. Others surprised me by their receptivity to my way of reading, while knowing where to draw the line I am trying to erase.

The School of Hebrew, Biblical, and Theological Studies at Trinity College, Dublin, was a stimulating and supportive place to write, thanks in particular to Sean Freyne. Later, Stuart Lasine made it possible for me to participate in the postmodernism seminar at Wichita State University. Two masked readers persuaded Yale University Press to take a chance on me; to one of them in particular I owe a debt of gratitude. My thanks, too, to Chuck Grench and Otto Bohlmann for needing so little persuasion. Then there was the "bad" crowd who were good enough to let me fall in with them, and who continue to challenge and inspire me: George Aichele, Fred Burnett, Elizabeth Castelli, David Jobling, and Tina Pippin, but above all Gary Phillips. To them this book is dedicated.

The English translation of the Bible most often quoted here is the New Revised Standard Version (New York: Oxford University Press, 1989), although I have sometimes found it necessary to modify it. All Greek quotations from the New Testament rely on the Nestle-Aland twenty-sixth revised edition (New York: United Bible Societies, 1983).

Introduction:

Before and After, or How Deconstruction

Made a de Man out of Mac

> Oh Mac, you are a real man after all!
> —Charles Atlas advertisement

> . . . and no one had the strength to subdue him.
> —Mark 5:4

Leaf through this book, recently a tree. Penned to its trunk are two readings. One is of Mark, "The Gospel of the Mark," the other is of Luke, "The Gospel of the Look." The two are alike, although they rarely acknowledge each other. Each wants to be read for itself alone. Thus they can be read in any order desired. Between them, Jesus hangs suspended. He may or may not have escaped decomposition, but how could he escape deconstruction?

Deconstruction—what will it have been? The studies it has spawned now run in their thousands across an astonishing array of fields—modern languages and comparative literature mainly, but also philosophy, psychology, cultural studies, linguistics, anthropology, political theory, historiography, legal studies, art theory, architectural theory, film theory, even theology and biblical studies—a gargantuan body of introductions and applications perched precariously atop the shoulders of a slight but slippery body of "exemplary" deconstructive texts, those of Jacques Derrida preeminently, but also those of Paul de Man. Derrida, a French philosopher revered, sometimes feared, more in the United States than in France, and better known to students of literature than to students of philosophy, continues to occupy a role of central importance in Anglo-American literary studies from a position out on its periphery.[1]

---

1. Derrida has even kept his distance from deconstruction, as we shall see. So how is it faring in the 1990s? I second Simpson's assessment, at least as regards literary studies: whereas deconstruction's challenges "remain urgent and . . . unignorable for the newly emergent moment

"With regard to this sect we know that everywhere it is spoken against" (Acts 28:22). How is deconstruction viewed in biblical studies—not in the outback of the discipline, where my own books have grown up, but in its centers of population and government?[2] Let us look at some examples. *Studying the Synoptic Gospels,* a 1989 textbook by E. P. Sanders and Margaret Davies, devotes a fifteen-page chapter to "Structuralism and De-Construction [*sic*]." Structuralism hogs fourteen of these pages. Still, a single page is not to be sneezed at if we turn to *The New Testament and Its Modern Interpreters,* a six-hundred-page volume edited by Eldon Jay Epp and George W. MacRae, also published in 1989, and "designed both to survey and to evaluate New Testament scholarship since World War II."[3] It deals with deconstruction in the course of a twenty-line entry on "Post-Structuralist Interpretation of the Parables."[4] In fairness, several of the essays in this volume appear to have been completed as early as 1980. But deconstruction does not receive more than passing mention even in later works, such as Terence Keegan's *Interpreting the Bible* (1985) or Robert Morgan's *Biblical Interpretation* (1988). Moreover, fleeting reference is the exception, not the rule. More commonly, the unwelcome stepchild is denied an allowance altogether, its status in biblical studies being such that most surveys need not mention it at all.[5] Stephen Neill and Tom Wright's *Interpretation of the New Testament, 1861–1986 (1988),* for example, manages not to mention it. So does the 750-page *Dictionary of Biblical Interpretation,* edited by R. J. Coggins and J. L. Houlden and published in 1990, although it has entries on structuralism, semiotics, narrative criticism, and reader-response criticism.

The silence has been even louder in Europe than in North America. Structuralism made significant inroads in biblical studies in the 1970s on both continents. But by then a multidisciplinary body of writing had emerged in and

---

that is constituted by cultural and gender studies, it is no longer the medium through which all debate within the elite sector of the profession must be conducted" (Simpson, "Paul de Man," 164). Standard introductions to it include Culler, *On Deconstruction*; Leitch, *Deconstructive Criticism*; and Norris, *Deconstruction.* I also recommend Norris, *Derrida*; and Kamuf, *A Derrida Reader.*

2. In the outback a trickle has become a stream that includes Aichele, *Limits of Story*; Crossan, *Cliffs of Fall*; Detweiler, "Derrida and Biblical Studies"; Jobling and Moore, "Poststructuralism as Exegesis"; Miscall, *1 Samuel*; Moore, *Literary Criticism*; Phillips, "Poststructural Criticism"; and Phillips and Moore, *Literary Theory.* Further examples are listed in Moore, *Literary Criticism,* 133n1, 149n23, 150n24.

3. Epp and MacRae, *New Testament,* xvii.

4. In Beardslee, "Recent Literary Criticism," 182.

5. Or else they mention it only to dismiss it in a sentence. I quote some such examples in my *Literary Criticism,* 150.

around French structuralism that American importers labeled *poststructuralism,* listing as its main ingredients Derrida's deconstruction; Jacques Lacan's "return to Freud" (faintly "poststructuralist" even while antedating structuralism); the Roland Barthes of *S/Z* and beyond (*The Pleasure of the Text, Barthes by Barthes,* and so forth); and the Michel Foucault of *Discipline and Punish* and *The History of Sexuality.*[6] Certain poststructuralists and liminal structuralists have addressed themselves to the Bible and the history of its interpretation—Barthes, Derrida, Lacan, Julia Kristeva, Michel Serres, and Jean-Joseph Goux, for example.[7] But French biblical scholars have shown little or no interest in what they have had to say, nor have German, British, or other European scholars (although a number of them do seem to have read Barthes's two biblical essays, written when he was on a tightrope between structuralism and poststructuralism).[8]

As regards deconstruction, then, biblical exegesis is still in the "before" stage. The sand repeatedly kicked in its face has so far had little effect. Meanwhile, titles in the "After Derrida" and "Beyond Deconstruction" mode have long been a familiar sight on the theoretical Muscle Beach that is American literary studies.[9] As is evident even with its jacket on, my own book boasts a "post" in its title. But the body of the book is not all equally developed.

Parts of the book have (been) worked out in a "During Deconstruction" phase. Time warps in the woof of my text, they were motivated by a certain melancholy. Quite simply, I should be sorry to see the deconstructive "icono-classics" of Derrida, de Man & Co. (*Of Grammatology, Allegories of Reading,* and so

6. Deconstruction is a species, then, and poststructuralism the genus. Leading poststructuralists are ably dissected in Descombes, *Modern French Philosophy,* and Harland, *Superstructuralism,* although Sarup, *Post-Structuralism and Postmodernism*, or Sturrock, *Structuralism and Since,* may be a better place to begin.

7. Barthes in "Structural Analysis" and "Wrestling with the Angel"; Derrida in "Tours de Babel," "Of an Apocalyptic Tone," *Writing and Difference,* 64–78, 294–300, and "Shibboleth" (cf. *Glas,* "Living On," and "No Apocalypse"); Lacan in several of his seminars (e.g., *The Seminar, Book II,* 309–14, *Le Séminaire, livre III,* 323–26, *Le Séminaire, livre VII,* 201–9, and "Names-of-the-Father," 90–95); Kristeva in "Discours biblique," *Language,* 98–103, "Lire la Bible," *Powers of Horror,* 56–132, and *Tales of Love,* 83–100, 139–50; Serres in *Le Parasite,* 207–19; and Goux in *Symbolic Economies,* 134–50. The list could, of course, be extended—Louis Marin, Luce Irigaray, Gillès Deleuze and Félix Guattari, Sarah Kofman . . . .

8. I know of only one biblical scholar in Germany seriously engaged with poststructuralism—Erhardt Güttgemanns, who has nothing left to lose (see, e.g., his *Fragmenta Semiotico-Hermeneutica,* "Gêmatriyya' und Lechëshbôn," and "Semiotik des Traums"). For a rare British example of deconstructive exegesis, see Clines, "Book of Job."

9. "Early" examples include Krupnik, *Displacement: Derrida and After*; Felperin, *Beyond Deconstruction*; and Ulmer, "Beyond Deconstruction" (in his *Applied Grammatology,* 3–153).

on) shuffle off, toothless, to the retirement home without having been properly introduced to the Gospels. It seems to me that they might have a lot to say to each other.

Other (body) parts bespeak a more recent American milieu that begins with deconstruction but does not end with it, that attempts to bend it without breaking it off, forcing it to come to grips with Derrida's more audacious texts, on the one hand—texts that push *him* "beyond deconstruction" (*Glas, Sign-sponge, The Truth in Painting, The Post Card*)[10]—and with issues such as gender, power, and the politics and ethics of reading, on the other hand.[11] If I begin by reading Mark over the shoulder of Derrida, I end by reading Luke over the shoulder of Foucault.

The visual arts have also colored my way of reading. Although the present book was largely formed before I stumbled on the following recommendation by Gregory Ulmer, much of it can be read as though it had been written in response to it:

> What is at stake in the controversy surrounding contemporary critical writing is easier to understand when placed in the context of modernism and postmodernism in the arts. The issue is "representation"—specifically, the representation of the object of study in a critical text. Criticism is now being transformed in the same way that literature and the arts were transformed by the avant-garde movements in the early decades of this century. The break with "mimesis," with the values and assumptions of "realism," which revolutionized the modernist arts, is now underway (belatedly) in criticism, the chief consequence of which, of course, is a change in the relation of the critical text to its object—literature.
>
> A rationale for this shift may be found in Hayden White's complaint that "when historians claim that history is a combination of science and art, they generally mean that it is a combination of late-nineteenth-

10. I am thinking primarily of Ulmer's *Applied Grammatology,* but also of Ronell's *Telephone Book,* Ulmer's *Teletheory,* Hartman's *Saving the Text,* and Stewart's *Reading Voices.* For a *Glas*-like experiment in biblical studies, see Hughes, "Framing Judas."

11. Diverse examples include Jardine, *Gynesis*; Miller, *Ethics of Reading*; Ryan, *Marxism and Deconstruction*; and Spivak, *In Other Worlds.* (Their closest counterparts in biblical studies are Belo, *Materialist Reading of Mark,* and Jobling, "Writing the Wrongs.") Then too there is the "Paul de Man Affair," the posthumous discovery in 1987 of some 170 articles written by de Man between 1940 and 1942 in occupied Belgium for the collaborationist newspaper *Le Soir.* Most of these articles (now in de Man, *Wartime Journalism*) are book or concert reviews; one of them is flagrantly anti-Semitic. Thirty-eight responses to the discovery (including Derrida's troubled "Like the Sound") appear in Hamacher et al., *Responses.*

century social science and mid-nineteenth century art" . . . . White suggests, instead, that historians of literature (or of any discipline, for that matter) should use contemporary scientific and artistic insights and methods as the basis for their work, pursuing "the possibility of using impressionistic, expressionistic, surrealistic, and (perhaps) even actionist modes of representation for dramatizing the significance of data which they have uncovered but which all too frequently they are prohibited from seriously contemplating as evidence."[12]

Ulmer contends that "post-criticism" (-structuralist, -modernist) "is constituted precisely by the application of the devices of modernist art to critical representations."[13] He is echoing the views of Rosalind Krauss and others, for whom the modernist revolution in the visual arts and literature, initiated in the nineteeth century but exhausted and at an impasse by the 1960s, has now erupted belatedly in *critical* discourse, catalyzed by French (post)structuralism.[14] When Barthes comes to stage "The Death of the Author" in 1968, for example, his firing squad includes a quorum of modernists (Mallarmé, Valery, Proust, and the Surrealists). Derrida too has apprenticed himself to modernist and postmodernist writers (as in *Writing and Difference, Dissemination, Glas, Signsponge,* and *Ulysse Gramophone*) and visual artists (in *The Truth in Painting*), not deconstructing them as he does the philosophers but culling strategies from them instead. Academe has at last been affected by the crisis of representation that rocked the arts more than a century ago.

Selecting pigments from the palette of Marcan and Lucan scholarship, I too have attempted to compose inventively. Sometimes my composition has taken the form of a collage—a surrealist collage, to be precise. Dissimilar materials have been combined so as to produce "surprising coincidences" and "bizarre overlappings."[15] This is where the colorful stacks of paper bearing the signatures of Jacques Derrida and Jacques Lacan, although also the more somber stacks bearing the signature of Michel Foucault, come into play. With these and other such writings, Mark, Luke, and their interpreters have been re(fr)a(me)d.

Deconstruction began not with a bomb but with a brushstroke. Prior

---

12. Ulmer, "Object of Post-Criticism," 83, quoting White, *Tropics of Discourse,* 42, 47–48. White himself does not act on his own suggestion, as Ulmer later points out (*Teletheory,* 19).

13. Ulmer, "Object of Post-Criticism," 83.

14. Cf. Krauss, "Poststructuralism and the 'Paraliterary.'"

15. Phrases lifted from H. Aram Veeser's description of the strategies of the New Historicism ("Introduction," xii)—although the similarities between its methods and mine do not extend beyond this.

readings were like so much pigment awaiting its flexible palette knife. Like the canvas, the critical page presents a spectacle of crucifixion, stretched and tacked as it is to institutional reading frames. Yet resourcefulness and nerve are the only limits to what can occur within the confines of a frame. Painters have known this for a very long time; critics are only beginning to discover it. The stretched surface that is the critical page demands an extension of critical language.

Graphic imagery, creative anachronism, sustained wordplay (wordwork, rather), and surrealistic stories of reading make up my method in this book. But if there is madness in my method, it is not without reason. Chapter 3, "The Lion('s) Unconscious: The Objest of the Pun(ch) in Exegesis," pauses between rounds to analyze strategy. My main tactic is a simple one. I am eager to reply to the Gospels in kind, to write in a related idiom. Rather than take a jackhammer to the concrete, parabolic language of the Gospels, replacing graphic images with abstract categories, I prefer to respond to a pictographic text pictographi- cally, to a narrative text narratively, producing a critical text that is a postmod- ern analogue of the premodern text that it purports to read. This strategy is elaborated at length in chapter 3, which is also the book's courtroom scene, the scene in which it attempts to defend itself.

First the reader will have been taken through chapters 1 and 2, the scene of the crime. I am the author of similar crimes in subsequent chapters, crimes some will view as serious, others as inconsequential. The plaintiff, in any case, is a certain reading practice. "To think *within* a practice," writes Stanley Fish, "is to have one's perception and sense of possible and appropriate action issue 'naturally'—without further reflection—from one's position as a deeply situ- ated agent. Someone who looks with practice-informed eyes sees a field already organized in terms of perspicuous obligations, self-evidently authorized pro- cedures, and obviously relevant pieces of evidence."[16] As the eldest son of an Irish farmer, I have long been on the run from fields, or at least from bogs.

"In [my] first book, O Theophilus . . ." (Acts 1:1). My first book, *Literary Criticism and the Gospels,* made much of Fish's reading theory.[17] Fish is an absent presence in the present book. Having assimilated his reading lesson, I no longer feel the need to keep reciting it. Still, a credal statement of the way I now see a text might be of interest to readers of my earlier book. The text for me is encrusted reading: an untotalizable sum of prior and potential readings, an unconscious reservoir. A pebble dropped in that reservoir will have a percepti-

---

16. Fish, *Doing What Comes Naturally,* 386, his emphasis.
17. See Fish, *Is There a Text?* and Moore, *Literary Criticism,* 112–30, 134–36, 167, 174.

ble ripple-effect, a boulder an effect that much greater. If I ascribe a great deal of power to the text in the present book—personifying it, fetishizing it, re-mythologizing it—it is not because I believe in the solidity of the text so much as in the solidity of the boulder. Fish would understand.

part one

The Gospel of the Mark

Mark the first page . . . with a red marker.
For, in the beginning, the wound is invisible.
—Edmond Jabès, *The Book of Questions*

I bear on my body the marks of Jesus.
—Galatians 6:17

The Lion Roars

Deconstruction was a child for which Derrida was unprepared, as he explains in the course of a colloquium:

> The word "deconstruction" has always bothered me. . . . When I made use of this word (rarely, very rarely in the beginning) . . . I had the impression that it was a word among many others. . . . It so happens . . . that this word which I had written only once or twice . . . all of a sudden jumped out of the text and was seized by others who have since determined its fate. . . . But precisely because of the . . .—how shall I put it?— negative connotations that it could have in certain contexts, the word by itself bothered me. . . .
>
> I love very much everything that I deconstruct . . . ; the texts I want to read from the deconstructive point of view are texts I love, with that impulse of identification which is indispensible for reading. They are texts whose future, I think, will not be exhausted for a long time. . . . My relation to these texts is characterized by loving jealousy and not at all by nihilistic fury (one can't read anything in the latter condition).[1]

But how does one read—or write—"deconstructively"?

"One must be several in order to write."[2] I shall be writing here in two directions at once, with two hands, writing sometimes so as to lay hold of Mark in the prescribed manner, with the right hand, but progressively putting to work more and more that which is still left out even when the right hand has

---

1. Derrida, *Ear of the Other,* 85–87.
2. Derrida, *Truth in Painting,* 152.

grasped all it can. I shall be writing with the left hand also, letting it meander into the margins of the page to pick up (on) things that Marcan scholars have yet to touch.

Mark can be trying, but so can Derrida. "She forced her mind through the labyrinthine sentences of . . . Jacques Derrida until her eyes were bloodshot and her head ached."[3] Lightning flashes across Derrida's page often enough to ensure its brilliance. But between these flashes one can sink into sentences so opaque, so turgid, indeed so pompous, that one doesn't know whether to laugh or to scream. Derrida is frequently impossible. And frequently he has every intention of being so. "For a deconstructive operation," he explains, "*possibility* would rather be the danger, the danger of becoming an available set of rule-governed procedures, methods, accessible approaches."[4] The rule is the lure to be avoided. Hence "deconstruction is inventive or it is nothing at all; . . . it opens up a passageway, it marches ahead and marks a trail; its writing is not only performative, it produces rules—other conventions."[5]

The points at which Derrida thinks through an innovative use of language are the points in his texts that most interest me. For reasons of temperament, the Derrida of my own text will be an inventive writer first and a philosopher second, although I recognize that he has smudged the line between the two, or put it "under erasure" altogether.[6] As my reading proceeds, I shall be shuttling from convention to invention, from conventional criticism, whether Marcan or deconstructive ("conventional deconstruction" is by now no oxymoron), to some of the stranger critical outworlds opened up by Derrida's writing.

DEMANIC READING: MARK'S DEATH-DRIVE

"How long has he had this?" . . .
"From childhood. And it has often cast him into the fire and
into the water, to destroy him."
—Mark 9:21–22

The impression they give is of being . . . possessed by some
"demonic" power.
—Sigmund Freud, *Beyond the Pleasure Principle*

3. Lodge, *Nice Work,* 46.

4. Derrida, "Psyche," 36, his emphasis.

5. Ibid., 42.

6. For a magisterial attempt to wrest Derrida from the literary critics and restore him to philosophy, see Gasché, *Tain of the Mirror.* Gasché's Derridean *summa,* however, depends on the exclusion of *Glas,* "Envois," *Signsponge,* and Derrida's other paraliterary experiments (see Taylor, "Foiling Reflection"), experiments that are crucial to my own project.

Traditionally, Mark's symbol has been the lion. And Mark's belly is bottomless. It devours the readings that we throw to it, ripping their pages to shreds. No man, ox, or eagle feeds with such ferocity.

But Mark is a lion with four or more tails. Three of them come off when pulled, the fourth is already a stump. First, there is 16:9–20, which scholars have dubbed "The Longer Ending of Mark." It comprises three resurrection appearances of Jesus, followed by his ascension. (A short addition to the Longer Ending is also known: the Freer Logion, or Codex W.) Second, there is "The Shorter Ending of Mark," which amounts to a thumbnail variant of the Longer Ending. On manuscript evidence, combined with such other criteria as patristic attestation, vocabulary, style, and content, most Marcan scholars now believe both these endings to be false appendages.[7] Was Mark's real ending lost in transmission, then? And if so, what was the carving knife that cut off this author's tale?[8] But what if this great cat were really a Manx all along? What if its stump were really a tail, 16:8 its intended ending—as most scholars now hold?[9]

Mark 16:8 reads: "So they [the women] went out and fled from the tomb, for terror and amazement had seized them; and they said nothing to any one, for they were afraid [*ephobounto gar*]." Their fear was contagious, it seems. And not surprisingly—for 16.8 appears to say that the empty tomb went unreported. To seize on 16:8 is to risk being savaged by the Lion. The pain inflicted by Mark's teeth was such that attempts to blunt his bite did not cease with Matthew and Luke,[10] nor with the Longer and Shorter Endings, nor with the advent of critical scholarship, an earlier generation of historians and philologists rising manfully to the challenge of writing amateur fiction. Here is Henry Barclay Swete, for example, writing in 1909:

> The picture is true to psychological probability. At first the Angel's words only increased their terror; they turned and fled from the tomb, trembling

---

7. See Farmer, *Last Twelve Verses*; Hug, *Finale de l'Evangile*; and Pesch, *Markusevangelium,* 2:544–59, for details.

8. Was the original manuscript mutilated? Did Mark expire before he could pen the final lines? Was he arrested in mid-sentence? An earlier generation of scholars did not hesitate to ask such questions.

9. Assorted examples include Aland, "Schluss der Markusevangeliums"; Boomershine and Bartholomew, "Apostolic Commission" and "Narrative Technique"; Crossan, "Form for Absence"; Lincoln, "Promise and Failure"; Magness, *Sense and Absence*; Myers, *Binding the Strong Man,* 397–404; and Petersen, "When Is the End?"

10. To Matthew and Luke, assuming that they relied on Mark, "this ending was intolerable," according to Taylor (*St. Mark,* 609). Robert Fowler remarks in a letter to me of 6 December 1989: "I tell my students in class that the best known 'endings' (or better, 'appendices') to Mark are Matthew, Luke, and even John. Mark's Gospel opens the floodgates to a hell of a lot of writing."

and unable for the moment to collect their thoughts or control themselves. . . . As they came to themselves and began to realize the truth, joy mingled with their fear and predominated . . . and their flight was changed into an eager haste to deliver their message. . . . But Mc.'s narrative comes to an abrupt end before this second stage of feeling has been reached; fear still prevails, and the shock has been too severe to permit them to say a word about what has occurred. . . . Until their terrors had subsided they had no thought for the angel's message and no tongue to tell it.[11]

One wonders who is the more terrified—the women or the Reverend Mr. Swete.

Mark 16:7 ("but go, tell his disciples and Peter that he is going ahead of you to Galilee; there you will see him, just as he told you") has often been read as signaling the restoration of the disciples following their desertion of Jesus at his arrest (14:50). Mark 16:8, then, is ironic, to say the least. The women "are to tell of a promise that failure is not the end, but then *they* fail to tell and that *is* the end—of the narrative!"[12] But that is only the beginning.

Each of the other canonical Gospels concludes with appearances of the risen Jesus to his disciples. In other words, each of them includes in its conclusion a germinal scene of which the given Gospel is the offshoot. This is clearest in Luke, although Matthew and John evince the same logic. Luke ends with Jesus saying to his disciples, "Thus it is written, that the Messiah is to suffer and to rise from the dead on the third day, and that repentance and forgiveness of sins is to be proclaimed in his name to all nations, beginning from Jerusalem. You are witnesses of these things" (24:46–48). Jesus' words have a double reference, pointing back to the Jewish scriptures ("thus it is written") but also pointing forward to Luke's second volume, the Acts of the Apostles ("repentance and forgiveness . . . is to be proclaimed . . . beginning from Jerusalem"—compare Acts 1:8). Carry on upriver from this commissioning scene at the end of Luke, exploring every tributary, and eventually you will arrive (back) at the beginning of the Gospel. Luke's opening sentence says as much: "Since many have undertaken to set down an orderly account of the events that have been fulfilled among us *just as they were handed on to us by those who from the beginning were eyewitnesses and servants of the word,* I too have decided . . . to write an orderly account for you" (1:1–3; compare 24:48; Acts 1:21–22, 10:39–41). From the commis-

---

11. Swete, *Commentary on Mark,* 398–99.

12. Lincoln, "Promise and Failure," 290. The irony cuts deeper, as Myers notes: "Whereas before the subjects had been commanded to silence but spoke nonetheless (1:44f., 7:36), here the women are commanded to speak but remain silent!" (*Binding the Strong Man,* 399). Tolbert makes a similar point (*Sowing the Gospel,* 295).

sioning scene at the Gospel's end, a narrative line snakes out in a great loop until its mouth closes around the Gospel's opening sentence. This loop is threaded through the Acts of the Apostles.

Mark has no such loop. Mark trails off before narrating "circumstances in which one could imagine something like the Gospel of Mark being narrated. The story *in* Mark's Gospel seems to preclude the telling *of* Mark's Gospel."[13] It is the story of a story that was never understood [see 8:31–33, 9:31–32] and therefore never told.[14] Mark's ending undercuts its beginning; it saws through the branch on which the book is perched. Outside the tomb, as the women flee and say nothing, Mark rips up its own birth record. In contrast to Matthew and Luke, each of which commences with a virginal conception, Mark concludes with a virginal conception—its own. Its tomb becomes a miraculous womb.[15]

Mark is by now in a state of collapse, and knows it: "If a kingdom is divided against itself, that kingdom cannot stand. And if a house is divided against itself, that house will not be able to stand" (3:24–25). Mark's demise clearly has demonic ramifications ("if Satan has risen up against himself and is divided, he cannot stand"—3:26); it also has de Manic ramifications. To adopt de Man's terminology, Mark by its ending "simultaneously asserts and denies the authority of its own rhetorical mode."[16] For de Man, every literary text turns on such moments of self-division, one hand stealthily withdrawing what the other straightforwardly extended: "The paradigm for all texts consists of a figure (or a system of figures) and its deconstruction."[17]

De Man's conception of the literary text bears a marked resemblance to the conception of the psyche that surfaces in Freud's later writings. As Fritz Wittels, Freud's first biographer, recounts: "In 1920 [in *Beyond the Pleasure Principle*], Freud astonished us with the discovery that there is in everything living, in addition to the pleasure principle which, since the days of Hellenic culture, has been called Eros, another principle: What lives, wants to die again. Originating in dust, it wants to be dust again. Not only the life-drive . . . but the *death-drive* as well."[18] Freud's later writings are haunted by a vision of the psyche as two elemental forces, Eros and Thanatos, locked in an unremitting struggle to the death.

Interestingly for our triadic analogy (Mark, Freud, de Man), Freud claimed

---

13. Fowler, "Reading Matthew Reading Mark," 14.

14. See Fowler, *Let the Reader Understand*, 250.

15. Cf. Cixous on *Finnegans Wake*, which has a similar nonending: "It is both mother and murderer of itself, giving both birth and death to itself" (*Exile of James Joyce*, 735).

16. De Man, *Allegories of Reading*, 17.

17. Ibid., 205.

18. Wittels, *Sigmund Freud*, 231, his emphasis.

figuratively to see the mark of the "demonic" in the self-de(con)structive aspects of human behavior that led him to posit a death drive (*Todestrieb*).[19] De Man does not see the mark of Freud on his own text, however. Or if he does, he is not saying.[20] For de Man, literature's self-deconstructing drive is to be explained not with reference to the psyche of an author or that of a reader, but with reference to language itself, of which literature is exemplary. Literature undoes itself because its parts and pieces are slippery tropes and figures, and its undoing "takes place independently of any desire; as such it is not unconscious but mechanical, systematic in its performance but arbitrary in its principle, like a grammar."[21] Slick to the touch, the text is a well-oiled machine.

Nevertheless, in erasing all records of its birth, does Mark show itself to be an organism that, as Freud might say, wants only to die in its own fashion?

THE WRITTEN V(O)ICE

> . . . you are a letter from Christ delivered by us, written not with ink but with the Spirit of the living God, not on tablets of stone but on tablets of human hearts. . . . For the written code kills, but the Spirit gives life.
> —2 Corinthians 3:3–6

> We can't help but agree, . . . but we should also like to know how the spirit could live without the letter. Even so, the pretensions of the spirit would remain unassailable if the letter had not shown us that it produces all the effects of truth in man without involving the spirit at all.
> —Jacques Lacan, *Ecrits*

Let us pull back from Mark's ending, its edge, for now. The women arrive there expecting to find Jesus. Apparently he has vanished over the edge, causing them to flee in distress. Searches are still under way for his body. But other explanations of his disappearance are possible. Could Mark not have staged Jesus'

19. See Freud, *Beyond the Pleasure Principle,* 15, 29–30. Lacan describes the unconscious as that which "escape[s] your vigilance. . . . It is as if a demon plays a game with your watchfulness" ("Of Structure," 189).

20. De Man frequently echoes Freud but seldom names him. Already in *Blindness and Insight* we find de Man preoccupied, in Freudian fashion, with the unconscious blind spots that regulate critical reading: "Critics seem curiously doomed to say something quite different from what they meant to say" (106).

21. De Man, *Allegories of Reading,* 298.

suicide in order to provide him with a new identity—that of a writer? What if "Mark" itself were but a pen name of Jesus, one of many?

> Instead of an image of an evangelist with pen in hand and ear cocked heavenwards waiting for his next line . . . imagine the Derridean counterpart: a large Jesus seated at a writing desk, while diminutive evangelists whisper in his ear; and not just the evangelists, but whole communities, churches, clusters of even more diminutive figures whose names and faces we cannot make out, feeding Jesus lines that grew out of oral traditions and liturgical practices, passed on and altered . . . and put in his mouth. The sayings of Jesus are dictated by those who followed him; the Teacher is the effect produced by those who are supposed to be receiving the teaching. You see the . . . reversal here; Jesus as effect, i.e., not an original content which is preserved and communicated . . . but a content which is produced by the followers; the founder is founded.[22]

Jesus indeed writes, and in more ways than one, as we are about to discover. But what does it mean to write?

"In the beginning was the *logos*. . . ." In the West, the spoken word has almost always been privileged over the written word. Writing has often been assigned a scapegoat role, akin to that of the wandering Jew. This has been a source of fascination for Derrida, himself of Algerian-Jewish extraction. (Writing as exile: the Jew "weeps for the lost voice with tears as black as the trace of ink.")[23] Derrida singles out Plato, Rousseau, Hegel, Saussure, and Husserl as exemplars of this unease with the written, "specific nuclei in a process and a system."[24]

But what could be more *natural* than so to privilege speech? "I would rather not use paper and ink; instead I hope to come to you and talk with you face to face, so that our joy may be complete," writes the Johannine elder to his "elect lady" (2 John 12). As I speak, my words appear to be one with my thoughts. My

22. Caputo, "Derrida and Religion," 22. Derrida and Bultmann merge in Caputo's description.

23. Derrida, *Writing and Difference*, 73, commenting on the work of the Jewish poet Edmond Jabès.

24. Derrida, *Margins of Philosophy*, 94. On Plato, see Derrida, *Dissemination*, 61–171; on Rousseau (with Lévi-Strauss), see *Of Grammatology*, 97–316; on Hegel, see *Dissemination*, 1–59, *Margins of Philosophy*, 69–108, and *Glas*; on Saussure, see *Of Grammatology*, 27–73, and cf. *Positions*, 17–36; and on Husserl, see *Edmund Husserl* and *Speech and Phenomena*. De Man's warning is apposite throughout: "Derrida uses Heidegger's and Nietzsche's fiction of metaphysics as a *period* in Western thought in order to dramatize, to give tension and suspense to the argument. . . . Neither is Derrida taken in by the theatricality of his gesture or the fiction of his narrative" (*Blindness and Insight*, 137, his emphasis).

meaning appears to be fully present both to me and to my hearer, provided I am speaking effectively, affectively. At such moments, the voice, the breath, appears to be consciousness itself, presence itself. "I breathe into the phone without saying anything and then you laugh and the Atlantic recedes. . . ."[25]

Voice, presence, truth. In the West, speech has always been the paradigm not only for every form of presence but also for every form of truth. All the names used to designate theological or philosophical fundamentals have always designated the constant of a presence: God, being, essence, existence, substance, subject, object, consciousness—the list is very long.

Writing as original sin: "We have ceased hearing the voice from within the immediate proximity of the garden. . . . The *difference* between speech and writing is sin . . . lost immediacy, work outside the garden."[26] Cut off from the *pneuma,* the breath, severed at its source from the authorizing presence of a speaker, writing has often been thought to threaten truth with distortion and mischief. To take a well-known example, *pneuma* also means "Spirit," and it is to this that Paul opposes the deadly *gramma* ("letter") in his celebrated antithesis, quoted as an epigraph above (compare Rom 7:6). Luther later elaborates: Moses' "pen is a dead and hollow reed. . . . But the tongue is solid and full flesh, and it produces living letters in the heart, with words that have been poured in through the ear. . . . Therefore the church does not acknowledge letters, nor the reed which draws them, but it acknowledges the spoken words which the tongue, or tongues, of fire produce."[27]

As lifeless written marks in place of present living speech, writing has seemed to be an inferior, if necessary, substitute for speech. An orphan, no sooner born than set adrift, cut loose from the author who gives birth to it, writing seems fated endlessly to circulate, if not from foster home to foster home, then from reader to reader, the best of whom can never be sure that he or she has fully grasped what the author intended to say. For authors have a way of being absent, even dead, and their intended meaning can no longer be directly intuited, or double-checked through question and answer, as in the face-to-face situation of speech. Writing defaces speech.

"The crack between the two is nothing. The crack is what one must

---

25. Derrida, *The Post Card,* 114. "My words are 'alive' because they seem not to leave me: not to fall outside me, outside my breath, . . . not to cease to belong to me" (Derrida, *Speech and Phenomena,* 76).

26. Derrida, *Writing and Difference,* 68, his emphasis. The crime of Cain follows: "speech, deluded into believing itself completely alive, and violent, . . . expelling the other, . . . throwing it *outside* and *below,* under the name of writing" (Derrida, *Of Grammatology,* 39, his emphasis).

27. Luther, *Lectures on the Psalms,* 399–400; cf. 211ff.

occupy."[28] Derrida deconstructs the opposition of speech and writing. But he does not simply declare writing the superior term. Rather than stand the opposition on its head, thereby inverting it but leaving it intact nonetheless, he shows how each term in the hierarchy is joined to the other by an intricate network of arteries. "Like Czechoslovakia and Poland, [they] resemble each other, regard each other, separated nonetheless by a frontier all the more mysterious . . . because it is abstract, legal, ideal."[29] Approaching the border between speech and writing, he asks: What if the illegal alien, the parasite, were already within? What if speech were already the host of writing? The details of his investigation need not concern us here.[30] Suffice it to note his conclusion: "One realizes that what was chased off limits, the wandering outcast . . . has indeed never ceased to haunt language as its primary and most intimate possibility."[31] Certainly it has never ceased to haunt the language of Mark.

JESUS AS A MAN OF LETTERS

I work every day alone at my big long wide high deep dense
prosework.
—James Joyce, *Letters*

And once more he bent down and wrote with his finger on
the ground.
—John 8:8

Mark's Jesus is a compulsive writer, as we are about to discover. His teaching suffers as a result. His career begins promisingly enough: "What is this? A new teaching [*didachē kainē*]—with authority!" (1:27). His public lectures attract record attendances: "He began to teach [*didaskein*] by the sea. Such a very large crowd gathered around him that he got into a boat on the sea and sat there, while the whole crowd was beside the sea on the land. He began to teach them many things in parables" (4:1; compare 3:8–9, 6:31–32). He dedicates himself to private tuition: "He explained everything in private [*kat' idian*] to his own disciples" (4:34; compare 3:13ff.). But a stormy relationship soon develops between Jesus and his private students: " 'Teacher, do you not care that we are perishing?' . . . . He said to them, 'Why are you afraid? Have you still no faith?' "

28. Derrida, *Glas,* 207b.
29. Ibid., 189b.
30. I have already summarized it in my *Literary Criticism,* 157–59 (cf. 132–33), as have hordes of others before me.
31. Derrida, *Of Grammatology,* 44.

(4:40). Following the first feeding miracle we are told that "they did not understand about the loaves, but their hearts were hardened" (6:52). Before long the teacher explodes: "Why are you talking about having no bread? Do you still not perceive or understand? Are your hearts hardened? Do you have eyes, and fail to see? Do you have ears, and fail to hear?"—like the "outsiders" of 4:11–12. The lesson ends on a note of frustration: "Do you not yet understand?" (8:17–18, 21; compare 7:18). They have a learning disability, as we shall see, probably dyslexia.

Three lessons on Jesus' impending passion follow (8:31, 9:31, 10:33–34). The first begins with a quiz: " 'Who do people say that I am?' And they answered him, 'John the Baptist; and others, Elijah; and still others, one of the prophets.' He asked them, 'But who do you say that I am?' Peter answered him, 'You are the Messiah' " (8:27–29). In response to the first passion prediction, however, Peter contradicts the teacher, and is sternly reprimanded: "Get behind me, Satan! For you are setting your mind not divine things but on human things" (8:32–33). Afterward Peter, accompanied by James and John, nervously submits his reading of the transfiguration to the master: "He did not know what to say, for they were terrified" (9:6). Down below, meanwhile, their classmates fail yet another test: "Teacher, I brought you my son; he has a spirit. . . . I asked your disciples to cast it out, but they could not" (9:17–18). Following the second passion prediction we are told that the disciples "did not understand what he was saying and were afraid to ask him" (9:32; compare 10:32). Later they squabble among themselves about which of them is the greatest (9:34). On being addressed as "Good Teacher [*didaskale agathe*]" by the rich young man, Jesus can only respond: "Why do you call me good?" (10:17–18). Following the third passion prediction, James and John have a request: "Teacher, we want you to do for us whatever we ask of you" (10:35). They demand seats of honor at the head of the class: "Grant us to sit, one at your right hand and one at your left" (10:37). "You do not know what you are asking," replies the weary teacher (10:38).

Jesus' pupils continue to disappoint him. Judas eventually betrays him (14:10–11); his other students doze during his final lesson ("could you not keep awake one hour?"—14:37); they abandon him when his classes are suspended (" 'Have you come out with swords and clubs to arrest me . . . ? Day after day I was with you in the temple teaching, and you did not arrest me. . . .' All of them deserted him and fled"—14:49–50); Peter denies ever having studied with him (14:66–72); and his women students fail their most important test (16:8).[32]

---

32. Mark's negative portrayal of the disciples has long been a central focus of Marcan studies, especially in North America. Weeden's *Mark: Traditions in Conflict* was an important catalyst in this

Right to the end of the Gospel, then, the insiders are on the inside looking in.[33] Contrasted as they are with "those outside [ekeinoi hoi exō]" (4:11), Jesus' disciples *must* be insiders. They do, after all, attend a private school ("privately to his own . . . he explained everything"—4:34; compare 10:10), a school whose entry requirements are notoriously stringent. Even Jesus' own family do not qualify: "And his mother and his brothers came, and standing *outside* [exō] they sent to him. . . . And a crowd was sitting around him, and they said to him, 'Behold, your mother and your brothers and sisters are *outside* [exō]. . . .' And looking around on those sitting about him in a circle [kyklō], he said, 'Behold my mother and my brothers!' " (3:31–35). And while outsiders are expected to see but not perceive, hear but not understand, elite insiders are by implication expected both to see and to perceive, to hear and to understand. But do they?

"When you make the inside like the outside and the outside like the inside . . . then will you enter [the kingdom]," explains *The Gospel of Thomas* (saying 22). In Mark the secret of the kingdom has been presented to Jesus' students (4:11). Its equations cover the blackboard. And yet the only thing that distinguishes disciples from outsiders is that disciples long to be inside, to *be* the insiders they are said to be. Between seeing and perceiving, hearing and understanding, something obtrudes, something that also keeps those explicitly labeled outsiders outside, something the teacher calls *parable*.

Between the parable of the Sower and its interpretation is Mark's so-called parable theory.[34] Jesus' listeners question him concerning the parables (4:10), but their eyes glaze over as he begins to theorize: "To you has been given the secret [to mystērion] of the kingdom of God, but for those outside everything comes in parables; in order that 'they may indeed look, but not perceive, and may indeed listen, but not understand; so that they may not turn again and be forgiven' " (4:11–12; compare Isa 6:10). What are Marcan parables that such abstruse things should be said of them?

Beginning with Matthew, who changed Mark's difficult "*in order that [hina] they may indeed look, but not perceive*" to "*because [hoti] seeing they do not see*" (Matt 13:13), countless readers have attempted to draw the sting from Mark's tale.[35] Let us beware of popularizing his parable theory, then. It says that

---

development, though his thesis that the disciples fill in for Mark's opponents commands little support today (see Dewey, "Recent Studies on Mark," 15).

33. See Kermode, *Genesis of Secrecy*, 27–47 passim.

34. See Räisänen, *Parabeltheorie im Markusevangelium*.

35. For a résumé of insider solutions, see Guelich, *Mark 1–8:26*, 209–12. For an outsider's view of such solutions, see Kermode, *Genesis of Secrecy*, 29–34. Kermode later warns that "*hina* is the inescapable shadow of *hoti*" ("Anteriority, Authority, and Secrecy," 165).

parables act to prevent sight from becoming insight in outsiders, and hearing from becoming understanding. But do theory and practice correspond in Mark?

Mark's theory has been challenged on the basis of 3:23–27 and 12:1–12, which suggest to some that the bafflement induced by parables is not complete. Mark 3:22ff. reads: "And the scribes who came down from Jerusalem said, 'He has Beelzebul, and by the ruler of the demons he casts out demons.'" And he called them to him, and spoke to them in parables, 'How can Satan cast out Satan?'" The parable of the binding of the strong man then follows, but it is not stated whether the scribes understand it. In 12:12, following Jesus' parable of the vineyard, we read: "And they [the chief priests, scribes, and elders] sought to arrest him, but feared the crowd, for they knew that he had told the parable against them." Should the *knowing* (*ginōskō*) in this statement be equated with the elusive *understanding* (*syniēmi*) of 4:12, 13? If the authorities had understood Jesus, would they still have sought to suspend his teaching? Or is it not that they themselves, here and in 3:23–37, have seen but not perceived, heard but not understood?[36] In seeking to arrest him they have been taken captive by his theory.

Mark's parable theory, however abstruse, helps to explain much in his Gospel. The expression "in order that 'they may indeed *see* [*blepontes blepōsin*], but not perceive'" (4:12), coupled with the expression "for those outside *all things happen in parables* [*en parabolais ta panta ginetai*]" (4:11), suggests that *parabolē* in Mark may mean more than just an oral didactic device adopted by the historical Jesus. The term may encompass Jesus' enigmatic ministry as such, a fusion of word and deed. Indeed, some have gone on to suggest that, given Mark's many startling features (not least its paradoxical ending), the Gospel as a whole can be said to function parabolically, parable being a genre of paradox.[37]

In fairness to the teacher, the simple fact of his parabolic words and deeds being obscure does not suffice to explain the depth of his pupils' ignorance. When Jesus begins "to teach them that the Son of Man must suffer many things, and be rejected . . . and be killed, and after three days rise again," thereby administering the coup de grace to their faltering understanding, the narrator adds: "And he said this plainly [*kai parrēsia ton logon elalei*]" (8:31–32). It seems

36. So Marcus, *Mystery of the Kingdom*, 103, 107, contra Räisänen, *Parabeltheorie im Mark-usevangelium*, 27–33, and Lambrecht, *Once More Astonished*, 139–43. Guelich too speaks of "opponents, 'those outside,' who seem to understand (*egnōsan*) 'parables' aimed at them (12:1–12)" (*Mark 1–8:26*, 209).

37. See Kelber, *Oral and Written Gospel*, esp. 216–17, and Donahue, *Gospel in Parable*, 194–99; cf. Williams, *Gospel against Parable*, esp. 178. Tolbert advances a similar argument: "The parables of the Sower and the Tenants [12:1–12] . . . function as plot synopses" (*Sowing the Gospel*, 125). A book-length appraisal of the role of 4:11–12 in Mark has now appeared (Beavis, *Mark's Audience*).

that the mystery of the kingdom can only meet with misunderstanding (at least for now), whether parabolic *or* plain speech be used in the classroom.

All of Jesus' speech and all of his actions in Mark quickly reduce to "parable" once they become vehicles of this mystery. "To those outside all things are in parables"—as they are to those "inside," who are caught in the schoolroom door, neither fully inside nor yet fully outside. Like the seed scattered by the sower, Jesus' parabolic speech falls ineffectually on rocky ground, unable to take root in the "hardened" hearts of his tough students, his undisciplined disciples.

Between speech and hearing, something obtrudes. Like a blade it severs the circle of understanding, the intimate circle of exchange ("looking around on those who sat about him in a circle [*kyklō*]"—3:34), within whose circumference Jesus' voice *should* circulate, coupling with the ears of his disciples, breath to flesh and nothing between. (Insemination is the desire of the Sower.)

Sliced through, Jesus' speech is unable to reach its mark. It falls to the ground and is picked up wrongly. It is as if Jesus were writing instead of speaking, as if his disciples were reading instead of listening. The severing blade can only be re(a)d; it makes no sound. Silently it makes its cut, forcing Jesus to write without a pen. And the blade appears to be wielded by Jesus' own Father, who wills that the disciples' ears not yet be impregnated with understanding (compare 6:52, 8:17c–18).[38]

Should not Jesus himself be a father? Traditionally the speaker is father of his speech. Unlike the written word, the spoken word is able to reach its target easily because it has a living father, a father who is present to it, who stands behind it, making sure that its aim is straight. Jesus cannot be such a father to his speech. The blade of his own Father has cut off that possibility, severing the "natural" bond that should exist between thought and voice, meaning and sound.

(Jesus: "I descend into writing; I approach its unendurable depth; a desert is revealed.")[39]

Mark's Jesus writes not with a pen but with a marker. Hampered by one of "those big felt-tipped tubes that are hard to hold in one's fingers,"[40] his scrawl is all but illegible. Upon the dark field of the disciples' understanding he writes,

---

38. Note the passive constructions (*pepōrōmenē*) in 6:52 and 8:17c (contrast 3:5), which seem, to me at any rate, to imply divine agency, especially in light of such texts as Luke 9:45, 18:34; John 12:40; Rom 11:7–8; and Deut 29:2–4, LXX. Cf. Quesnell, *Mind of Mark*, 180–90; Myers, *Binding the Strong Man*, 225.

39. Barthes, *Barthes by Barthes*, 137. Jesus is not the speaker in Barthes's text. However, the Jesus of my own text models himself on Mark's Jesus, which is to say that scraps of the tradition that has fed the text that sustains him invariably end up on his lips.

40. Derrida, *Signsponge*, 6.

although not in luminous letters. "The alphabet of stars alone does that," Mallarmé somewhere says. But if the disciples' understanding is dark, it is due to the inky blackness of the letters it must soak up—blue-black letters that release little light. "A writing in my sense is made not to be read."[41]

But is the disciples' illiteracy also due to repression? What is it about Jesus' words that makes his disciples turn away as if from a bad smell? Is it that these undigested words, on falling to the ground, become turds? As Freud observed, that which we feel most impelled to bury, to repress, "stinks just as an actual object may stink."[42] "Those who are ashamed of me and of my words . . ." (8:38). The scatology of the cross.

Writing as death: Jesus writes to please his Father.[43] And so he writes in earnest only when he begins to speak of his own death (8:31ff.; compare 14:36). "He seizes himself, cuts into himself, and signs himself to death."[44] That of which Mark's Jesus writes, therefore, is not disembodied knowledge. Rather, it is (a) body (of) knowledge: the knowledge of one marked out for death, whose flesh must be engraved (entombed) with the tools of execution. "Watch the inscription taking form on the body. Wouldn't you care to come a little nearer and have a look at the needles?"[45] Lost in a book, the disciples don't want to know.

If the Johannine Jesus is modeled on the spoken word ("in the beginning was the *logos*"), the Marcan Jesus is modeled on the written word. Not only does Jesus write in Mark; he is himself a species of writing—literally, since we know him only through the letter. Jesus is a man of letters.

As writing, Jesus is censored by his disciples. "Words, whole clauses and sentences are blacked out so that what is left becomes unintelligible."[46] Faced with a script that they have rendered illegible, the disciples flee the set when Jesus is arrested (14:50). Later, in a scene the scholars have tried to censor, the writer returns as analyst to attack the resistance of his analysands: "He appeared to the eleven . . . as they reclined [on couches?] at table [*anakeimenois autois*]; and he upbraided them for their unbelief and hardness of heart" (16:14). (Did each of them end by confessing: "The unconscious is that chapter of my history that is marked by a blank or occupied by a falsehood: it is the censored chapter. But

---

41. Lacan, *Le Séminaire, livre XI,* 251.

42. Freud, *Origins of Psychoanalysis,* 232.

43. "*One begins to want to write in the presence of the father,* before the symbolic father, before the absent father . . . in order to please him" (Cixous, "Scene of the Unconscious," 4, her emphasis).

44. Derrida, *Signsponge,* 6–7, on the poet Francis Ponge.

45. Kafka, "The Penal Colony," 200.

46. Freud, *Origins of Psychoanalysis,* 273.

the truth can be rediscovered . . . written down elsewhere. Namely:—in monuments: this is my body"?)[47]

Like Jesus, who drifts from misunderstanding to misunderstanding across the surface of Mark's page, writing has always been a wandering outcast, drifting from (mis)reading to (mis)reading. At least since the time of Plato, writing has also been read as an orphan or delinquent: "Once a thing is put into writing, the composition . . . drifts all over the place, getting into the hands not only of those who understand it, but equally of those who have no business with it; it doesn't know how to address the right people, and not address the wrong. And when it is ill-treated and unfairly abused it always needs its parent to come to its help."[48] But "the specificity of writing [is] intimately bound to the absence of the father."[49] The present writer is always absent. The orphaned word must circulate without its parent's protective presence, vulnerable to mishandling and misreading. Without its father it is, in fact, "nothing but . . . writing."[50]

As letter, Mark's Jesus is "delivered into human hands" (9:31; compare 10:33). As writing, he is penned to the cross, cut off from his Father ("my God, my God, why have you forsaken me?"—15:34), exposed to the casual violence of any reader who happens by ("those who passed by derided him, shaking their heads and saying, 'Aha!'"—15:29ff.). As writing, Jesus is crucified, stretched out on the wood, the rack, the reading frame, with all the associated risks ("a 'stretched' sense always risks being empty, floating, slackened").[51] Mark's Jesus does transgress the common law of writing by finally uniting with his Father. But even then his status remains more that of an inscription than of a logos, marked as it is by absence ("he has been raised; he is not here"—16:6) and exposure to the accidents of (mis)reading ("they said nothing to anyone, for they were afraid"—16:8).

As writing, Jesus must contend with invisible forces other than demons. As writing, he must be delivered up to powers other than the Jewish and Roman authorities. This force, this power, is the reader. Temma F. Berg asks: "Who is the reader?" She replies: "The reader is legion ['for we are many'—Mark 5:9]. And to give oneself to readers, to allow strange others the power of breathing life into you, is to deliver yourself into the unknown. It is to take the greatest chance of all, the risk of annihilation, of death."[52] But if to write is to run the

---

47. Lacan, *Ecrits,* 50.
48. Plato, *Phaedrus,* 275d–e.
49. Derrida, *Dissemination,* 77.
50. Ibid.
51. Derrida, *Archeology of the Frivolous,* 133.
52. Berg, "Reading (Derrida) Reading," 338.

risk of death, it is also to seize the chance of a life after death (undead, the author lives on in his or her tome). Although Mark condemns Jesus to death by making him write, Mark *as* writing also offers him a body to live on in.

MARK AND JACQUES READ EACH OTHER WITHOUT REALIZING IT

> I am trying, precisely, to put myself at a point so that I do not
> know any longer where I am going.
> —Jacques Derrida, "Structure, Sign, and Play"

Mark's Jesus can be read on the model of the written mark, then. (And what is Jesus in Mark but a series of written marks, a marked man?) But Jesus' status in Mark prefigures Mark's own status. Mark's Jesus is a writer, himself inscribed in a text, but so inscribed as to prefigure the fate of that text. Mark's own destiny as a writing is adumbrated in the way it writes up the story of Jesus, as we shall see.

Mark pilfers fabric from other texts and pegs it to its own lines. Take the quotation with which Mark opens, for example: "See, I am sending my messenger ahead of you, who will prepare your way; the voice of one crying in the wilderness: 'Prepare the way of the Lord, make his paths straight'" (1:2–3). Here verses have been clipped from their original contexts (Exod 23:20; Mal 3:1; Isa 40:3). They have been trimmed,[53] pasted, and affixed to Mark's page.

As Derrida points out, however, the capacity of writing to break with its context is not an incidental predicate, an accident or mishap to which writing is prone, but is instead its very structure. Writing can always readdress itself to addressees that its producer(s) could not have foreseen. Even in the case of a communication between two people in a code of their own devising, the possibility of a third party cracking the code and redeploying it in ways unforeseen by its inventors can never be ruled out. In order to be what it is, writing must always be able to operate in the absence of any specific addressee(s). Hence Derrida's hyperbole: "If I say that I write for dead addressees, not dead in the future but already dead at the moment when I get to the end of a

---

53. Especially Isa 40:3, which, in Mark's rendition, corresponds exactly neither with the Hebrew text nor with the Septuagint, the Greek version of the Hebrew (see Mann, *Mark,* 195; Pesch, *Markusevangelium,* 1:77–78). Mark's scissors might not have been the only pair at work here, moreover. Some commentators have suspected v. 2 of being a copyist's gloss (see Taylor, *St. Mark,* 153).

sentence, it is not in order to play."[54] Or again: "The possibility of the 'death' of the addressee is inscribed in the structure of the written mark."[55]

Let us trim and reframe this last sentence: *The possibility of the death of the addressees is inscribed in the structure of Mark.* Mark is a writing in virtue of its iterative capacity to function in the absence of its target audience. In the scene at the tomb, a "young man [*neaniskos*]" fills in for Jesus, speaks for him in his absence, signs with his signature (16:5–7)—but so does Mark itself. Jesus' absence is the pretext for the young man's presence at the tomb ("he is not here"). But it is also the pretext for the Marcan text itself. "The absence of the referent constructs the mark."[56] Yes, and the Gospel of (the) Mark also.

But there is another more interesting way in which the possibility of the death of the addressees is inscribed in the structure of Mark. The story told in Mark can be read as a parable of the destiny of every written mark. Here is Derrida again, clipped from his page and pasted to my own, so that his text becomes a reading of Mark. (More than a demonstration of the truth of Derrida's hypothesis, and more than a Derridean reading of Mark, this is a Marcan reading of Derrida; recall Mark's strategy in his opening quotation.) Derrida asks:

> Is this general possibility [of misreading] necessarily that of a failure or trap into which [Jesus' speech] might *fall* [in Mark], or in which [his] language might lose itself, as if in an abyss situated outside or in front of it? . . . . In other words, does the generality of the risk . . . *surround* [his] language like a kind of *ditch,* a place of external perdition into which [his] locution might never venture, that it might avoid . . . ? Or indeed is this risk, on the contrary, its internal and positive condition of possibility? this outside its inside? the very force and law of its emergence?[57]

Jesus' address to his disciples in Mark—more a species of writing than of speech, no sooner uttered than utterly misread—graphically illustrates the condition and destiny of every written mark or series of marks, including the Gospel of (the) Mark in which it is inscribed. A figure in a writing, Jesus is also a figure *of* writing. Derrida again: "This essential drifting, due to writing as [a]

---

54. Derrida, *The Post Card,* 33. And what of the author? "I hardly have the time to sign than I am already dead . . . because the structure of the 'signature' event carries my death in that event" (Derrida, *Glas,* 19b).

55. Derrida, *Margins of Philosophy,* 316.

56. Ibid., 318.

57. Ibid., 325, his emphasis.

structure cut off from . . . *consciousness* as the authority of the last analysis, writing orphaned and separated at birth from the assistance of its father, is indeed what Plato condemned in the *Phaedrus*."[58] If Plato's gesture is, as Derrida suspects, the metaphysical gesture par excellence in which living, present truth is coupled with the voice, one sees what an unlikely source for Christian metaphysics Mark is. De Man's remarks on Rousseau apply mutatis mutandis to Mark: although Mark itself stands in little need of deconstruction, the established tradition of Marcan interpretation stands in dire need of deconstruction.[59]

Derrida has long been infatuated with the term *mark* (to the point of causing his needle to become stuck in *Positions*: "A mark marks both the marked and the mark, the re-marked site of the mark").[60] This is more than a mere stylistic trademark. "I suggest this word *mark,*" he explains, "in order to avoid saying 'say,' 'show,' 'represent,' 'paint,' so many words that this system works to deconstruct."[61] Admittedly, the Gospel of (the) Mark hardly begins to disturb "all the strongholds, all the out-of-bounds shelters that [watch] over the field of language,"[62] to whose gates Derrida has dragged an impressive array of siege-weapons. Nevertheless, in writing on the written mark, Derrida performs an insightful reading of the Gospel of Mark, no less so for being unwitting. And the more he unknowingly reads Mark, the more evidence he amasses for his assertion that the possibility of being read in ways unintended and unimaginable is the ineradicable birthmark of the written.

Derrida himself would hardly be surprised to hear what he has done. He writes: "Thus does a text become infatuated. With another."[63] And again: "One text loves another."[64] A brief exchange of letters (*mark*, *Mark*) is all that is required for a meaningful encounter to take place. A telephone connection would also suffice, one text hooking itself up to the other by means of "blanks, shifts of accent, lines skipped or moved out of place, as if they reached us over a broken-down teletype, a wiretap in an overloaded telephone exchange."[65] In

58. Ibid., 316, his emphasis.
59. De Man, *Blindness and Insight,* 139.
60. Derrida, *Positions,* 46.
61. Derrida, *Truth in Painting,* 342.
62. Derrida, *Of Grammatology,* 7.
63. Derrida, *Glas,* 168b.
64. "A text can stand in a relationship of transference (primarily in the psychoanalytic sense) to another text! And, since Freud reminds us that the relationship of transference is a 'love' relationship, stress the point: one text loves another" (Derrida, "Living On," 147).
65. Derrida, *Glas,* 196b.

what follows, I wish to make my own page available whenever possible as a place where such texts can spend a few hours together.

MARK'S POISONOUS CURE FOR IGNORANCE

> Avoid understanding too quickly.
> —Jacques Lacan, *Le Séminaire, livre XX*

Reading writings *on* writing by Plato, Rousseau, Mallarmé, and others, Derrida finds that the terms used by each writer to describe writing—*pharmakon* in Plato, *supplement* in Rousseau, *hymen* in Mallarmé—have a contradictory, double sense.[66] (To take the simplest example, *pharmakon* means both *poison* and *cure* at once.)

What of Mark? Mark isn't explicitly about writing, of course. But a speech deeply scored with the traits of writing does figure in it. Interestingly, Mark has a term for such speech. He calls it *parabolē* ("parable"), a graphic mode of discourse whose peculiarities we must now examine more closely.

The prefix *para* itself behaves rather strangely, as J. Hillis Miller has observed:

> "Para" is a double antithetical prefix signifying at once proximity and distance, similarity and difference, interiority and exteriority, something inside a domestic economy and at the same time outside it, something simultaneously this side of a boundary line, threshold, or margin, and also beyond it. . . . A thing in "para," moreover, is not only simultaneously on both sides of the boundary line between inside and out. It is also the boundary itself, the screen which is a permeable membrane connecting inside and outside. It confuses them with one another, allowing the outside in, making the inside out, dividing them and joining them. It also forms an ambiguous transition between one and the other.[67]

Has Miller too laid hands on Mark without realizing it?

Parabolai in Mark are a partition, screen, or membrane designed to keep insiders on one side, outsiders on the other. Outsiders are those for whom "everything comes in parables," parables that they find incomprehensible

---

66. On the *pharmakon* see Derrida, *Dissemination*, 61–171; on the *supplement*, *Of Grammatology*, 141–64; and on the *hymen*, *Dissemination*, 172–286.

67. Miller, "Critic as Host," 219. *Parasite* is the "para-" word of choice for Miller, though he does list *parable* among his other examples (220). He addresses himself to the gospel parable in *Tropes, Parables, Performatives*, 135–50, and "*Heart of Darkness* Revisited," 210ff.

(4:11–12). At the same time, *parabolai* are what rupture that membrane, render it permeable, infect the opposition with contradiction: those who should be on the inside find themselves repeatedly put out by Jesus' parabolic words and deeds. Appointed to allow insiders in and to keep outsiders out, parables unexpectedly begin to threaten *everyone* with exclusion in Mark, even disciples seeking entry. Deranged doormen, parables threaten to make outsiders of us all.[68]

Like *pharmakon, supplement, hymen,* and Derrida's other "undecidables,"[69] *parabolē* refuses to be laid to rest within the narrow framework of a classic binary opposition—here, that of inside versus outside. *Parabolē* turns language inside out like a pocket, threatening to empty it of its content(s). Indeed, *parabolē is* a pocket in Mark, one that turns (the) inside(r) out. Possibly *parabolē* is the key to this pocket book, Jesus' address book, the book of his enigmatic addresses ("with many such parables he spoke the word to them"—4:33). But does the key unlock the book or ensure that it stays shut? Could the author have used it to lock the book, and then thrown the key away—into the book? If so, Mark cannot be contained in the pocket we cut for it; Mark is what makes a hole in our pocket (see 2:21–22).[70]

Perhaps Mark is not so much a pocket (book) as a shoe—a laced shoe, double-knotted.[71] Through Mark's eyelets, ever watchful, disciples and readers are threaded relentlessly: outside, then inside, then outside again; left, then right, then left (clueless) again.

With what can we compare Mark, or what parable shall we use for it? It is like a bottle with no inside or outside, what mathematicians call a Klein bottle. The Klein bottle was one of the parabolic objects that Lacan liked to bring to his famous seminar.[72] "There was a jar of mustard, half full, that lasted a whole

68. Cf. Kermode, *Genesis of Secrecy,* 27: "Being an insider is only a more elaborate way of being kept outside." Burton Mack's assessment is similar; the Marcan parables were "claimed as esoteric teaching, yet placed outside the boundaries of understanding in order to precipitate the very events they encoded" (*Myth of Innocence,* 171).

69. "Non-terms" to which he assigns a strategic role. See Derrida, *Positions,* 43, and "Ja, ou le faux bond," 103.

70. Reflections inspired by Taylor, *Tears,* 13–14; Hartman, *Saving the Text,* 105; and Derrida, *Glas,* 170b.

71. Cf. Derrida, *Truth in Painting,* 229.

72. The seminar began in 1951 and ran for almost thirty years. Althusser, Barthes, Derrida, Kristeva, Lévi-Strauss, Merleau-Ponty, and Ricoeur were among those who came to sit at Lacan's feet—although "some . . . were sitting there, questioning in their hearts, 'Why does this fellow speak in this way?'"

year,"[73] there was "the period of the Borromean knots," there was a bottle opener, a Moebius strip, and many other such items, exotic or quotidian, all subpoenaed to testify to "the theory of the unconscious as he conceived of it: specifically, he wanted to show that the unconscious is a structure with neither an outside or an inside."[74] He might well have called on Mark as his expert witness. Moreover, if Lacan was himself a messiah, as some of his disciples seem to believe, he was a messiah in the Marcan mold—a messiah with a secret: "If they knew what I was saying, . . . they would never have let me say it."[75] As a teacher, too, Lacan did not lag far behind Mark's Jesus: "We thought about what he had said but even more about the enigma of what he might have meant."[76] For those inside, all things are in parables.

Inside/outside: the wall that separates the two is as thin and fragile as a slash mark. It leans precariously, undermined by *parabolē,* slashed by Mark. "Hidden in the recess, between outside and inside," is a figure the narrator brings into play—a figure Barthes calls *paradoxism,*[77] but which we are content to call *parabolē.*

Parabolē takes a voice that issues from the intimacy of an inside, from the interiority of a speaker, Jesus, a voice that should easily be able to leap the distance separating it from the ear of the hearer, and turns it into an unincorporable exteriority. Too blunt to penetrate the ear, it cannot fit inside. "Let anyone with ears to hear listen!" cries Jesus (4:9; compare 4:23), but nobody has ears big enough.

Parabolē unsettles speech. It inhabits the oppositions of inside and outside, speech and writing, but only that it might disrupt the order of the house, rock the foundation in which these oppositions are embedded, shake the interpretive (bed)frames so as to keep the interpreters restlessly turning over.

Parabolē is duplicitous. It is of the same stock as *parabolos,* which has "counterfeit" and "false" among its senses. *Parabolē* positions itself between opposing terms, ostensibly to pull them apart, all the while sowing confusion between them.

73. "It is like a mustard seed, which, when sown upon the ground. . . ."

74. Clément, *Lives and Legends,* 160.

75. Lacan, as quoted in Schneiderman, *Jacques Lacan,* 11.

76. Clément, *Lives and Legends,* 13. Lacan was a speaker, not a writer (the title of his *Ecrits* is intended ironically, he tells us), and the founder of an oral tradition. The editor's note on *Le Séminaire, livre XI* would be worthy of the first evangelist: "My intention here was to . . . obtain from Jacques Lacan's spoken work an authentic version that would stand, in the future, for the original, which does not exist" (J.-A. Miller in Lacan, *Le Séminaire, livre XI,* 249).

77. Barthes, *S/Z,* 27.

Parabolē is prudent. It inflicts a grievous wound on common sense, but takes care to leave it untended. It stays away from the pharmacy, the *pharmakon*. It is wary of the cure that might turn out to be a poison. And it is suspicious of the get-well gift that the critic brings to Mark's bedside. "What if the gift were always poisoned . . . ?"[78]

Yet it is not as though the outsiders in Mark never get a look in(side). Jesus is identified as Son (of God), not only by God himself (1:11, 9:7) and by the narrator (1:1),[79] but also by the demons (3:11, 5:7; compare 1:24, 34) and by the centurion at the foot of the cross (15:39; compare 14:61). But although the demons do have inside information on Jesus, they can hardly be said to be insiders. And among the human characters, only the centurion, a gentile and hence an outsider, is allowed to look inside. Assigned to dispatch Jesus (see 15:44–45), he executes a reading as well: "Truly this man was God's Son!" The women disciples do advance steadily toward the inside (15:40–41, 47, 16: 1ff.)—until *parabolē* leaps out to greet them from the interior of the tomb, driving them back outside: "So they went out and fled, for terror and amazement had seized them" (16:8). But what of the Syrophoenician woman (7:25– 30)? Or Bartimaeus (10:46–52)? Assuredly they have faith, but would they accept that Jesus must suffer? And until we know that they would, can they be said to be insiders? In short, there are no insiders in Mark who are not at the same time outside.

The contradiction obtains until the end, and beyond. Mark 16:7 does seem finally to promise the long-deferred establishment of the insiders *as* insiders: "He is going ahead of you to Galilee; there you will see him." But 16:8, the Marcan nonending, parablelike in its demolition of narrative conventions, threatens to leave the disciples stranded yet again in a liminal zone that is neither fully inside nor yet fully outside.

Mark: the story of a story ("the Son of Man must suffer") that was never understood and therefore never told.[80] No real insiders but one, and he is an outsider. The centurion who oversees Jesus' execution is an outsider abruptly pulled inside to substitute for the disciples (insiders become outsiders), who should themselves have been at the foot of the cross, if not hanging on other crosses round about (see 8:34b, 10:38–39, 14:31). But what has aroused the

78. Derrida, *Limited Inc,* 75. *Gift* means "poison" in German.

79. "Son of God" is lacking in Mark 1:1 in certain manuscripts. See Metzger, *Textual Commentary,* 73, for a discussion.

80. Cf. Fowler, *Let the Reader Understand,* 250.

centurion to utter his climactic confession (15:39; compare 1:1)?[81] Is it something that Jesus has said? Privately to his own disciples Jesus has explained everything (4:34), and they have understood nothing. But his public cry of abandonment, coupled with his inarticulate scream as he expires ("Jesus gave a loud cry [*apheis phōnēn megalēn*] and breathed his last"—15:37), succeeds where his private teaching could not. Paradoxically, the centurion's recognition of Jesus as Son of God follows on Jesus' anguished declaration that God has cut him adrift ("my God, my God, why have you forsaken me"—15:24).[82] It is the declaration of the book after the Author has expelled it from his body. Having read the book, the centurion believes ("now when the centurion . . . saw that in this way he breathed his last"—15:39; compare 13:14). A writing of absence and inarticulation accomplishes what "plain" speech (8:32) could not, speech that should have been laden with present, self-evident meaning. Jesus' living presence and plain speech fail to evoke understanding in Mark. Understanding occurs only at the moment when Jesus becomes absent, and when his speech decomposes as it is delivered up to death.[83]

MARK'S INDIGESTION

What if what cannot be assimilated, the absolute indigestible,
played a fundamental role in the system . . . ?
—Jacques Derrida, *Glas*

One is tempted to conclude that there is no idealization of speech in Mark, only speech's de-idealization; that in Mark, contrary to the general thrust of Greco-Christian metaphysics, the voice is *not* an instrument enabling truth to be grasped as presence; and that to grasp Mark in this fashion is to have its fabric come apart in one's hands ("the patch pulls away . . . , the new from the old, and a worse tear is made"—2:21).

81. Mark 15:39 is generally taken to be the climax of the Gospel. For discussion of this, and of the ambiguous phrase *huios theou* (lit. "a son of God"), see Gnilka, *Evangelium nach Markus*, 2:324–25; Pesch, *Markusevangelium*, 2:499–502; and Taylor, *St. Mark,* 597–98.

82. Kelber remarks: "It is one thing to have death reversed by the epiphany of resurrection, but quite a different matter to locate epiphany at the point of absence. The former had been foretold, but the latter had not" ("Narrative and Disclosure," 17; cf. Via, "Irony as Hope," 24–25).

83. Alternatively, the centurion's confession is provoked not by Jesus' limit language but by an entirely different text, one ripped from top to bottom: the centurion has seen the temple veil (the one that covered its entrance) torn in two. For the latest version of this argument, see Ulansey, "The Heavenly Veil."

Such a conclusion, however, might end up wide of the mark. Speech has another face in Mark, although its features are not as plain as some have supposed. It has often been argued—on the basis of 9:9 and 16:7, for example—that the resurrection is an epistemological watershed in Mark: once Jesus is risen, his words will no longer be unintelligible.[84] Mark 9:9 simply says: "As they were coming down the mountain, he ordered them [Peter, James, and John] to tell no one about what they had seen, until after the Son of Man had risen from the dead." And 16:7 has the young man say to the women: "Go, tell his disciples and Peter that he is going ahead of you to Galilee; there you will see him, just as he told you." But when we couple the male disciples' clueless response to Jesus' charge to secrecy ("they kept the matter to themselves, questioning what this rising from the dead could mean"—9:10) with the silence of the women disciples (16:8), which stands in the way of Peter and his companions ever receiving an answer to their question, we begin to wonder whether Jesus' resurrection in Mark can really effect the epistemological breakthrough that is claimed for it.

Mark 13:31 represents a more telling plea for speech: "Heaven and earth will pass away, but my words will not pass away" (compare 13:23, 1:22, 27). A more thoroughgoing idealization of speech can hardly be imagined. To the spoken word, that most ephemeral of substances, a status of pure transcendence is attributed. As indestructible as they are unintelligible, Jesus' words are seeds that are unable to die, even though they fall on the most inhospitable rock (see 4:5–6, 16–17, 6:52, 8:17—"Are your hearts hardened"?). But although his words are unable to die, they are not alive, either. "For what is death," asks Jean-Joseph Goux, "if not the absence of any bodily ties—an absolute detachment, a supersensible position beyond matter."[85] Neither dead nor alive, Jesus' words are the living dead whose return from beyond the grave ("just as he told you," says the apparition at the tomb—16:7; compare 14:28) will cause the women to flee in terror.

Nevertheless, however much certain scenes in Mark appear to delete the authority of Jesus' word, it is never simply erased. Mark both idealizes speech and de-idealizes it, undermining its argument even as it erects it. In and through its remarkable ending, Mark narrates the flight of meaning—the meaning of Jesus' death fleeing with the women disciples, threatening to sink into silence. But this does not prevent Mark's own meaning from being incessantly in flight

84. I take the term *epistemological watershed* from Marcus, *Mystery of the Kingdom,* 120n175, although the hypothesis goes back to Wrede's *Messiasgeheimnis* (1901).

85. Goux, *Symbolic Economies,* 146.

from itself.[86] Mark incorporates contradiction into the body of its diction, where, like some vital internal organ, it sits undigested and unexpelled. Yet legions of Marcan scholars, able to construe contradiction only as blockage, have been only too eager to help the Lion complete its "unfinished" business— to unstop its blockages, cause the streams of sense to flow, give this Gospel of enigma an enema.

86. Cf. de Man, *Allegories of Reading,* 78.

777

The Lion S(pr)ings

A deconstructive machine that sings. . . .
—Geoffrey Hartman, *Saving the Text*

What if literature were always a jump ahead of criticism? Then the critic, while appearing to comprehend a literary text from a position outside or above it, would in fact be comprehended, grasped, by the text. He or she would be unwittingly acting out an interpretive role that the text had scripted, even dramatized, in advance. He or she would be enveloped in the folds of the text even while attempting to sew it up.

In "Le Facteur de la vérité" Derrida has occasion to ask: "What happens in the psychoanalytic deciphering of a text when the latter, the deciphered itself, already explicates itself? When it says more about itself than does the deciphering . . . ? And especially when the deciphered text inscribes in itself *additionally* the scene of the deciphering?"[1] And in *Glas*: "What is poetry . . . if it prescribes, inscribes and comprehends and in advance overflows, engulfing in its abyss, hermeneutic and doctoral discourse"?[2] In *The Truth in Painting* he confesses: "So I yielded, even before knowing it, as if I were read in advance, written before writing, prescribed, seized, trapped, hooked."[3] The myth of the prescient text.[4]

1. Derrida, *The Post Card,* 414, his emphasis.
2. Derrida, *Glas,* 214b; cf. 42b, 150b, 219b.
3. Derrida, *Truth in Painting,* 156, responding to Valerio Adami's *Study for a Drawing after Glas.* Although Derrida protests that he has "never wanted to abuse the abyss" (*The Post Card,* 304), many other such examples could be cited (*Dissemination,* 290ff; *The Post Card,* 293ff.; etc.).
4. Also the founding myth of deconstruction in America. De Man: "The text . . . tells the story, the allegory of its misunderstanding" (*Blindness and Insight,* 136); Miller: "Any terminology of analysis or explication is already inextricably folded into the text the critic is attempting to see from without" ("Ariadne's Thread," 162); Johnson: "Literature stages the modes of its own misreading" (*Critical Difference,* xii); Felman: "Through its very reading, the text . . . acts itself out" ("Turning the Screw," 101).

THE CRITIC POSSESSED BY THE TEXT

He would not permit the demons to speak, because they knew
him.
—Mark 1:34

It would no longer be clear who is analysing and who is being
analysed.
—Paul de Man, *Blindness and Insight*

The early history of Mark's reception is prefigured in Mark's own story. Jesus' message to his disciples about the way in which his mission must end is no sooner heard than buried. Mark's own end(ing) proved no less scandalous than that of Jesus, swiftly eliciting cover-ups. But those who undertook to rewrite the ending of the Lion's Gospel from a position outside its cage only succeeded in taking up a position within it: they reenacted the response of the disciples to Jesus. The desire of Peter and his companions (Jesus "began to teach them that the Son of Man must undergo great suffering. . . . And Peter took him aside, and began to rebuke him"—8:31–32), displaced by the traumatic event of the crucifixion, makes a powerful return in the Longer Ending of Mark (16:9–20).

The Longer Ending embodies the desire whose power over the disciples eclipsed that of Jesus (see 15:50, 66–72)—the desire to circumvent physical pain and death: "And these signs will accompany those who believe: by using my name . . . they will pick up snakes in their hands, and if they drink any deadly thing, it will not hurt them" (16:18). It is a dream of the Marcan disciples as they sleep fitfully in Gethsemane (14:37, 40–41). Everything that Mark's "premature" ending (16:8) seemed to thwart—desire for closure, for the circumvention of contingent human response (epitomized in the silence of the women), for the unambiguous presence of Jesus (compare 16:20, "the Lord worked with them")—declares its strength in the speed with which that ending was covered over in the tradition.

No element in Mark has been the object of more resolute cover-ups than 16:8. Is the Longer Ending a toupee, then, designed to hide Mark's baldness? Or is it simply another braid in his tale, the outgrowth of certain forces at work in it? But if it is a toupee, why should so many scholars want to tear it off? And if it is a braid, why should they want to shear it off?

You may be sorry you asked. "We know the symbolism of the braid," says Barthes, although that is not going to stop him from telling you. "Freud, considering the origin of weaving, saw it as the labor of a woman braiding her pubic hairs to form the absent penis."[5] But the text too is a braid—a braid of

5. Barthes, *S/Z*, 160. See Freud, *New Introductory Lectures*, 132.

voices. Thus "the text . . . is a fetish; and to reduce it . . . is to *cut the braid,* to sketch the castrating gesture."[6] It is also to reveal what the braid had obscured. It is to usher in the apocalypse.

"*Apokalypto,* I disclose, I uncover, I unveil, I reveal the thing that can be a part of the body, the head or the eyes, a secret part, the genitals or whatever might be hidden."[7] Marcan scholarship, long intrigued by Mark's apocalyptic desire (8:39, 9:1, 13:1–37, 14:62), has let itself be possessed by a similar longing (contagion is always a risk in textual encounters). It has longed to see the secret thing uncovered or unveiled, the hidden Marcan ending, for example.

"Apocalyptic unveiling, the disclosure that lets be seen what up to then remained enveloped, . . . for example, the body when the clothes are removed or the glans when the foreskin is removed in circumcision."[8] Believing Mark to be a man writing, not a woman weaving, the deft, critical knife has circumcised his small corpus (a mere sixteen chapters) with a re(a)d blade, the blade of reading, thereby uncovering its ending.

But perhaps the critical knife has simply cut away the counterfeit ending, the fake foreskin intended to disguise the real ending. When it was still permissible to talk about a lost original ending of Mark (the result of an accident, perhaps), phrases such as "the mutilation of the original papyrus" were not uncommon.[9] In the Hellenistic world, where circumcision tended to be regarded as a disfigurement, some male Jews felt impelled to disguise their circumcision ("they removed the mark of circumcision"—1 Macc 1:15; compare 1 Cor 7:18). Was (the) Mark too Semitic for Greek taste, necessitating prosthetic additions?[10]

MARK AS STRIPTURE

Truth did not come into the world naked.
—*The Gospel of Philip* 67,9

Another of Mark's more perplexing scenes likewise concerns uncoverings and fumbled cover-ups: "A certain young man [*neaniskos*] was following him, wear-

6. Barthes, *S/Z,* 160, his emphasis.

7. Derrida, "Of an Apocalyptic Tone," 64.

8. Ibid., 65.

9. The example is taken from Taylor, *St. Mark,* 610. Mark might also have been capable of self-mutilation. Two ancient sources, the *Anti-Marcionite Prologue* and Hippolytus, *Refut.* 7.30, describe Mark as *kolobodactylus*—"stumpy-finger(ed)," or "deformed in the finger." The term "can be taken metaphorically," meaning "that Mark was no stylist. It can also be taken literally, with the suggestion that Mark deliberately mutilated himself to avoid serving as a priest . . . or to avoid military service" (Kealy, *Mark's Gospel,* 14).

10. In a de Manian reading, however, one in which Mark would also be said to have (under)cut

ing nothing but a linen cloth [*sindōn*]. They caught hold of him, but he left the linen cloth and ran off naked" (14:51–52). Who is the young man in question? How best to tackle that fleeing figure?

In the 1909 edition of his Marcan commentary, Swete cites with approval the hypothesis of "many recent commentators" that the fleeing young man is none other than the evangelist himself.[11] The pericope would then be an auto-biographical recollection, tantamount to the author's personal signature within the text.

Commentators today accord little credence to this hypothesis. "The unfacts, did we possess them, are too imprecisely few to warrant our certitude."[12] What fascinates me, however, is the way a discredited hypothesis such as this one hits the mark in one sense while missing it in the sense in which it was aimed. However poor their marksmanship as conventional historians might be, those who ventured to describe Mark 14:51–52 as an authorial signature deserve excellent marks for their aim. For the flight of the naked young man would be an uncannily apt signature left behind by the author, a glimpse of the author's vanishing behind.[13]

Again, the scene is of apocalypse, of uncovering—"for example, the body when the clothes are removed."[14] It suggests that if you attempt to grasp Mark—and among the "crowd with swords and clubs" that advance on him do we not detect a detail of Marcan scholars armed with the tools of exegesis?—

---

itself, Mark's ending would not be a disfigurement so much as a *disfiguration*—de Man's term for the gesture "by which language performs the erasure of its own positions" ("Shelley Disfigured," 119).

11. Swete, *Commentary on Mark,* 354. Swete's contemporary, Theodor von Zahn, probes this consensus (*Introduction,* 2:490–92), but agrees that Mark "paints a small picture of himself in the corner of his work" (494).

12. Joyce, *Finnegans Wake,* 57.16–17. As late as 1966 Vincent Taylor could write: "No good reason can be suggested for the recording of the incident unless it rests on a genuine reminiscence" (*St. Mark,* 561), although by then caution had set in. For Taylor, as for Lagrange and others, the reminiscence is more likely that of an eyewitness known to the evangelist (see Lagrange, *Saint Marc,* 397). Caution has since advanced into skepticism; for the state of the question by the late 1970s, see Gnilka, *Evangelium nach Markus,* 2:271–73, and for an index of its complexity today, see Meyer, "The Youth." Refreshingly different is Kermode, *Genesis of Secrecy,* 49–73, who connects Mark's *neaniskos* with the mysterious man in the macintosh in *Ulysses.*

13. But does the author vanish only to reappear in 16:5, the one other place in Mark where *neaniskos* occurs? The young man in the tomb fills in for Jesus, speaks for him in his absence, as does Mark itself. Yet, with the sole exception of J. H. McIndoe ("Young Man," 125), no historical critic has ever ventured to suggest that the *neaniskos* in the tomb might be the evangelist himself (so Pesch, *Markusevangelium,* 2:402n23). The insight of blindness has its limits, apparently.

14. Derrida, "Of an Apocalyptic Tone," 65.

you will be left holding the cloth, the covering, whatever has been added on to make him seem respectable, while he slips away naked into the night.

"Fascination by a figure inadmissible in the system."[15] Although it seemed once or twice as if they had him, the fleeing youth has managed to give the slip to the most determined systematizers of his Gospel. With his back(side) always turned to them, he vanishes into the darkness. He is a figure of the outside within, the bit that will never fit, the bit that will always sit undigested in the scholar's belly.[16]

Not only a marked man, then, but a masked man, who coolly gives the slip to the police. As Barthes has remarked: "The text is (should be) that uninhibited person who shows his behind to the *Political Father*."[17] Bar(r)ed a(cce)ss—Mark bares only to bar, embarrassing his interpreters.

This book of reveilation reviles all who would arrest it. It leaves them with a fistful of fabric and the fetishistic compulsion to unravel and reweave it. Mark revels in concealment, revealing everything only as it vanishes into the night, its nakedness reveiled by the darkness. But does Mark escape uninjured? What if its reveilation were misunderstood, mutilated by the exegete, its left *i* poked out by the exegete's pen in an attempt to read it as revelation?

Mark does protest that an apocalyptic unveiling is imminent (9:1, 13:14ff., 14:62). But does apocalypse, uncovering, yield *parousia*, or presence, in Mark? The *parousia* of the thing sought can be glimpsed, but can it ever be grasped? Something will certainly be exposed, but will anyone be able to seize it? Jesus, risen or returned, will certainly rendezvous in Galilee (14:28, 16:7), but will anyone be there to meet him (see 16:8b)?

"They caught hold of him, but he left the linen cloth and ran off naked." Is not criticism itself a form of denuding?[18] Clearly scholars have but one thing on their minds. They are always eager to undress a work—to expose an original content concealed beneath secondary revisions, for example, as in their handling of Mark's (rear)ending. But Mark cannot be stripped with ease, and that has been the tease for so many Marcan scholars. Mark has never failed to send the ink coursing through their pens. Sacred scripture as "secret stripture,"[19] Mark has been invigoratingly hard to pen down.

Denuding, undressing, exposing, unveiling: these are the prurient gestures of

15. Derrida, *Glas,* 151a.

16. But "what if what cannot be assimilated, the absolute indigestible, played a fundamental role in the system, an abyssal role rather . . . ?" asks Derrida (*Glas,* 151a; cf. Derrida, "Economimesis," 21–25). That is what I want to examine.

17. Barthes, *Pleasure of the Text,* 53, his emphasis.

18. Cf. Derrida, *The Post Card,* 415–19.

19. Joyce, *Finnegans Wake,* 293n2.

scholarship in search of truth. "They caught hold of him, but he left the *sindōn* and ran off." Mark's *sindōn,* Swete tells us, is "not a close-fitting garment" but "a rectangular wrap."[20] Its page-shaped form is like a re(a)d rag to a critic. Add to this the semantic interpenetration of cloth, textile, and text ("etymologically the text is a cloth; *textus . . .* means 'woven' "),[21] and the disrobing of the young man can be read as having text and critic as its theme: at the moment when the critic, seeking to arrest the movement of its meanings, lays rough hands on the text, it exposes the truth of criticism as a form of denuding, and denuding as a form of violence. Criticism (st)rips the page.

Citation is a case in point. To cite is to bite, and not always gently. Such bites can be pleasurable: what author has not experienced pleasure on seeing himself or herself cited? Yet even gentle bites of the sort protected by copyright can puncture the delicate skin of a text. And at its most predatory, citation can take advantage of a loophole in copyright not just to *read* a text but to *raid* it, to (st)rip (search) it without a warrant, to bag samples from it that can be used as evidence against it.

The critic, as judge (*kritēs*), longs to pronounce sentence(s) on the text. But the text invariably walks free. "The rare force of the text," notes Derrida, "is that you cannot catch it (and therefore limit it to) saying: *this is that. . . .* There is always some question of yet something else."[22] Indeed, it *is* a text only "inasmuch as it lays itself open to the grip and weight of two readings, that it to say, lets itself be struck with indetermination."[23] Struck open with a pen or truncheon, the text gives itself up to the grip of two readings, two hands, two heavy policeman's hands. It will slip out of its jacket and flee.[24] But will it escape unharmed?

Should we speak instead of the blushing retreat of truth, its modest veil, paper-thin, torn and crumpled so as to be nearly illegible? Of *inter*pre*tation* as a sublimated form of *penetration* (letting the anagram think for us), or of *pen*-etration, as here? Does the fleeing youth show a *bloody* behind to his interpreter? ("I bleed at the bottom of my text.")[25] If so, the young man's page has been

20. Swete, *Commentary on Mark,* 354.

21. Barthes, "From Work to Text," 76. Cf. Barthes, *Pleasure of the Text,* 64: "*Text* means *Tissue*; but whereas hitherto we have always taken this tissue as a product, a ready-made veil, behind which lies, more or less hidden, meaning (truth), we are now emphasizing . . . the generative idea that the text is . . . worked out in a perpetual interweaving. . . ."

22. Derrida, *Glas,* 198b–99b, his emphasis.

23. Ibid., 199a.

24. "The more the policemen act like policemen the less they'll find," says Lacan (*The Seminar, Book II,* 186–87).

25. Derrida, *Glas,* 84b.

torn, his veil pulled back, his mask ripped off, his makeup wiped clean. And his laugh is not a laugh of glee but of hysteria.

"His attire would excite attention," observes Swete.[26] Critics tend to gang up on texts that have *gaps* in their fabric. "Is not the most erotic portion of a body *where the garment gapes?*" asks Barthes. "It is intermittence . . . which is erotic: the intermittence of skin flashing between two articles of clothing . . . ; it is this flash itself which seduces."[27] Mark's weave is riddled with such gaps, causing the critics to gape and reach excitedly for their pens.

To read is perhaps to reap (compare Mark 4:8, 20). But is it not also to raid? And even to rape? Joyce's *Finnegans Wake* offers a s(l)ob(b)ering parody of critical reading's (unconscious?) aggressiveness. "Man to man," the narrator urges a more gentle(manly) approach. The *letter* of the text should be treated with respect, after all—"sound sense" demands it. But by the end of his speech the narrator is himself drooling for what he imagines to be behind the letter:

> Has any fellow, of the dime a dozen type, it might with some profit some dull evening quietly be hinted—has any usual sort of ornery josser, flatchested fortyish, faintly flatulent and given to ratiocination by syncopation in the elucidation of complications, . . . only another the son of, in fact, ever looked sufficiently longly at a quite everydaylooking stamped addressed envelope? Admittedly it is an outer husk: its face, in all its featureful perfection of imperfection, is its fortune: it exhibits only the civil or military clothing of whatever passionpallid nudity or plaguepurple nakedness may happen to tuck itself under its flap. Yet to concentrate solely on the literal sense or even the psychological content of any document to the sore neglect of the enveloping facts themselves circumstantiating it is just as hurtful to sound sense . . . as were some fellow in the act of perhaps getting an intro from another fellow turning out to be a friend in need of his, say, to a lady of the latter's acquaintance . . . straightaway to run off and vision her plump and plain in her natural altogether, preferring to close his blinkhard's eyes to the ethiquethical fact that she was, after all, wearing for the space of the time being some definite articles of evolutionary clothing, inharmonious creations, a captious critic might describe them as, or not strictly necessary or a trifle irritating here and there, but for all that suddenly full of local colour and personal perfume and suggestive too, of so very much more and capable of being stretched, filled out, if need or wish were, of having their surpris-

26. Swete, *Commentary on Mark,* 354.
27. Barthes, *Pleasure of the Text,* 9–10, his emphasis.

ingly like coincidental parts separated don't they now, for better survey by the deft hand of an expert, don't you know?[28]

This man(ner of) reading can also be (that of) a woman—the adoption of a textual position traditionally coded as male. Mark's distress at being man-handled even by women interpreters finds displaced expression in the *Testament of Joseph* 8:2–3 (a text to which Mark 14:52 is related by way of Genesis 39:12): "At last, then, she laid hold of my garments, forcibly dragging me to have connexion with her. When, therefore, I saw that in her madness she was holding fast to my garment, I left it behind, and fled away naked."[29]

"Psychoanalytically," as Jane Gallop notes, "interpretation is always moti-vated by desire and aggression, by desire to have and to kill"[30]—desire to possess the object, to appropriate its meaning, and to slay one's rivals through the force of one's arguments. "The violent truth of 'reading.' "[31] Must it ever be so? Is to read always "to ask for identity papers, for an origin and a destina-tion,"[32] as it so often has been in biblical studies? Must a letter always be *opened*—torn, cut, unglued? Might it not be *unbound* instead, as in Greek: "*epistolēn luein,* to open a letter, to unbind the strings of a letter."[33] Untying Mark, unfastening its letter, unchaining the Lion and running with it—is that what we should be about instead?

Even in "playful" *interpretation*, however, *penetration* also occurs. To wrestle with a text is to bring one's own style to bear on it. And "in the question of style there is always the weight or *examen* of some pointed object. At times this object might be only a quill or a stylus. But it could just as easily be a stiletto, or even a rapier. Such objects might be used in a vicious attack against [some] matter or matrix, an attack whose thrust could not but leave its mark."[34] Mark must be tattooed from head to toe with such marks, given the armies of readers who

28. Joyce, *Finnegans Wake,* 109.1–30. Later the letter, become a "new book of Morses," is found to be "punctured (in the university sense of the term) by numerous stabs and foliated gashes made by a pronged instrument. These paper wounds, four in type, were gradually and correctly understood to mean stop, please stop, do please stop, and O do please stop respec-tively" (123.31–124.5).

29. Translation from Charles, *Apocrypha and Pseudepigrapha.* To resort to Gen 39:12 (cf. Amos 2:16) in order to unlock Mark 14:51–52 is "desperate in the extreme," says Taylor (*St. Mark,* 561). But is it the interpreter or Mark who is desperate?

30. Gallop, *Reading Lacan,* 27, glossing Kristeva, "In the Microcosm," 33.

31. Derrida, "Living On," 152.

32. Derrida, *Glas,* 7b.

33. Derrida, *The Post Card,* 165.

34. Derrida, *Spurs,* 37. Cf. Derrida, *Glas,* 5a: "A deciphering cannot be neutral, neuter, or passive. It violently intervenes." Hence the problem posed by Derrida in "Living On": "How can

have brought their pointed instruments to bear on it through the centuries. "The stylate spur rips through the veil."[35] But when the young man's paper veil is torn open, what is actually revealed? Does the ga(u)ze part only to reveal other veils, other (em)b(r)o(i)d(er)ies of writing, infinitely layered, the penprick scars left by countless others who have written on this text? To be solicitous for Mark's integrity is perhaps to underestimate its defenses. And to overlook the fact that it too is armed. As a violent reading of an older body of writing (Jewish scripture), an exercise in "stolentelling,"[36] Mark is not itself without (a) style. Nor is its protagonist, Jesus, a raider of scripture any less violent than Mark. Style is the Son of Man.

Style is also an umbrella. "The style-spur, the spurring style, is a long object, an oblong object, a word, which perforates even as it parries. It is the oblongi-foliated point (a spur or a spar) which derives its apotropaic power from the taut, resistant tissues, webs, sails and veils which are erected, furled and unfurled around it. But, it must not be forgotten, it is also an umbrella."[37] Mark's writing instrument is Jesus, as we have seen, a Jesus who writes. Jesus, as writer and as writing, has the aggressive-defensive, hermaphroditic design of an umbrella, able to thrust, to parry, and to penetrate, but also to open, to enfold, and to conceal. And Mark itself, which applied the final stitches to this umbrella, is a sewing machine, one that also sows (see 4:3ff.). For the Surrealists, beauty was the chance meeting upon a dissecting table of a sewing machine and an umbrella.[38] On the dissecting table that is the critical text, this chance encounter is endlessly restaged.

The youth is armed with an umbrella, then. He too is the victim of a chance encounter, not with a sewing machine but with a lynch mob. His undressing also is accidental. Those who seize him intend only to arrest him, not to strip him. But an accident is what we are here to investigate—the accident through which the discredited hypothesis identifying the young man as Mark lays bare a truth it did not reach for: the truth that criticism is a fantasy of violent possession instead of the young man's true identity, the truth of criticism instead of critical truth. "Truth grabs error by the scruff of the neck in the

---

one text . . . give or present another to be read, without touching it, without saying anything about it, practically without referring to it?" (80).

35. Derrida, *Spurs,* 107.

36. Joyce, *Finnegans Wake,* 424.35.

37. Derrida, *Spurs,* 41.

38. This definition of beauty originated with Isadore Ducasse, poet, anarchist, and self-styled Comte de Lautréamont, and was embraced by André Breton, Surrealism's leading theorist and spokesperson. See Balakian, *Surrealism,* 191, and cf. Derrida, *Spurs,* 129f.

mistake," says Lacan.[39] But where do we ourselves lie in relation to this truth? In attempting to pronounce the truth of this scene, what have we effected? A denuding of criticism as denuding? If so, we ourselves stand exposed. The text has slipped away, having stripped *us* on its way out, and whether it flees naked or clothed we cannot tell. The more one appears to be the master, "the more one presents one's rear."[40]

Another possibility is more unnerving still. What if the secret of this scene were precisely that it *had* no secret? What if it were "only . . . simulating some hidden truth within its folds"?[41] The proposition that truth entails unveiling would then be unveiled as untrue. Run after the young man and you might end up in the abyss.

(The young man to his critics: "The truth, in this sense, is that which runs after truth—and that is where I am running, where I am taking you, like Actaeon's hounds, after me."

The critics: "All [we] can do is tell the truth. No, that isn't so—[we] have missed it. There is no truth that, in passing through awareness, does not lie. But one runs after it all the same.")[42]

Tracking meaning can be a tricky business. Frequently we (t)read (upon) a piece of cloth or text that has been cunningly placed in our path, only to feel it give way beneath us. "Save oneself from falling into the bottomless depths by weaving and folding back the cloth to infinity," advises Derrida.[43] Can our fascination with the young man's loincloth, after the Lion has bolted, save us from the bottomless lion pit?

The sound of cloth being sundered is also heard at Jesus' trial. "Are you the Messiah, the Son of the Blessed One?" the high priest asks. "I am," replies Jesus, "and 'you will see the Son of Man sitting at the right hand of the Power,' and 'coming with the clouds of heaven'" (14:61–62; compare Dan 7:13). Apocalypse, unveiling, tearing aside to uncover or reveal. On hearing Jesus' blasphemy, the high priest ritually tears his own garment (*diarēxas tous chitōnas autou*), inadvertently miming the apocalypse that his adversary has just predicted. He pronounces its name while refusing to hear it.

Jesus' death too provokes an apocalpytic rending/reading: "And the veil of

39. Lacan, *The Seminar, Book I*, 265.

40. Derrida, *The Post Card*, 453, as he exposes Lacan's reading of Poe. Later Barbara Johnson will denude Derrida's reading of Lacan. The main players in this game of strip poker are now gathered in Muller and Richardson, *The Purloined Poe*.

41. Derrida, *Spurs*, 133.

42. Lacan, *Four Fundamental Concepts*, 188, vii.

43. Derrida, *Truth in Painting*, 37.

the temple was torn in two [*eschisthē eis duo*], from top to bottom" (15:38).[44] Which veil? The temple had two veils, or curtains: an outer one, which covered its main entrance, and an inner one, which covered the entrance to the Holy of Holies. The Greek term used here, *to katapetasma,* suggests the second veil to most scholars (compare Exod 27:16, LXX), the inner one that separated the awesome presence of Yahweh from those outside. But when at Jesus' death the veil of the temple is torn in two, it reveals the presence of God as—absence.

According to Josephus, the first-century Jewish historian, whose description of the Herodian temple is the most detailed we possess, the Holy of Holies contained "nothing at all [*ouden holōs en autō*]."[45] Derrida comments:

> The structure encloses its void within itself, shelters only its own proper interiorized desert, opens onto nothing, confines nothing, contains as its treasure only nothingness: a hole, an empty spacing, a death. . . . Nothing behind the curtains. Hence the ingenuous surprise of a non-Jew when he opens . . . or violates the tabernacle . . . and after so many ritual detours to gain access to the secret center, he discovers nothing—only nothingness. . . .
>
> One undoes the bands, displaces the tissues, pulls off the veils, parts the curtains: nothing but a black hole. . . . It is the experience of the powerful Pompey at the end of his greedy exploration. . . .
>
> The tent of the tabernacle, the stone of the temple, the robe that clothes the text of the covenant—is finally discovered as an empty room, is not uncovered, never ends being uncovered, as it has nothing to show.[46]

You undo the bands, unfurl the cloth or shroud, pull back the veil—endlessly. You wait endlessly for apocalypse.

JESUS' POSTCARDS

When I enter the post office of a great city I tremble as if in a
sacred place.
—Jacques Derrida, *The Post Card*

44. His career ends as it began; cf. 1:10: "As he was coming up out of the water, he saw the heavens torn asunder [*schizomenous tous ouranous*]." On the connection between the two tearings, see Malbon, *Narrative Space,* 187n93, and more recently, Ulansey, "The Heavenly Veil."

45. Josephus, *Jewish War* 5.5.4.219. A contemporary of Josephus, the author of 2 Baruch (on the dating, see Collins, *The Apocalyptic Imagination,* 170), also alludes to this empty interior, recounting how an angel descended into the Holy of Holies of the first temple prior to its destruction and removed its contents for safekeeping (6:7–8; cf. 2 Macc 2:4–8).

46. Derrida, *Glas,* 49a–50a. A no less remarkable reading/raiding of the empty sanctuary can be found in Goux, *Symbolic Economies,* 146–47, 243–44.

On Golgotha, too, God's presence, in his Son, is disclosed as the sun is eclipsed (15:33), as the Son absents himself. Of course, it is not that Jesus' absence as such triggers understanding in Mark. The subsequent announcement of the *neaniskos* at the empty tomb, a jubilant proclamation of absence—"he has been raised; he is not here"—merely triggers confusion: "They went out and fled from the tomb, for terror and amazement had seized them" (16:6–8). Jesus' living presence among his disciples precipitated confusion; the absence of his dead body at the tomb precipitates confusion. The climactic scene of comprehension in Mark—the centurion's confession (15:39)—follows Jesus' desolate cry of abandonment at the apparent absence of God (15:34). At the moment in which Jesus departs his body, becoming absent, the centurion realizes in whose presence he has been, recognizes Jesus as an absent presence.

Like those who attempt to seize the young man, the centurion must be content with a bare, tantalizing glimpse of Jesus as he slips away. No immediate consummation comes with the rupturing of the temple veil, Yahweh's hymen, which is coupled with the centurion's penetrating (g)lance ("the curtain of the temple was torn in two. . . . And when the centurion . . . saw that in this way he breathed his last. . . ." The consummation of presence must await Jesus' *parousia,* his coming in glory (9:1, 13:26, and so forth). Full presence is subject to postponement, deferral, detour in Mark. And detour—the mandatory detour through Galilee, for example ("he is going ahead of you to Galilee; there you will see him," 16:7)—is always subject to the risk of accident, of nonarrival: "They said nothing to anyone, for they were afraid" (16:8).

In short, Jesus' message in Mark is subject to the postal principle—"postal maneuvering, relays, delay, anticipation, destination, telecommunicating network, the possibility . . . of going astray."[47] Indeed, Jesus' message *as* mark is already subject to that principle. If, as Saussure assures us, language is a differential system that depends for its intelligibility on the differences that distinguish each of its elements from all the other elements in the system,[48] then "within every sign already, every mark . . . , there is distancing, the post, what

---

47. Derrida, *The Post Card,* 66. Sadly, Avital Ronell's *Telephone Book* (complete with Yellow Pages) came my way too late to color the midrash that follows.

48. Saussure, *Course in General Linguistics,* 120. The relationship between a signifier and its referent is arbitrary (as in *tree, arbre, Baum*). What is not arbitrary, however, but necessary in order that a signifier be intelligible, are the *differences* that distinguish it from every other signifier in language. *Tree* is intelligible not because of what it is, strictly speaking, since there is no resemblance between the sound *tree* (or its appearance when written) and the leafy object it designates. *Tree* is intelligible, rather, precisely because of what it is not—*three, tea, see,* and every other sound in language.

there has to be so that it is legible for another."[49] Nothing, therefore, "neither among the elements nor within the system, is anywhere ever simply present or absent. There are only, everywhere, differences and traces of traces."[50] *Trace*: reshuffle its letters and you are dealt a *carte*, perhaps a *carte postale*.

Critical writing bearing the post-age stamp is only now being delivered in biblical and theological studies.[51] This newborn writing is nothing if not eclectic—"my name is legion, for we are many"—cautiously assuming flesh in the form of the Work, although also willing to risk embodiment in the Text. (The Work is object-ive, meaning-full—I can heft its weighty meaning in my hand. The Text is what throws all such proprietary logic into question.)[52]

Post-age writing should prefer the postcard even more than the Text. A depthless object, the postcard is a hopeless container. It cannot retain meaning; meaning plays over its surface and splashes off. Hardly object-ive, barely meaning-full, it gives little satisfaction to the Book lover. The disinterested posture is foreign to the postcard; it is the most personal (and personable) of communications. It can also be the most cryptic.

Ever the nonbook, the postcard begs to be judged by its cover. Evaluating the collection *Writing and Sexual Difference*,[53] Gallop is as intrigued by its cover as by its contents. In other words, she reads it like a postcard. The cover has

> pictures of people writing: on the front a woman, on the back a man. Together they compose a particularly well-articulated illustration of "writing and sexual difference." The woman is writing a letter; the man a book. Women write letters—personal, intimate, in relation; men write books—universal, public, in general circulation. The man in the picture is in fact Erasmus, father of our humanistic tradition; the woman, without a

49. Derrida, *The Post Card*, 29. Saussure's *Course*—suitably boosted—is part of the Derridean can(n)on. See Moore, *Literary Criticism*, 132–33, 157–58.

50. Derrida, *Positions*, 26.

51. See, e.g, Burnett, "Postmodern Biblical Exegesis"; Burnham, *Post-Modern Theology*; Fowler, "Postmodern Biblical Criticism"; Griffin et al., *Varieties of Postmodern Theology*; McKnight, *Postmodern Use*; Moore, "The 'Post-' Age Stamp"; Phillips, "Exegesis as Critical Practice"; and cf. Breech, *Jesus and Postmodernism*.

52. See Barthes, "From Work to Text." Derrida, following Blanchot, prefers the term *Book* to *Work*: "The idea of the book is the idea of a totality. . . . It is the encyclopedic protection of theology and of logocentrism against the disruption of writing" (*Of Grammatology*, 18; cf. *Dissemination*, 44–47; *Writing and Difference*, 294ff.). A/theological texts include those of Mark Taylor—*Erring*, *Altarity*, and *Tears*. Even less bookish is Kirk Hughes's "Framing Judas," each page of which is arranged in four columns, the pages folding out so that what begins as an article ends up as an artifact: a large paper cross.

53. Edited by Elizabeth Abel.

name. In the man's background: books. The woman sits against floral wallpaper, echoed in reverse by her patterned dress.[54]

The woman could just as easily be writing a postcard, that most decorative and undecorous of texts. The same cannot be said of Erasmus. We do not know what Erasmus is writing, but we suspect that it is no longer addressed to us. The postcard is the stamp of our post-age system in a way that Erasmus's book no longer can be, a system of mass communications in which informal, anecdotal address is everywhere juxtaposed with graphic imagery—look no further than the network news and the advertisements around which it is structured.[55] And thanks to feminism and poststructuralism, the personal, the anecdotal, and the graphic are now to be heard and seen with unprecedented frequency in academic discourse as well.

The postcard is a postmodern text, then. But that is not to say that there are no ancient postcards. If the postcard can be said to contain the recipe for the texts that many of us are now eager to produce, it also contains the recipe for the texts that some of us are still willing to devour—the biblical texts, for example.[56] This is the case whether we choose to read the Bible as a love letter from God to his people, a cryptic missive, admittedly, but one strategically left open for all the world to see (a postcard, in other words); or whether we choose to read it instead as a miscellaneous collection of all-too-human communications, all too closely tied to local particulars of time and place, accident and circumstance ("when you come, bring the cloak that I left with Carpus at Troas"—2 Tim 4:13). They are communications exposed to the pious, prurient gaze of a readership populous beyond the wildest nightmares of the senders, communications nearly always unsigned, addressed to persons almost never named and long since dead[57]—a bundle of yellowed and tattered postcards on which depend our very life (if we happen to be believers) and livelihood (if we happen to be biblical scholars).

54. Gallop, *Thinking through the Body*, 163.

55. Advertisements that themselves tend to be structured around puns. The pun is the trope of our age. It bombards us from every billboard, every newspaper stand, every television screen. Its irruption in academic discourse represents a fusion of popular and elite cultural forms— although we find the pun already rumbling in such texts as Lacan's "Seminar on 'The Purloined Letter' " (1955), and exploding in Derrida's *Glas* (1974), long before taking the media by storm. Popular-elite conflation, in any case, is often regarded as an index of postmodern culture (see Huyssen, *After the Great Divide*, viii-x).

56. "I never dramped of prebeing a postman," says Joyce's idiot Christ in *Finnegans Wake* (488.19). Some of the earliest postcards were written in the language of the New Testament: *card* comes from the Greek *chartes* by way of the Latin *charta*, a leaf of papyrus.

57. "Letters open, but like crypts" (Derrida, *The Post Card*, 53).

"The guardians of tradition, the professors, academics, and librarians, the doctors and authors of theses are terribly curious about correspondences," Derrida notes, "private or public correspondences (a distinction without pertinence in this case, whence the post card, . . . half-private half-public, neither the one nor the other . . .)."[58] We biblical scholars earn our living by peeking into other people's mail. Working long shifts in the Dead Letter Office we examine the writings of the dead for clues of their identity and whereabouts. We perform postmortems on dead letters. The blades of our letter-openers run red.

(The scholar's defense: "Everything is opened and read in order to divine, with the best intentions in the world, the name of a sender or of an addressee. When I came . . . into possession of these letters . . . they had in effect been opened. Once more become the post cards that at bottom they already were.")[59]

Throughout the Dead Letter Office, the Book of Life lies scattered as leaves, *chartae,* cards, postcards. We call it the Book of Life because we depend on it for our living—depend, that is, on its remaining scattered. But the office also runs a bonus system. Those willing and able to trace the postcards back to their putative points of origin merit the postmasters' stamp of approval, and amass substantial material benefits as a result. Fortunately for us, the postcards are sufficiently decipherable (public) to keep the bonus system operable, but sufficiently indecipherable (private) to ensure that we never work ourselves out of a job.

In Mark the message, the letter, that Jesus mails and remails to his disciples (although marked urgent, it is repeatedly returned unopened) is eventually read at the foot of the cross—by a third party (the centurion) to whom it had not been addressed. "We are . . . dealing with a letter which has been diverted from its path," as Lacan remarks of another purloined letter, "or, [in] the language of the post office, a *letter in suffrance.*"[60] No sooner does Jesus absent himself than the centurion reads his letter of suffering. Here, however, the intrusion may be desired.

(Jesus' love for the centurion: "They will have only post cards from me, never the true letter, which is reserved uniquely for you.")[61]

But the centurion is able to read the letter only when Jesus has left the room.

---

58. Ibid., 62.
59. Ibid., 50.
60. Lacan, "The Purloined Letter," 43, his emphasis.
61. Derrida, *The Post Card,* 81. Do I still need to add that Jesus is not the speaker in Derrida's text?

Could the letter have been mailed, opened, and read while Jesus was physically present to his disciples? After all, letters normally presuppose the physical dissociation of addresser and addressee(s). Jesus' message in Mark functions like a letter: it makes more sense when Jesus is away.

(Jesus to his disciples: "Do I write to you in order to bring you near or in order to distance you . . . ? The question is posed when you are in the next room, or even when in the same room, barely turning my back to you, I write to you again, when I leave a note under your pillow or in the letter box upon leaving, the essential not being that you are absent or present at the moment when I write to you but that I am not there myself, when you are reading."

The disciples' desire for Jesus: "To have the other within oneself, right up close but stronger than oneself, and his tongue in your ear before being able to say a word while looking at yourself in the depths of the rearview mirror."

Jesus: "I want you to look at the envelope for a long time before you open me."[62]

But will the envelope contain anything other than a postcard, or open crypt?)

Terrorized, the disciples suspect Jesus' message of being a lethal letter bomb ("those who followed were afraid"—10:32; compare 9:32). Rejected, Jesus' emitted sense, his seed, falls along the path, on rocky ground, among thorns: "postmark, stamp, and return to sender."[63] His discarded love letters litter the landscape ("how is it that, under certain circumstances, you return your letters to the person who, for a period in your life, bombarded you with them?").[64] His postcards are returned unread—except by strangers, of course; such is the exposed condition of the postcard. Although he wants to keep them private, he cannot: "He said to him, 'See that you say nothing. . . .' But he went out and began to proclaim it freely" (1:44–45; compare 7:36). (Derrida too exclaims: "The secret of the post card burns—the hands and the tongues—it cannot be kept.")[65] Moreover, everything that passes between Jesus and his disciples is surreptitiously rerouted to us. Indeed, even while he is in the very act of writing them, Jesus' postcards are already being intercepted, already being readdressed. "Let the reader understand," urges Mark sotto voce (13:14), interrupting Jesus in mid-sentence.

But is Jesus reading from a teleprompter as he delivers his eschatological

---

62. Ibid., 79, 60, 110.

63. Ibid., 24.

64. Lacan, *The Seminar, Book II,* 197–98.

65. Derrida, *The Post Card,* 188. The secret circulates openly: "this is what I call a post card" (185).

address (13:5–37)? Did the speech have a ghost writer? Certain scholars claim to have seen the ghost,[66] suggesting that a Jewish apocalyptic broadsheet or flysheet underlies this address—and so it does. "A letter is precisely speech which flies," says Lacan—"a letter is a fly-sheet"[67]—and here, as always, Jesus' speech is in full flight even as it leaves his lips. Its paper wings bear it to the reader, but so swiftly that its meaning cannot be caught by Jesus' hapless hearers. His flysheets, like his postcards, are un-enveloped, nude, but their sense is just as hard to uncover.

(Jesus to himself: "I am suffering . . . from a real pathology of destination: I am always addressing myself to someone else (no, to someone else still!), but to whom? I absolve myself by remarking that this is due, before me, to the power of . . . the 'first' mark, to be remarked, precisely, to be repeated, and therefore divided, turned away from whatever singular destination."[68]

The reader to herself: "I receive as a present the chance to which this card delivers itself. It falls to me. And I choose that it should choose me by chance, I wish to cross its path."[69]

Mark to itself: "I am somewhat hung up on post cards: so modest, anonymous, . . . stereotyped . . .—and absolutely indecipherable, the interior safe itself that the mailmen, the readers, the collectors, the professors finally pass from hand to hand with their eyes, yes, bound."

Jesus to Mark: "There is nothing I fear more than this exposition without envelope.")[70]

Mark's epistemology is thus an epistle-ology. And his hermeneutic is a postal hermeneutic, which is to say a hermetic hermeneutic, Hermes the messenger being the patron not only of interpreters but also of postmen. But to be (a) postman is to be past the age of man. Is Mark really (a) postman or just another male man?

It all depends on where you stand—at the foot of the cross or in the empty tomb. Mark 15:40–41 states: "There were also women looking on from a distance. . . . These used to follow him and provided for him when he was in Galilee; and there were many other women who came up with him to Jerusalem." Mary Ann Tolbert comments: "They have not betrayed, denied, and

66. See Kümmel, Promise and Fulfillment, 98, for a report on these sightings. Today they would be greeted with skepticism, and indeed Kümmel himself is unconvinced.

67. Lacan, The Seminar, Book II, 198.

68. Derrida, The Post Card, 112.

69. Derrida, "Telepathy," 6. "Telepathy" is a postscript to The Post Card, a late delivery, published separately.

70. Derrida, The Post Card, 47, 68.

fled, as did the male disciples, but have remained with Jesus through tribulation and persecution. Although some scholars treat the women basically as surrogates or stand-ins for the disciples, . . . *how* they are described, and their identity *as women* all depict a group similar to but *much better than* the Twelve. They are not surrogates but superiors."[71]

Tolbert is surely right. But is excellence rewarded in the Marcan workplace? Mark is hardly a manifesto for equal-opportunity employment. Jesus' final message addressed to the eleven, collected by the mysterious young (mail)man and carried to the tomb or office where everything *should* be sorted (out), threatens to become yet another card adrift in a bag, yet another victim of a strike or a sorting accident. And thanks to whom? Mark's female postal workers? Mark has used his author-ity over these women to place them in a compromising position. His(s)tory recounts that they resigned without notice just when they were most needed. Tolbert confesses as much: "The seed has fallen on rocky ground once again, as fear, not faith, motivates their actions. Like the Twelve before them, the women too flee in silence."[72]

(The women on their failure to become the readers Mark will not let them be: "What does a post card want to say to you? On what conditions is it possible? Its destination traverses you, you no longer know who you are. At the very instant when from its address it interpellates, you, uniquely you, instead of reaching you it divides you or sets you aside.")[73]

Letters are always at risk, as Derrida (himself a post-philosopher) reminds us: "A letter does *not always* arrive at its destination, and from the moment that this possibility belongs to its structure one can say that it never truly arrives, that when it does arrive its capacity not to arrive torments it with an internal drifting."[74] This risk, this internal capacity for going astray, is what Mark will not erase from its own letter. The disciples *may* eventually get Jesus' note to meet him in Galilee (16:7). Indeed, they *must* get it, even if he has to deliver it in person. But *will* they eventually get it, even if he does deliver it by hand? Person-to-person delivery has proved astonishingly ineffective throughout this Gospel. Possibly they may never get it at all. Mark keeps this possibility open, holds its legs apart, not caring whom it frustrates or offends.

(Mark to itself: "I love the delicate levers which pass between the legs of a

---

71. Tolbert, *Sowing the Gospel,* 291–92, her emphasis.

72. Ibid., 295. Other feminist critics give Mark the benefit of the doubt, interpreting the role given to the women in 16:8 more benignly. See, e.g., Fiorenza, *In Memory of Her,* 320ff., and Malbon, "Fallible Followers."

73. From the statement on the back of *The Post Card.*

74. Derrida, *The Post Card,* 489, his emphasis.

word, between a word and itself to the point of making entire civilizations tremble.")[75]

The possibility, although open, is nevertheless closed to investigation. And the way that Mark has signed off, the way he has sealed his legacy, crossed his own legs, suggests that it will ever remain so.

(Mark to the executors of his estate: "I have enclosed everything in a virgin envelope. I [have] signed on the borders, on the V, you know, where the two parts stick to each other, the lips, the one on the other, such that the letter [cannot] be opened without deforming my signature.")[76]

The disciples' fate is sealed, then, forever tucked away out of sight. But this does not mean that Mark lacks a resurrection appearance. Is not Mark itself Jesus' resurrected body, the reappearance that its ending predicts but does not depict? Jesus' corpse, soon to become a colossal literary corpus—"the world itself could not contain the books that would be written" (John 21:25)—is raised up in the very act of being read. So the body of Christ can indeed now be eaten, but only as one would devour a book. And the tomb is indeed empty ("look, there is the place they laid him"—Mark 16:6), but only as a bookshelf might be empty, empty of the very book whose flesh the reader is in the act of ingesting.

(Mark to Jesus: "Your absence is reality for me, I don't know any other."

Jesus to Mark: "You mark for me both reality and death; . . . you mark me.")[77]

What of Jesus' remains? Mark tells us that the tomb was vacant. Yet there must have been a remains, a residue. If Jesus had been *totally* translatable he would have vanished into Mark, utterly become Mark. He would have been completely devoured and digested, nothing remaining. Tradition does insist that Mark was a skilled *hermēneutēs* ("interpreter," "translator").[78] But that Mark could not totally translate Jesus is attested to by the fact of subsequent Gospels. Mark must have left something to be desired, to be devoured, to be digested— some uneaten scraps on the mortuary slab. (No longer a letter, Jesus is become litter.) But if Jesus had been totally *un*translatable, he would simply have remained, untouched, in the tomb, a cryptic and unappetizing remains. As

---

75. Ibid., 78.

76. Ibid., 137.

77. Ibid., 181.

78. "Mark, having become the *hermēneutēs* of Peter, wrote down accurately all that he remembered of the things said and done by the Lord" (Papias, as quoted in Eusebius, *Hist. Ecc.* 3.39.15).

writing, as text, Jesus *is* translated, not totally, yet triumphantly. "Triumphant translation is neither the life nor the death of the text, only or already its living *on,* its life after life, its life after death."[79] "It lives and lives on in mutation."[80] This, in so many words, is what the angel tells the women at the mortuary, now become a library. Jesus is no longer stored in the tomb; instead, he is storied in the tome. He has risen to an eternal (shelf)life. But he can no longer be read in the original. Like Enoch of old, a type(script) of the book Jesus has become, Jesus can only be found in translation: "By faith Enoch was translated [*metetethē*] that he should not see death; and he was not found because God had translated him" (Heb 11:5, KJV). Unable to read the translation, the women run from the library.

Or is it that they have been unable to locate the volume—precisely because the mortuary has become a library, precisely because Jesus has become a book. "He is not here." The book "is *missing from its place,*" says Lacan, "as the call slip puts it when speaking of a volume lost in the library." Even if the volume were "on an adjacent shelf or in the next slot," it would be no less hidden, "however visibly it [might] appear."[81] Confronted with it, the women might not recognize it—John and Luke tell us as much: "She . . . saw Jesus standing there, but she did not know that it was Jesus" (John 20:14; compare 21:4); "Jesus himself came near . . . , but their eyes were kept from recognizing him" (Luke 24:15–16).

At his baptism the Son is accepted for publication by his Father ("with you I am well pleased"—Mark 1:11), although he goes into production only as he dies. The event is announced in *The Gospel of Truth*: "Jesus appeared; he put on that book; . . . he published the edict of the Father on the cross" (20,24–25; compare Col 2:14). Writ(h)ing in pain on his cross, Jesus can at last be read: "Truly this man was God's Son" (Mark 15:39). He is in the process of becoming a book. Nailed, grafted onto the tree, Jesus' body is becoming one with the wood. His flesh, torn and beaten to a pulp, joined by violence to the wood, is slowly being changed into processed woodpulp, into paper, as the centurion looks on. As tree and budding book, Jesus is putting forth leaves, the leaves of a gospel book, whose opening sentence the centurion has just read: "The beginning of the good news of Jesus Christ, Son of God" (1:1).

Doubled over in pain, folded like a stack of leaves, Jesus is bound to a hard

---

79. Derrida, "Living On," 102–3, his emphasis.
80. Derrida, "Tours de Babel," 183.
81. Lacan, "The Purloined Letter," 40, his emphasis.

wooden spine. Graphted onto the tree, he is leafing his body, in order to readturn as a book. He will spend tree days in the tome. But in death his voice will acquire the volume that it lacked in life.

(Jesus: "My foos won't moos. I feel as old as yonder elm. . . . My ho head halls. I feel as heavy as yonder stone. . . . Lsp! I am leafy speaking. Lpf! . . . . Not a sound falling. Lispn! No wind no word. Only a leaf, just a leaf and then leaves.")[82]

"From the fig tree learn its lesson: as soon as its branch becomes tender and puts forth its leaves, you know that summer is near. So also, when you see these things taking place, you know that he is near, at the very gates" (13:28–29). What is the lesson of that other, newly sprung tree (the cross) in whose bark Mark has carved his Gospel (for this is a book that bleeds)? Is it that Jesus' body, grafted onto the cross, become one with it, and thus become branch, tree, book, and leaf, inscribed with letters of blood, can now at last be read, no longer an indecipherable code but an open codex? And that in its (now) re(a)d(able) ink, lately invisible, the message that was scratched into the fig tree is transcribed: outside the gates, but only just, the summer Son is shining in full strength?

But what if the Sun were really a black hole, a gigantic vacuum cleaner, a S(p)on(ge)?

THE SPONGE OF GOD

He who will drink from my mouth will become like me.
—*The Gospel of Thomas* (saying 108)

I sink I'd die down over his feet, humbly dumbly, only to
washup.
—James Joyce, *Finnegans Wake*

Mark 15:36 reports: "And someone ran, filled a sponge [*spoggos*] with sour wine, put it on a reed [*kalamos*], and gave it to him to drink. . . ." What did Jesus read in this sponge swollen with *oxos* (cheap, sour wine, or wine vinegar), poised to assault his palate? Himself God's own Sponge, destined to wipe away sin (14:24; compare 10:45) and soak up readings insatiably, did he see a simulacrum of himself in the body of this prodigy: a zoophyte with wine for blood?

The sponge is supported on a reed, or reading.[83] Being overheavy with liquids (vinegar, wine, blood), it is fated to bend and break every reading, every

---

82. Joyce, *Finnegans Wake*, 215.34–36, 216.1, 619.20–23.
83. A reading that is also a rewriting. The *kalamos* was an ancient writing instrument (see Ps 44:2, LXX; 3 Macc 4:20).

reed. Grotesquely swollen, nonsaturable, the sponge drips continually, incurably, incontinently. It finds "its irreducible force in a passivity without limit, absorbing everything":[84] clean or filthy water, fine wine or rotgut, strong or insipid readings. "It is a remarkable figure for a receptacle," remarks Derrida.[85]

What must be wiped clean in order that Derrida's Sponge (the antihero of his nonbook *Signsponge*) may be resurrected as Mark's Son? The pge, seemingly, or page. But if we erase Derrida's p(a)ge, it is only in order to clear a space for Mark within its margins, and thereby to read a christography where none was intended.

Now, it is not that Derrida's *Signsponge*—the spongy, sticky text I am re(kne)ading here, devoted to the poet Francis Ponge—is itself entirely bereft of references to the gospel story. Derrida notes that Ponge once signed himself "Franciscus Pontius, . . . through a fabulous affiliation with Pontius Pilate."[86] As Ponge himself explains, this gesture of signing himself "Pontius" had to do "with soap and the washing of hands, after the fashion of my forefather Pontius Pilate [*Ponce Pilate*], of whom I am so proud of his having—after saying 'What is truth?'—washed his hands of the death of the Just Man (or the fanatic) [*ou de l'exalté*], and thus become the only person in the story to have gone into history with pure hands."[87]

In my own cross-reading of Mark and *Signsponge,* certain scenes of cross-dressing will be staged, the self-absolving Ponge Pilate, protagonist of *Signsponge* ("l'éponge est Ponge"),[88] being examined as if *he* were Jesus. In other words, Derrida's statements about (the S)Ponge will be treated as if they were statements about the Son. Thus, Pilate, as (S)Ponge, will try on the tattered robe of Christ all the better to posture as the pure-handed man. And I in turn try on the now discarded robes of the examiner Ponge Pilate, becoming the one who asks "What is truth?" Derrida's (S)Ponge swells to become an even bigger (S)PUN(GE), able to absorb more than we can ever pour into it.

We thus have Jesus as S(p)on(ge) of God, the apocalyptic punchline held in reserve by God to bring hi(s)story to a shattering climax. As God's parabler, and as such his wordsmith, Jesus is himself a punster; to pun "is to pound words, to beat them into new senses, to hammer at forced similes."[89]

---

84. Derrida, *Signsponge,* 66.
85. Ibid.
86. Ibid., 110.
87. Ibid., quoting Ponge, *Le Savon*.
88. Ibid., 73. *Signéponge/Signsponge* is a dual-language edition, French on one side, English on the other.
89. Skeat, *Etymological Dictionary,* cited in Culler, "Call of the Phoneme," 1–2. Skeat's dictionary was the Bible of another well-known punster, James Joyce.

The Father is content to let Jesus sponge off him, for he means to mop up using Jesus as the stake. The demons know that they are about to be cleaned out: "What do you want with us, Jesus of Nazareth? Have you come to wipe us out [*ēlthes apolesai hēmas*]?" (Mark 1:24). But for those who long to be clean, the Sponge overflows with compassion: "A leper came to him begging him, and kneeling he said to him, 'If you choose, you can make me clean [*dunasai me katharisai*].' Moved with pity, Jesus stretched out his hand and touched him, and said to him, 'I do choose. Be made clean.' Immediately the leprosy left him, and he was made clean" (1:40–42). "Receptive, open, welcoming . . . ready, in its guile, to receive all impressions, the sponge"[90]—God's beloved Sponge. Like any medical sponge, Jesus absorbs bodily spillages, drying them up with a touch: "Now there was a woman who had had a flow of blood for twelve years. . . . She . . . came up behind him in the crowd and touched his cloak, for she said, 'If I but touch his clothes, I will be made well.' Immediately the flow of blood dried up [*exēranthē hē pegē tou haimatos*]" (5:25–29).

The Sponge is of course closely associated with water, as we might expect. God's initial acclamation of Jesus as S(p)on(ge) occurs only after he has been thoroughly doused in water: "And just as he was coming up out of the water, he saw the heavens torn apart. . . . And a voice came from heaven, 'You are my Son, the Beloved' " (1:10–11). The sponge is "able to hold gases or liquid alternatively, 'to fill itself with wind or water.' "[91] The Sponge thus has power over these elements. "Who then is this, that even the wind and the sea obey him?" exclaim the disciples as the sea grows calm (4:41; compare 6:48b).[92] Moreover, the destiny of those who follow the Sponge is reward by reason of water, or punishment by means of it: "Whoever gives you a cup of water to drink because you bear the name of Christ will by no means lose his reward. If any of you put a stumbling block before one of these little ones who believe in me, it would be better for you if a great millstone were hung around your neck and you were thrown into the sea" (9:41–42).

The Sponge cleans deep to remove dirt and stains. As a result, it can itself appear to be a source of filth: "They noticed that some of his disciples were eating with defiled hands [*koinais chersin*], that is, without washing them [*tout estin aniptois*]. (For the Pharisees, and all the Jews, do not eat unless they thoroughly wash their hands . . . and they do not eat anything from the market

90. Derrida, *Signsponge*, 80.
91. Ibid., 70.
92. The Sponge in turn meets his double in this scene—the "cushion" or "pillow" (*proskephalaion*) on which he has been asleep (4:38).

unless they wash it; and there are also many other traditions that they observe, the washing [*baptismous*] of cups, pots, and bronze kettles.) So [they] asked him, 'Why do your disciples not live according to the tradition of the elders, but eat with soiled hands?' " (7:2–5). The Pharisees fail to see that this is no ordinary sponge. It does not simply clean hands and eating utensils (of foodstains and other blemishes); it cleans the food itself. Any further washing is unnecessary: "Do you not see that whatever goes into a person from outside cannot soil, since it enters, not the heart, but the stomach, and goes out into the sewer?' (Thus he cleansed all foods [*katharizōn panta ta brōmata*])" (7:18–19). The Sponge attacks stains at their source. A more dazzling demonstration is in store, however. On the mount of transfiguration, as the p(a)ge is finally peeled back and the S(p)on(ge) is revealed for what it has been all along—a Son—its "clothes bec[o]me dazzling white, such as no fuller on earth could bleach them [*stilbonta leuka lian hoia gnapheus epi tēs gēs ou dunatai houtōs leukanai*]" (9:3).

Disciples of the Sponge are challenged to match him drink for drink, even if it kills them: " 'Are you able to drink the cup that I drink, or be baptized with the baptism that I am baptized with?' They replied, 'We are able.' Then Jesus said to them, 'The cup that I drink you will drink; and with the baptism with which I am baptized, you will be baptized' " (10:38–39). But eventually even the Sponge has one drink too many and can barely keep the last one down ("Abba, Father, for you all things are possible; remove this cup from me"— 14:36), after having had "an alabaster flask of ointment of pure nard, very costly," poured over him to anoint him for burial (14:3–9), having secured a room in which to celebrate Passover by the novel (but not unspongely) device of having his disciples tail a man "carrying a jar of water" (14:12–16), and having had his half-oblivious followers finally drink him under the table ("this is my blood . . . which is poured out for many. . . . I will never again drink . . . until . . . I drink . . . in the kingdom of God"—14:23–25).

In short, more can be squeezed out of the sponge of 15:36 than Mark has seen fit to give us—Jesus erected on a stake, his features sculpted in a sponge, itself erected on a reed, or reading, also a writing. Yet that excess can easily be wrung out of what has been hung out to dry on Mark's other lines, taut lines or lines of thought, lines dripping water and wine, pus and blood.

"Insofar as it ingests, absorbs, and interiorizes everything, proper or not, the sponge is certainly 'ignoble,' " remarks Derrida[93]—but its ignobility is what makes it serviceable. Indeed, the Sponge is designed to serve and not to be

93. Derrida, *Signsponge,* 72.

served (10:45), as we shall see. "It can also, when applied to a surface, expunge, wipe, and efface." Moreover, it "is also the chance for purification, something which sponges away the stain, and even . . . expunges the debt ('the slate')."[94]

Unquestionably, our insatiable Sponge has begun to overflow even Mark's margins by now (although this is a Gospel written on blotting paper)[95] to mop up John, Paul, and other texts round about. It wipes off their dusty surfaces to uncover fresh inscriptions: "Behold the Sponge of God who wipes away the sin of the world," for example, or "I am the Sponge of life" (John 1:29, 36, 6:35ff.). Jesus, endlessly read and reread, is also bread, the bread of life. But note that "crumb has a texture akin to that of sponges."[96] Thus it is not surprising to find that the bread of life satisfies thirst as well as hunger: "I am the bread of life. Whoever comes to me will never hunger, and whoever believes in me will never thirst [ou mē dipsēsei]" (John 6:35). The Sponge of God is kneaded (needed) dough. Yet it is only through pain that this pain de vie is made edible. More precisely, since the word sponge is used technically of leavened dough prior to kneading, the kneady pain of the cross is what causes the S(p)on(ge) to rise. Crushed or violently compressed, the Sponge always regains its form, always resurrects.

(Am I wringing this metaphor dry? Or, situated as it is on the seabed of language, does the Sponge not refill faster than I can compress it?)

(S)pun(ge)-diving in these texts (in the depths of their ink, superficial yet abyssal), we find that the Sponge partakes of more than one substance. A taxonomic anomaly, it is "neither simply a thing, nor simply vegetal, nor simply animal."[97] Neither simply divine nor simply human, the S(p)on(ge) is an animal plant, a divine human being. It has emptied itself, humbled itself, to take on a form that is serviceable (compare Phil 2:7–8). John recounts how the S(p)on(ge), on the night before he suffered, "knowing that the Father had given all things into his hands, and that he had come from God and was going to God, got up from the table, took off his outer robe, and tied a towel [lention] around himself. Then he poured water into a basin and began to wash [niptein] the disciples' feet and to wipe [ekmassein] them with the towel that was tied around him" (13:3–5). Arguably, by this symbolic act of wiping, the Sponge reveals that he is also a towel. From the preexistent Sponge, or raw material, "will have been cut, to give it form, a serviette-éponge [sponge-towel]," says Signsponge.[98] "Be-

94. Ibid.
95. Or "drinking paper," as in French (papier buvard).
96. Derrida, Signsponge, 84.
97. Ibid., 72.
98. Ibid., 84.

cause it is less natural—it comes from a factory, a process of production can be read in it—it also comes closer to us."[99]

The eminently serviceable sponge-towel (as a towel, the Sponge is able to clean still deeper to remove stubborn stains) can be said, not without injustice, to be "the very example of the worthless, of the no-thing or the such-a-little-thing, the no-matter-what of low price, the nameless or nearly so in the mob of small things."[100] The *serviette-éponge* is the thing of low extraction. And what of the *bloody* S(p)on(ge)-towel, said by some to have emerged from between the immaculate thighs of a virgin?[101] Virtually without value, it is practically priceless. The exaltation of the *serviette-éponge* (on a reed, or reading, for example, to assuage the thirst, perhaps to mop the brow, of the suffering Son of God, now wrung out so that his perforated body streams cleansing blood and water) is therefore a scandal of particularity. Why the S(p)on(ge-towel) in particular? And why *this* S(p)on(ge-towel) on its particular (towel-)rack of pain?

Thus perforated, dark squiggles of blood adorning his stretched skin, the S(p)on(ge) is again writing. Although only a muscle filled with wind (*pneuma*), the Sponge can absorb anything that is poured into it. So too the text (a prosthetic organ designed to reproduce vocal sounds, and hence an artificial windmuscle, or sponge) can soak up readings endlessly. However grotesquely bloated it becomes, neither the S(p)on(ge) nor the text ever appears in danger of bursting.

(The Sponge remembers: "Bursting with emotion, I wanted to swallow myself by opening my mouth very wide and turning it over my head so that it would take in my whole body, and then the Universe, until there would be nothing more than a ball of eaten thing which little by little would be annihilated; that is how I see the end of the world.")[102]

And so, as S(p)on(ge), Jesus is once again writ(h)ing, this time with a wooden pen too massive for him to maneuver (and to which he is in any case pinned, fingers clenched around other pens whose nibs have been hammered through his palms), his own nib dipped in perspiration, in vinegar, in blood.

"And someone ran, filled a sponge with sour wine, put it on a reed, and gave it to him to drink. . . ." As the unweaned sponge rears up on its reed, impatient to drink from Jesus even as he drinks from it, and then to suck down the entire Gospel in long swallows, Mark's fabric parts to reveal a cleavage, or abyss. "In

99. Ibid., 82.
100. Ibid., 88.
101. Cf. ibid., 104.
102. Derrida, *Glas,* 198b.

order to be abyssal, the smallest circle must inscribe in itself the figure of the largest."[103] The sponge is such an inscription.

But the name *Mark* is an abyssal inscription of another sort, as we are about to see.

THE GOSPEL OF (THE) ~~MARK~~

[M]ark an X on the foreheads of those who moan and groan.
—Ezekiel 9:4 (NAB)

Afeard themselves were to wonder at the class of a crossroads
puzzler he would likely be.

O, you were excruciated, in honor bound to the cross of your
own cruelfiction!
—James Joyce, *Finnegans Wake*

Presence in Mark promptly absents itself whenever anyone tries to grasp it. "We are dispossessed of the longed-for presence in the gesture . . . by which we attempt to seize it."[104] To this extent, the flight of the naked young man, an apocalyptic unveiling, a (lightning) streak or flash, can fittingly be read as the signature of the author of this Gospel, a Gospel of absent apocalypse, a mark of an emptiness. "Supreme form of the sacred: the mark and the void."[105]

It can, moreover, be read as a special kind of signature, a mark—recall that the signature hypothesis identified the young man as Mark. Now, a signatory mark is a written character in the form of an X, or cross. And Mark's theology is commonly said to be a *theologia crucis*, a theology of the cross, a theology in which life and death crisscross. Jesus, having cross-examined his dyslexic disciples ("who do people say that I am? . . . who do you say that I am?"), announces: "If any want to become my followers, let them deny themselves and take up their cross and follow me. For those who want to save their life will lose it, and those who lose their life for my sake, and for the sake of gospel, will save it" (8:27–29, 34–35). In Mark, the signature of the disciple can only ever be that of a crisscross, or Christcross, which my *O.E.D.* defines as "the figure or mark of a cross in general; esp. that made in 'signing' his name by a person who cannot write." But a person unable to write is generally unable to read, and in Mark the disciples, generally at cross-purposes with Jesus, are singularly unable

---

103. Derrida, *Truth in Painting,* 27. Elsewhere he writes of "an internal pocket larger than the whole" ("Law of Genre," 206).

104. Derrida, *Of Grammatology,* 141.

105. Barthes, *Barthes by Barthes,* 79.

to read. Jesus must speak cross words to his puzzled disciples (8:33; compare 8:17–21).

A cross is also a chiasmus, a crosswise fusion: "Whoever would *save* their life will *lose* it, and whoever *loses* their life . . . will *save* it." Central to Mark is the fact of the crucifiction, a fiction structured like a cross, or chiasmus. Mark's structure is that of a post, complete with crossbeam, to which his hero is pinioned. Hence, poststructuralist Mark.

Closely related to the chiasmus is the *inclusio,* or "envelope construction," in which a key term, image, or motif introduced at the beginning of a narrative (or narrative unit) is repeated at the end, generally as a mark of closure. Into Mark's envelope construction ("Son of God . . . Son of God"—1:1, 15:39) Jesus, as writing, is inserted, although without closure (sealing) taking place. Jesus' message in Mark is an open letter or postcard.

Chiasmus comes from the Greek verb *chiazein,* "to mark with the letter X," or *chi.* And *chi* is an anagram of *Ich,* which is German for the personal pronoun *I* and the technical term in Freud that English translators render as *ego.* (This is the Freud who proclaimed: "Speak of chance, gentlemen, if you like. In my experience I have observed nothing arbitrary in this field, for it is *cross-checked* in such a way that it escapes chance.")[106] And Jesus, who identifies himself to his terrified disciples in Mark 6:50 with the words *egō eimi* ("I am," or "it is I"), himself possesses a name that is an echo of the French *je suis* ("I am"), the single superfluous letter being the *I* (or ego), which is thus marked out for deletion: "Father, . . . not what I [*egō*] want, but what you want" (14:36).

I, the first-person pronoun, blinks uncertainly, and not without reason. Once written, "I am" would be legible even if the *I* in question were dead. "My death is structurally necessary to the pronouncing of the *I,*" notes Derrida. " 'I am' or 'I am alive' . . . is what it is . . . only if . . . I can be dead at the moment when it is functioning. . . . This is not an extraordinary tale by Poe but the ordinary story of language."[107] It is also the story of Mark. Just as the eventuality of my own death "is structurally necessary to the pronouncing of the *I,*" so too is the eventuality, indeed the inevitability, of Jesus' death fundamental to his own identity in Mark (8:29ff.). Jesus is *je suis* without an *I,* always already written.

To be marked with the X, the cross, is painful, for *chiazein* also means "to cut." "Pronounce it *qui* or *khi,* breathing out, groaning or scraping a little, with an extra *r* in your throat, almost *cri* [cry, shout]."[108] Jesus lives by writing (*écriture*), but he dies with a terrible cry (*cri*). Another meaning of *chiasma* is

---

106. Quoted in Lacan, *Four Fundamental Concepts,* 45, emphasis mine.
107. Derrida, *Speech and Phenomena,* 96–97.
108. Derrida, *Truth in Painting,* 165.

"piece of wood." And the chiasma on which Jesus writhes is a lectern as well as a writing desk. Dying, he opens the book to Psalm 22 and reads the first verse: "My God, my God, why have you forsaken me?" *Chi,* the first letter of *Christos,* is also the twenty-second letter of the Greek alphabet.

But *chi,* as *Ich,* is also *ichthus.*[109] And *ichthus* ("fish" in Greek) was an early christological acronym: *Iēsous Christos Theou Huios Sōtēr* ("Jesus Christ Son of God, Savior"). Now, "vowels, as they are written, resemble the mouths of fish out of water pierced by the hook," as Edmond Jabès notes. And "consonants resemble dispossessed scales. They live uncomfortably . . . in their hovels of ink. Infinity haunts them."[110] It is in such a habitat that Jesus-*Ichthus* dwells: the Gospel of Mark, God's pool of muck.[111] Dragged from the muddy river in 1:10 ("and when he came up out of the water"), Jesus slithers across the surface of the text. Who can ever grasp him? Mark itself comes closest. Mark's plotlines are fishing lines, as are the lines of its page. And its genre is that of the fishing manual: "I will make you fishers of men" (1:17). Caught and taught by these fishermen, Jesus' followers will be a school of fish.

But first Jesus himself must be caught ("they . . . seized him"—14:46), and so Mark's book becomes a hook, a clawed fishhook or X. From the four sharp corners of its page Jesus-*Ichthus* dangles, gasping for air.[112] At the end of the narrative line, Jesus writhes helplessly. His tale thrashes furiously as its climax approaches. But he is not yet in the net. As fish, Jesus will never be eaten; at the Last Supper (no fish supper) wine replaces the fish of the feeding miracles (6:38, 41, 43, 8:7, 14:23–25). Jesus can only be eaten as bread. In short, Mark is a standard (ev)ang(e)ler's tale about the one that got away: "He is not here. Look, there is the place they laid him" (16:6).

Chiasma: put out its *i* and you are plunged into the darkness of a *chasma,* or "chasm," here a marine abyss. In Mark, the tomb is the most dangerous of holes. Into this hole Jesus must swim, dragging Mark's plotline with him. At precisely this point, the line breaks (off). Derrida inadvertently picks up the thread: "The volume, the scroll of parchment, was to have insinuated itself into the dangerous hole, was to have furtively penetrated into the menacing dwelling

---

109. As Derrida reminds us (*Truth in Painting,* 157). Taylor approaches it from a different angle: "While *pêche* means fishing or angling [in French], and *pêcher* is to fish for, fish up, drag out and get hold of, *péche* means sin, trespass, and transgression, and *pécher* is to sin, transgress, offend, and to be deficient" (*Altarity,* 295n52).

110. Jabès, *Book of Questions,* 68, quoted in Derrida, *Writing and Difference,* 72.

111. "It's the muddest thick that ever was heard dump" (Joyce, *Finnegans Wake,* 296.20–21).

112. To die of crucifixion was to die of asphyxia, frequently, the torso slumping forward in exhaustion until the contraction on the lungs gradually cut off respiration.

place with an animal-like, quick, silent, smooth, brilliant, sliding motion, in the fashion of a serpent or fish. Such is the anxious desire of the book."[113] In order to achieve (r)e(sur)rection and (over)come in the hole, Jesus had to adapt himself to the phallic, fishlike form of a scroll ("the Son of Man goes as it is written of him"—14:21; compare 9:12), sheets of skin glued together with blood, rolled up around a rod or backbone. His seed is deposited in the tomb (womb). It will reemerge as a codex,[114] and will be christened Mark.

Of course, he will also turn up on the communion table. "It is an attractive-looking fish," admits Lacan, "and if it is presented, as is the custom in restaurants, under a thin gauze, the raising of this gauze creates a similar effect to that which occurred at the culmination of the ancient mysteries. To be the phallus, if only a somewhat thin one."[115] Wafer-thin, as a matter of fact. Otherwise, how can it be (b)read?

"Mark the first page of the book with a red marker. For, in the beginning, the wound is invisible."[116] But by the end, the wound is festering. The *chi* cuts a deep gash in Mark, one that never closes. As we have seen, Mark holds opposites in painful tension: inside/outside, presence/absence, speech/writing. And this takes place within a book whose ending precludes its ever having been able to begin. In Mark's case there is no origin, at least no simple origin. The nonsimple origin Derrida terms the *trace*. In Greek, trace would be rendered as *ichnos: ich, chi, son*. Trace is also an anagram of *écart,* "gap" in French, and so we are thrust once more into the gap that closes this Gospel by opening it up. This gap is marked by a *gar,* Mark's last word,[117] the Greek r (*rho*) being written like our *p,* as every beginning student of Greek knows to his or her cost.

Stealing a stratagem from Heidegger,[118] Derrida puts concepts "under erasure" (*sous rature*). He crosses them out, deletes them without erasing them, as in "The Outside ✖ the Inside,"[119] for example—what better epigraph for

113. Derrida, *Writing and Difference,* 297–98.

114. "In the . . . scroll, individual papyrus sheets were glued together and rolled up on a rod. . . . In contrast, a codex was made by folding leaves, stacking them in layers, and then binding them. . . . NT manuscripts . . . are available only in codex form" (Conzelmann and Lindemann, *Interpreting the New Testament,* 18–19).

115. Lacan, *Ecrits,* 262; cf. 288.

116. Jabès, *Book of Questions,* 13, quoted in Derrida, *Writing and Difference,* 69 (translation modified).

117. " . . . for they were afraid [*ephobounto gar*]" (16:8). Marcan scholars have often debated whether or not a book can close with a *gar* (see, e.g., Horst, "Can a Book End with *gar*?"; he decides that it can).

118. See Heidegger, *Question of Being,* 80–83.

119. Derrida, *Of Grammatology,* 44.

Mark? These are concepts that are inadmissible in his text, yet indispensible to it (~~presence, being, origin~~). "I do not believe in decisive ruptures," he explains, "in an unequivocal 'epistemological break.' . . . Breaks are always, and fatally, reinscribed in an old cloth that must continually, interminably be undone."[120] This unending reinscription Derrida dubs the "structure of the *double mark*."[121] Mark breathes equivocality, speaks with two different voices, writes with two different hands, deletes without erasing, writes his entire Gospel *sous rature,* under the sign of the cross, the *chi,* the chiasmus, the mark (X). A writing that "marks and goes back over its mark with an undecidable stroke,"[122] Mark can more aptly be written ~~Mark~~.

(Mark to himself: "I write folded in two with a double, bifid, perfidious, perjuring instrument. I scratch and I erase everything with the other hand.")[123]

Faced with the mystery of Jesus, Mark can only (double) cross itself. Faced with the hit-and-misstery of exegesis, the critic can only repeat the gesture. One thing is certain, however: Mark is a cross-disciplinary text/book ("let them . . . take up their cross and follow me"—8:34), which demands a cross-disciplinary reading.

But the real double cross in Mark is the kiss that draws blood, the savage kiss of Judas that initiates Jesus' passion ("and he kissed him"—14:45), the lewd X near the end of Mark's letter. Mark writes under the sign not of one but of *three* crosses, then: the cross of Jesus, coupled with the colossal double cross of Judas. The latter looms over the story almost from the start (see 3:19), driving its action onward and bringing it to an inexorable climax (14:10–11, 18–21, 43–46). This sign of the triple cross is marked by a threefold crucifixion: "And with him they crucified two robbers, one on his right and one on his left" (15:27). Jesus' cross, soon to become a book, is placed between two cross-shaped bookends.

In short, the author of this Gospel has disseminated his autograph, his signature, (his) Mark, in the text—a name he does not yet know is his, since it will only be assigned to him posthumously. This author's real name is lost to us. Did the text deliberately drop it? Did it murder its father and bury his body in an unmarked grave, knowing that it no longer needed him? "Once it is *possible* for X to function under certain conditions (for instance, a mark in the absence . . . of [an author's present] intention), the possibility of a certain non-

---

120. Derrida, *Positions,* 24.

121. Derrida, *Dissemination,* 4, his emphasis. "Every concept necessarily receives two similar marks . . . one mark inside and the other outside the deconstructed system" (ibid.).

122. Derrida, *Positions,* 193.

123. Derrida, *The Post Card,* 143.

presence . . . pertains to the structure of the functioning under consideration, and pertains to it *necessarily.*"[124] Did this parricidal text always know itself to be the mark in Derrida's example? At first it circulated anonymously, only later revealing its self-chosen name, branding it on its forehead like the mark of Cain. This name, Mark, appears to have been pilfered from certain neighboring texts (Acts 12:12, 25, 15:37–39; 2 Tim 4:11; 1 Pet 5:13) that feature a (John) Mark who was a companion of Peter and Paul.

Did (John) Mark write the first Gospel? Most scholars today doubt that he did. However, the hypothesis that he did write it might not be altogether amiss. Like the reading that turns the fleeing young man into the author's signature, it seems to hit (the) Mark a stunning blow while missing it. And it is the striking, "other" logic of that missterious hit which fascinates me—how, flying wide, it nevertheless connects with a truth that conventional historiography would not think to target.[125] Missunderstanding's underestimated striking power has made an accurate miss-ile of an inaccurate reading, "truth . . . misfiring—sure as clockwork," as Lacan says.[126]

But just how wildly can truth misfire? "Reading a dismembered or disseminated proper name in a text can . . . be an interesting . . . exercise," Derrida confesses,

> a more or less fascinating piecing together of clues. But it can also be a total trap. In effect, once one has reconstituted, for example, the name of Francis Ponge disseminated in his text . . . perhaps one has gotten off on altogether the wrong track. And this because Francis Ponge has perhaps a secret or unconscious name which has nothing at all to do with either Francis or Ponge. Perhaps all the poetic work he does in order to mark his patronym in his text . . . is a means not only of misleading the reader or the detectives—the critical detectives—but also of losing himself.[127]

What should we conclude? That this Gospel, text, cloth, *sindōn* (see 14:51–52), covered with a profusion of scribbled Marks, is simply a cloak or cover-up

---

124. Derrida, *Limited Inc,* 57, his emphasis.

125. "The mark is hit only because one remains blind to the law of one's own address," says Barbara Johnson (*World of Difference,* 115). Blind sharpshooting is also the spectator sport of choice in Johnson, *The Critical Difference;* de Man, *Blindness and Insight;* and Felman, *Literary Speech Act.* Derrida too writes of "decrees involving *mis,*" "utterances that . . . tend to produce . . . effects often quite different from those apparently intended" (*Limited Inc,* 39).

126. Lacan, "Television," 41. Cf. "Truth Emerges from the Mistake," in Lacan, *The Seminar, Book I,* 261–72.

127. Derrida, *Ear of the Other,* 105–6, commenting on his *Signsponge*.

designed to divert our attention while the bearer of a name that we can never know loses himself—or herself—in the night? But for us the unknown name is the *public* one, whereas the *unconscious* name, planted in our text, has pushed its way up through the title page—*Kata Markon,* "[the Gospel] according to Mark." It is "as if someone would scatter seed . . . , and would sleep and rise day and night, and the seed would sprout and grow, he does not know how" (4:26–27).

One final twist. What is Derrida's term for the unconscious name that always gives the slip to the analyst? Will we be surprised to find that he calls it *the secret mark*?[128] In the patois of New Testament scholarship, *Secret Mark* is short for the *Secret Gospel of Mark,* which was discovered in the Greek Orthodox monastery of Mar Saba in the Judean desert in 1958.[129] The purpose of *Secret Mark,* according to the letter of "the most holy Clement" that frames it, is to "lead the hearers into the innermost sanctuary of the truth hidden by seven veils." *Secret Mark* is thought by some to be the parent text of *Public Mark*[130]—a parent the public Gospel would have dismembered privately, scattering the evidence throughout its own textual domain.[131]

"Silently, laboriously, minutely, obsessionally," like a thief in the night, the author of Mark has set his signatures in place. "In the morning . . . you find his name all over the place. . . . He is no longer there, but you live in his mausoleum or his latrines."[132]

(Mark to himself: "At the limit of the text, of the world, there would remain nothing more than an enormous signature, big with everything it will have engulfed in advance, but pregnant with itself alone.")[133]

The cross-stitching in this text is elaborate and delicate: from Mark, who signs his name with the sign of the cross, also the sign of erasure, to Jesus who(se name—*Je suis*) is put to death on the cross (thereby deleting the *I* it contains), through an intricate pattern of crosslike marks, crosswise fusions, and *cruces criticorum,* all enacted in the shadow of a colossal double-cross. To begin to unravel it is to take hold of an Ariadne's thread that leads not *out* of a labyrinth but *into* one.

But whose labyrinth is it?

128. Ibid., 107.

129. See Smith, *The Secret Gospel,* for details of the find. For a résumé of the controversy and debate surrounding it, see Meyer, "The Youth in the *Secret Gospel of Mark.*"

130. See, e.g, Crossan, *Four Other Gospels,* 108, and Koester, "Development of Mark's Gospel," 56. Crossan uses the term *Public Mark* of "our present canonical Mark" (98).

131. See Crossan, *Four Other Gospels,* 111.

132. Derrida, *Glas,* 41b–42b.

133. Ibid., 39b.

The Lion('s) Unconscious:

The Objest of the Pun(ch) in Exegesis

Here . . . the pun is analyzed as much as practiced.
—Jacques Derrida, "Proverb"

Midway through "Plato's Pharmacy," his reading of the *Phaedrus,* Derrida stops to ask who the owner of the many meanings coursing through its corridors might be:

> Like any text, the text of "Plato" couldn't not be involved, at least in a virtual, dynamic, lateral manner, with all the words that composed the system of the Greek language. Certain forces of association unite—at diverse distances, with different strengths and according to disparate paths—the words "actually present" in a discourse with all the other words in the lexical system. . . . The textual chain we must set back in place is thus no longer simply "internal" to Plato's lexicon. But in going beyond the bounds of that lexicon, we are less interested in breaking through certain limits . . . than in putting in doubt the right to posit such limits in the first place. In a word, we do not believe that there exists, in all rigor, a Platonic text, closed upon itself, complete with its inside and its outside. Not that one must then consider that it is leaking on all sides and can be drowned confusedly in the undifferentiated generality of its element. Rather, provided the articulations are rigorously and prudently recognized, one should simply be able to untangle the hidden forces of attraction linking a present word with an absent word in the text.[1]

Other passages could be cited which suggest that Derrida does not dispense with authorial intention altogether.[2] What *is* being called into question, how-

1. Derrida, *Dissemination,* 129–30. Parallel statements occur in *Dissemination,* 95–96, 225, and *Of Grammatology,* 158ff., 329n38; cf. *Limited Inc,* 142ff.
2. Notably, *Of Grammatology,* 158ff.

ever, is the power often attributed to authors—and nowhere more insistently than in biblical studies—to bend the language of texts to their will, to use language only and not be used by it, to keep its seething semantic potential at a controlled heat so that a unity of meaning can form in it, to prevent the text from boiling over with scalding force, spoiling the author's recipe. In response, Derrida gestures to a "structural" or textual unconscious,[3] an unpredictable and hence uncontrollable excess of meaning that simmers within any linguistic production, ever ready to spill over.

The ways into Derrida's own labyrinthine oeuvre are many—doors marked *Heidegger* ("what I have attempted to do would not have been possible without the opening of Heidegger's questions"), *Husserl* ("all of the problems worked on in [my] Introduction to [Husserl's] *The Origin of Geometry* have continued to organize the work I have subsequently attempted"), and *Hegel* ("we will never be finished with the reading and rereading of Hegel, and, in a certain way, I do nothing other than attempt to explain myself on this point").[4] A door no less serviceable, although less often used, is the one marked *Freud*.[5]

(W)RI(O)TING WITH PLATO'S POETS OUTSIDE THE CITY

[A] riot of blots and blurs and bars and balls and hoops and
wriggles and juxtaposed jottings linked by spurts of speed.
—James Joyce, *Finnegans Wake*

As the century that opened with Freud's *Interpretation of Dreams* draws to a close, Freud's message still sits undigested in our bodies of writing. "It is essential to abandon the overvaluation of the property of being conscious," wrote Freud. "The unconscious is the larger sphere, which includes within it the smaller sphere of the conscious."[6]

3. For example, in *Limited Inc*, 18, 73–74.

4. See Derrida, *Positions*, 9, "Time of a Thesis," 39, and *Positions*, 77, respectively. Then, of course, there is Nietzsche, with whom Derrida obviously identifies; see, e.g., *Of Grammatology*, 19, and *Margins of Philosophy*, 305.

5. Derrida's analyses of (with) Freud and selected Freudians begin with his 1966 essay, "Freud and the Scene of Writing," and continue in "Facteur de la vérité," "Fors," "To Speculate—on 'Freud,'" "Du Tout," "Me—Psychoanalysis," "My Chances," "Géopsychanalyse," and "Let Us Not Forget." *Ear of the Other*, "Envois," "Telepathy," and several other texts also have much on psychoanalysis.

6. Freud, *Interpretation of Dreams*, 5:612–13. Lacan, of course, agrees: "Psycho-analysis regards the consciousness as irremediably limited" (*Four Fundamental Concepts*, 82).

Derrida has been critical of certain forms of psychoanalysis.[7] But he has sought help from the Viennese doctor nonetheless. In *Of Grammatology* he wrote: "To make enigmatic what one thinks one understands by the words 'proximity,' 'immediacy,' 'presence' . . . is my final intention in this book. This deconstruction of presence accomplishes itself through the deconstruction of consciousness . . . as it appears in both Nietzschean and Freudian discourse."[8] And later: "A certain privilege should be given to research of the psychoanalytic type."[9] But if metaphysics is unable to duck out of the analyst's waiting room, neither does psychoanalysis itself escape Derrida's couch.[10]

Derrida is a stern analyst, neither "yung nor easily freudened."[11] What might he say to biblical criticism should it come to him for a consultation? What forms of analysis might it pursue? What he would *not* recommend, very likely, is that it immerse itself in psychobiography, that brand of psychoanalytic literary criticism launched by Freud himself that reads literary texts as case histories or authorial symptoms, disguised or sublimated reworkings of repressed material.[12] Psychobiography has often been applied to biblical authors, Paul in particular.[13]

In France the innovative rereading of Freud long associated with Lacan, although more recently with Derrida as well, has effected a dramatic realignment of the old Oedipal triangle of psychoanalysis, literary criticism, and literature. Pschoanalytic literary critics who take their lead from French Freud show little interest in authorial neuroses. They look to psychoanalysis not just for a new way of reading but also for a new way of writing—a reinvigorated academic writing that would take its lead from an observation implicit in early Freud[14] but neglected by Freudian literary critics, Freud himself included. "If you open a book of Freud," notes Lacan, "and particularly those books which

---

7. See, e.g., Derrida, *Of Grammatology,* 159–61, *Positions,* 107–13 (his critique of Lacan, elaborated in "Facteur de la vérité"), and "Géopsychanalyse."

8. Derrida, *Of Grammatology,* 70. Cf. Derrida, *Margins of Philosophy,* 16ff., 299ff.

9. Derrida, *Of Grammatology,* 88. Cf. ibid., 21, and Derrida, *Writing and Difference,* 230–31.

10. Cf. Derrida, *Positions,* 83–84, and *Writing and Difference,* 196–97.

11. Joyce, *Finnegans Wake,* 115.22–23.

12. Psychobiography is the term that Derrida and others use. Freud's own term, coined in his *Leonardo da Vinci,* was *pathography*.

13. Beginning with Freud's friend, Oskar Pfister, in "Entwicklung des Apostels Paulus." More recently Gerd Theissen has put Paul on the couch in his *Psychological Aspects.*

14. Most especially in the three books Lacan calls "canonical with regard to the unconscious—*The Interpretation of Dreams, The Psychopathology of Everyday Life,* and *Jokes and Their Relation to the Unconscious*" (*Ecrits,* 170).

are properly about the unconscious, you can be absolutely sure . . . to fall on a page where it is not just a question of words . . . but words which are the object through which one seeks for a way to handle the unconscious. Not even the meaning of the words, but words in their flesh, in their material aspect. A great part of the speculations of Freud is about punning in a dream, or *lapsus,* or what in French we call *calembour, homonymie,* or . . . the division of a word into many parts with each part taking on a new meaning after it is broken down."[15]

In short, the unconscious is irreducibly literary in its workings. It is a realm of metaphoric condensations, metonymic displacements, graphic images, startling associations, surrealistic spectacles, bad jokes, and Joycean multilingual puns. It is a tasteless assemblage of "alphybettyformed verbage," "messes of mottage," "quashed quotatoes," and "once current puns."[16] Elsewhere Lacan remarks, speaking in the name of that "goddess" (the unconscious) whose mystique drew the respectable Viennese professor into a scandalous, lifelong pursuit: "I wander about in what you regard as being least true in essence: in the dream, in the way the most far-fetched witticism, the most grotesque nonsense of the pun [*calembour*] defies sense, in chance, not in its law, but in its contingency. . . ."[17]

What *are* puns, and why do we belittle them?[18] Could we put the question to the Puntiff, the Puntriarch himself (Joyce, of course), how might he reply?[19] "The pun is letter-day apocalyptic," he might begin, "a quivering tic of the pen or lip, a pen or lip trick, apocalipstick." But why should it induce such apoplectic reactions? "Because its babelings illicit an epiphony of chaosmic upevil."

Imagine that you have encountered a word "in a severely impoverished context," and let that word be *God.* "It appears on a scrap of paper pushed under the door, for instance, or is spoken in a dream."[20] The word's normal range of meanings, ample but orderly, thereby broadens uncomfortably. "No longer is language's potential for semantic expansion hinted at but simulta-

15. Lacan, "Of Structure," 187.

16. Joyce, *Finnegans Wake,* 183.13, 22–23.

17. Lacan, *Ecrits,* 122, translation modified.

18. Two book-length answers to that question are now available: Culler, *On Puns,* and Redfern, *Puns.*

19. Joyce anticipated Lacan in jettisoning the notion that the workings of the unconscious are primitive. "To imitate the sophistication of word- and image-formation in the unconscious mind, he [Joyce] took settled words and images, then dismembered and reconstituted them" (Ellmann, *James Joyce,* 716).

20. Attridge, "Unpacking the Portmanteau," 142. Attridge's example is not *God,* however, but *port.*

neously kept at bay; it has become threatening and confusing. Remove even more of the context and the expansion accelerates rapidly: imagine the word being encountered by someone who knows no English, or no Indo-European language, or no human language. Eventually its meaning becomes infinite and, at exactly the same moment, disappears."[21] "God" would become everything and nothing at once.

On the brink of this I-splitting silence (cataracts of sense falling away into nonsense) the pun is s(l)i(p)tuated. Puns are slits in the great body of discourse that we erect in order to protect ourselves from the unconscious. But puns are not only the female parts of language. If on hearing a pun we groan, as we are meant to, it is because our unconscious has been stroked by the pun's (secret) point. To dismiss a pun as pointless by moaning is both to miss and to point to its other meaning. Puns babel obscenely of what they have seen: an ecstasy of meaning so immense that one could forever lose one's self in it.

To the extent that homophonic writing is writing with a point, a point that ought not to be missed, a point intended for the reader (to impale himself or herself on), it is a patriphallocentric writing. But to the extent that it is an unweaned writing, it is a writing that threatens the paternal regimen: it seeks to (re)inscribe the (M)other.[22] It is at once tormented with phallacious fantasies and (b)re(a)stless longings. Both aspects surface in Derrida's description of his dredging operation in *Glas*:

> I am seeking the good metaphor for the operation I pursue here. I would like to describe my gesture, the posture of my body behind this ma-chine. . . . I see . . . a sort of dredging machine. From the dissimulated, small, closed, glassed-in cabin of a crane, I manipulate some levers and, from afar, I saw that done at Saintes-Maries-de-la-Mer at Eastertime, I plunge a mouth of steel in the water. And I scrape the bottom, hook onto stones and algae there that I lift up in order to set them down on the ground while the water quickly falls back from the mouth.

21. Ibid.

22. Cf. Barthes, *Pleasure of the Text*: "The writer of this text employs an unweaned language" (5). It is for Hélène Cixous, however, although also for Luce Irigaray and Julia Kristeva, that the body of the mother matters most: "There is always within [woman] at least a little of that good mother's milk. She writes in white ink" (Cixous, "Laugh of the Medusa," 251). Kristeva, Irigaray, and Cixous have also addressed themselves to the Bible and/or theology (e.g., Kristeva, "Discours biblique," *Language*, 98–103, "Lire la Bible," *Powers of Horror*, 90–132, and *Tales of Love*, 83–100, 139–87, 234–63; Irigaray, *Marine Lover*, 164–90, "Equal to Whom?" "Femmes divines," "Les femmes, le sacré," and *Speculum*, 191–202; and Cixous, "Morceau de Dieu").

And I begin again to scrape, to scratch, to dredge the bottom of the sea [*mer*], the mother [*mère*]. . . .

The toothed matrix only withdraws what it can, some algae, some stones. Some bits [*morceaux*], since it bites [*mord*]. Detached. But the remain(s) [*reste*] passes between its teeth, between its lips. You do not catch the sea. She always re-forms herself.

She remains. There, equal, calm. Intact, impassive, always virgin.[23]

In Derrida's more audacious texts (paraliterary or paraphilosophical, as you prefer—*Glas* and *Signsponge*; "Envois" from *The Post Card* and its postscript, "Telepathy"; "+ R" and "Cartouches" from *The Truth in Painting*; *Dissemination*'s title piece; "Hear Say Yes in Joyce"; and so on), he would appear to be miming the movements of the unconscious, exploiting chance associations between words across several languages—associations traditional scholarship would disregard as inconsequential—performing interpretations that engage in textual congress with the *letter* of the text being read—its accidents of expression, the minutiae of its style, the look of its words as well as their sound—as opposed to the ideality of its content.[24] (Needless to say, the firm distinction of letter and idea is the first casualty of these readings.)

Apocalapse: Derrida's project in such writings can be understood in part as an attempt to extend to the domains of philosophical and critical analysis Freud's pioneering explorations of dreams, slips of the tongue and pen, lapses of memory, and all the other "accidents" of conscious life that we ordinarily shunt into the margins.[25] "The whole domain of verbal wit is put at the disposal of the dream-work," wrote Freud.[26] Why should it not be put at the disposal of academic work also? As Derrida remarks rather cruelly in *Signsponge*, "We must decide to scandalize those illiterate scientisms . . . shocked by what can be done

23. Derrida, *Glas,* 204b-205b. Hartman remarks: "It would be a vulgar though affective simplification to say that Derrida is exhibiting in *Glas* the difficulty of bringing a truly womanly speech to light" (*Saving the Text,* 82). Too vulgar for Derrida, certainly, and suspect for many feminists, yet not without a grain of truth. On Derrida and feminism, see his "Choreographies," *Spurs,* and "Women in the Beehive"; also Jardine, *Gynesis,* 178–207. "I would love to write like (a) woman. I try . . . ," Jardine quotes Derrida as saying (187n43).

24. "This is in effect a species of midrashic play," as Susan Handelman notes (*Slayers of Moses,* 170). Her thesis is that "there are striking and profound *structural* affinities between the work of some of our most influential (Jewish) thinkers like Freud, Derrida, and Bloom, and rabbinic models of interpretation" (xv, her emphasis). Others have reiterated (e.g., Faur, *Golden Doves*) or contested (e.g., Green, "Romancing the Tome") that thesis.

25. Cf. Derrida, *Writing and Difference,* 230.

26. Freud, *Interpretation of Dreams,* 5:340.

with a dictionary. . . . We have to scandalize them, make them cry out still louder—in the first place because it is fun to do so, and why deny ourselves the pleasure."[27]

Ulmer prefaces his important study of Derrida with this comment: "His detractors accuse him of superficial wordplay, and sometimes even the deconstructors consider the images and puns as nonfunctional subversion of academic conventions. What I had not expected, what in fact astonished me, is the fully developed homonymic program at work in Derrida's style, a program as different from traditional academic discourse and assumptions as it is productive in its own terms of knowledge and insight. I say I was astonished because it is one thing to engage in wordplay, but another thing to sustain it and extend it into an epistemology."[28] Derrida's principled refusal to pull his punches causes Ulmer later to announce: "The extent of his reliance on . . . puns for the generation of his strategies can never be overestimated."[29] Derrida himself would seem to agree; the dust jacket of Ulmer's book sports a glowing endorsement by him ("I read this book with recognition and admiration"). According to Ulmer, Derrida's wordplay works from the assumption "that language itself is 'intelligent,' hence that homophones 'know' something."[30] And Ulmer says of Lacan (whose late style is even more pun-ishing than Derrida's) that "he adopts a manner of speaking . . . which allows language to say what it knows."[31] "Let that be our first assignment," urges Ulmer, "to let language do some thinking for us."[32]

Such a project would entail the disorganization of a cluster of oppositions that happen—not by chance—to form the foundations of academic discourse, the discourse of biblical scholarship included: rational/irrational, intended/ unintented, essential/accidental, motivated/arbitrary, necessary/ contingent, serious/trivial, central/marginal, content/form, idea/ornament, literal/ metaphorical, primary text/secondary text, creative writing/critical writing. . . . As

27. Derrida, *Signsponge,* 120. The dictionary is the "most beautiful objest [*objeu*], made for sinking all illiterate scientisms into the greatest confusion" (42). And in *Glas:* "Thus words are unchained. They drive the dictionary wild" (8b). See too Derrida's "Proverb: 'He That Would Pun. . . .'"

28. Ulmer, *Applied Grammatology,* xi–xii.

29. Ibid., 19.

30. Ibid., 46.

31. Ibid., 201.

32. Ibid., 315. Despite its difficulty, Ulmer's is the one study of Derrida that I return to again and again. I am less convinced by Richard Rorty's elucidation of Derrida's paraliterary strategies (*Contingency, Irony, and Solidarity,* 122–37).

with all such conceptual pairs, the second term is deemed inferior to the first. These hierarchies tend to be accepted as natural and self-evident, as though they had not been established at certain junctures, as though they had no history. Frozen, reified, they paralyze thought even as they enable it. But take, for example, the exclusion of noninferential associations[33] from the Western intellectual tradition—the homonymn, homophone, or garden-variety pun. This exclusion can be traced back to such contingencies as Aristotle's strictures against homonyms,[34] and Plato's exclusion of poets from his ideal state.

For the serious scholar, puns and anagrams are jest a joke. Language should be heard and not seen. ("I have a disease," moans Barthes; "I *see* language.")[35] But it is precisely at such points that deconstruction sets up camp and begins to dig: where what is *written* (for example, "his story") is not identical to what is *heard* ("history"), where writing flaunts an excess that is irreducible to speech, and where the history that enslaves writing to the voice begins to flounder before our very eyes (history, his story, hystery, herstory, mystery, mystory . . .).[36]

Texts such as *Glas* give us a glimpse, a whiff, a taste, and a touch of an academic writing no longer fixated on the voice. (Smell, taste, and touch figure in this new writing along with sight, as we shall discover when we come to read Luke.) Homophonic and other associative clusters, moreover—recall the *chi*-cluster whose inky footprints we tracked through Mark—disrupt binary thinking. A thinking that lives in vertical, two-tiered, oppositional, hierarchical structures is necessarily unsettled by a nomad thinking that picks its steps through horizontal, single-tiered, associative, open-ended word clusters. Outside the city, with Plato's poets, on ground that academe has long deemed a swamp, there is ample room for a different academy that would house alternative approaches to reading and writing.[37] What might the city council say to a Babelian edifice in its own back yard? "Shun the Punman!" advises Shem the Penman, author of *Finnegans Wake*.[38] "What [an] institution cannot bear is for anyone to tamper with language," adds Derrida, in an essay that does just that. "It can bear more readily the most apparently revolutionary ideological sorts of

33. I borrow the term from Rorty ("Deconstruction and Circumvention," 12).

34. Cf. Derrida, *Margins of Philosophy,* 240–41, 247ff., 271.

35. Barthes, *Barthes by Barthes,* 161, his emphasis.

36. For *mystory,* see Ulmer, "Mystory" and *Teletheory,* 82ff.

37. The idea is not as utopian as it sounds. Derrida has been a coordinator of the International College of Philosophy in Paris, which fosters crossdisciplinary research in areas not accommodated in conventional curricula (see Derrida, *Du droit,* 551–618).

38. Joyce, *Finnegans Wake,* 93.13.

'content,' if only that content does not touch the borders of language and all of the juridico-political contracts that it guarantees."[39]

MARK'S NIGHTMAZE:
WRIT(H)ING ON A BED OF PAPER

And they heard a voice out of the heavens crying, "Thou
hast preached to them that sleep," and from the cross there
was heard the answer, "Yea."
—*The Gospel of Peter* 10:42

I have put the language to sleep.
—James Joyce to Samuel Beckett

What does Mark, or any other Gospel, have to do with the language of the unconscious, epitomized by the language of dreams? Quite a bit, as a matter of fact. Listen to Temma F. Berg, as she picks her way through Mark:

> At one point the text takes, for me, a peculiarly metonymic turn. Jesus has just been asked to lay hands on a little girl who is at the point of death (5:22–24), when the narrative suddenly . . . deviates to narrate a different miracle: "And there was a woman who had a flow of blood for twelve years. . . ." The text goes on to tell us that the blood stops when she touches Christ. . . . The narrative then returns to the dying girl, whom Jesus also heals: "And immediately the girl got up and walked; for she was twelve years old." What an odd placement for the statement "for she was twelve years old"! It almost seems to be brought forward as the reason for her walking. She walks because she is twelve years old. That's what twelve year olds do. But of course, she walks because she has been healed by Jesus. But, then, why bring in the detail of twelve years old? Well, I believe it has a metonymic relation to the story of the woman that interrupted the story of the girl. While the girl was twelve years old, the woman bled for twelve years. The narrative, at this point, begins to take on the qualities of a Freudian dream landscape, where linguistic logic rather than narrative logic causes things to happen.[40]

Mark's linguistic logic is capable of more involved inferences. How does language behave in dreams? Freud's *Interpretation of Dreams* spills over with

---

39. Derrida, "Living On," 94–95.
40. Berg, "Reading in/to Mark," 199–200.

dream reports and dream analyses, much in the manner of the following analysis (although it is not from Freud's dreambook but from Mary Ann Tolbert's *Sowing the Gospel,* and the narrative being analyzed is not that of a dream but that of Mark):

> The Greek word naming the curtain [of the temple], *kata*petasma (lit.: something spread out *down*), and the Greek description of the tear, ap anōtherr heōs *katō* (from top to *bottom*), in Mark 15:38 form the culmination of a whole series of plays (paronomasia) on words—mainly verbs—compounded with *kata* (down) prefixes that runs throughout the central portion of the crucifixion episode to contrast this generation's view of salvation and Jesus' view. In Mark 15:29–30, passers-by ridicule Jesus by insisting that as one who could tear *down* (*kata*luōn) the temple, he ought to be able to save himself by coming *down* (*kata*bas) from the cross. Similarly, in 15:32 the chief priests and the scribes taunt him to come *down* (*kata*batō) from the cross so they can see and believe. Even later, after Jesus' cry from the cross, bystanders hope to see divine aid in the form of Elijah take Jesus *down* (*kath*elein) off the cross in 15:36. Alternately, Jesus' own words in 15:34 question in the strongest possible way why God has left him *behind* (*egkat*elipes). . . . In the blind view of Jesus' human opponents, for him to be saved (15:30) would require that he come *down* from the cross to rejoin the human world; however, Jesus' cry implies that his heartfelt desire is to rejoin God in the divine realm instead of being left *down* here. . . . Reporting the splitting of the curtain from top to bottom (15:38) immediately after Jesus' death as the conclusion of this series of wordplays connects the tear with Jesus' cry and further supports its symbolic role as an image of transportation from realm to realm.[41]

Tolbert does not claim to be offering a psychoanalytic reading here.[42] Yet *kata*'s obsessive behaviour as she reads it, its insistent repetition and return (*kata*luōn, *kata*bas, *kata*batō, *kath*elein, *egkat*elipes, *kata*petasma, heōs *katō*), would enable it to slip unnoticed between the covers of *The Interpretation of Dreams* as yet another example of what Freud calls *displacement*—movement along an associative chain

41. Tolbert, *Sowing the Gospel,* 282. Cf. ibid., 145–46, also on Marcan wordplay. Frederick Ahl notes: "Greek and Roman writers were more sensitive to the possibilities—including what they took to be the scientific, even divine possibilities—of wordplay than we are" ("Ars Est Caelare Artem," 43). On the widespread use of wordplay in the Hebrew Bible, see Glück, "Paronomasia in Biblical Literature," and Watson, *Classical Hebrew Poetry,* 237–50.

42. Although her earlier book, *Perspectives on the Parables,* did offer a Freudian interpretation of the parable of the prodigal son (93–114).

linked by associative pathways,[43] a process he describes as "nothing less than the essential portion of the dream-work."[44]

But has Tolbert connected with Mark's conscious intentions? The deadly serious wordplay in these sentences of Holy W(r)it (which tell, after all, of an execution) should not be downplayed in our reading of them. Yet Tolbert's reading will strike some as "implausible" (wide of the evangelist's intentions)— in which case it becomes a striking disclosure of the Gospel's textual unconscious. Tolbert too will have succeeded in hitting the mark even if she has managed to miss it.

Mark's affinity with the dreamwork extends beyond local examples of linguistic logic or punning algebra. Abstract expression is alien both to the Gospel and to the dream. That the pictorial language of a Gospel is not the propositional language of a theological monograph is a truism. A Gospel is more like a dream than a dissertation. "Abstract expressions offer the same kind of difficulties to representation in dreams as a political leading article in a newspaper would offer to an illustrator," notes Freud,[45] and what is true of the illustrator and the dreamer is also true of the evangelist. Like the cartoon, the dream or Gospel must render in concrete terms a subject matter that is generally "colorless and abstract."[46] But biblical scholars and theologians are, for the most part, neither dreamers nor cartoonists, preferring to take a pneumatic drill or jackhammer to the concrete language of the Gospels, to replace graphic images with abstract categories.

A Gospel is a nocturnal writing, then. Mark is a Gospel of the dark, close kin to the oneiric writing that finds its most daring model in Joyce's *Finnegans Wake*. If Freud's *Interpretation of Dreams* is a respectable *Traumbuch, Finnegans Wake* is a see-through "nightynovel."[47] It shows that of which Freud can only tell. "One great part of every human existence is passed in a state which cannot be rendered sensible by the use of wideawake language, cutanddry grammar and goahead plot," explains Joyce.[48] And again: "In writing of the night I really could not . . . use words in their ordinary connections. Used that way, they do not express how things are in the night."[49]

---

43. A minimal definition, admittedly; see further Laplanche and Pontalis, *Language of Psychoanalysis,* 121–24.

44. Freud, *Interpretation of Dreams,* 4:308.

45. Ibid., 5:340.

46. Ibid., 5:339.

47. Joyce, *Finnegans Wake,* 54.21.

48. Joyce, *Letters,* 3:146.

49. Quoted in Ellman, *James Joyce,* 546. In *Finnegans Wake,* as in the dream, "we find

We moderns have poor night vision. We demand sharp outlines, unambiguous boundaries, plain definitions, lucid analyses, clear answers, and brilliant solutions. "But this is a vision of truth which *occludes* our experience with shadows and shades (of meaning)," as David Michael Levin argues.[50] It forgets and suppresses "a night where our vision subsides into a different logic, the intertwining of opposites, a 'confusion' of identities and difference." We tend to see "with a vision of the head, the disembodied mind, the pure intellect, reason and rationality: a vision for which the values of clarity and distinctness are supreme and exclusive; a vision of instrumentality, calculation, analysis, and power of domination; . . . a vision which happens only during the day."[51] What the glare of the Enlightenment has occluded is an unconscious knowledge whose paradigm would be our experience with the night—"an experience with absence, with fusion and indistinctness, with ambiguity, shifting boundaries, elusive and transitory presences. . . . Under the spell of the night, our vision goes *down* into the body."[52]

How are things in the *Marcan* night—a night which finds us puzzling over a linen cloth or shirt (*sindōn*—14:52) that has mysteriously appeared in our hands; a cloth or text made from linen sheets, covered with illegible writing, which later becomes a grave cloth ("he wrapped him in the linen shroud [*sindōn*]"—15:46); a text whose meaning sleeps the sleep of death between linen sheets, whose author has sunk into the ink of the text as into the darkest night?

I have tried to suggest, or rather to sketch, how things might look in such a night, a night that comes at the end of a long journey: "They were on the road, going up to Jerusalem, and Jesus was walking ahead of them; they were amazed, and those who followed were afraid" (10:32). In his dreambook, Freud tells of another road, a road that seems to me to intersect with that on which Mark's Jesus walks, so as to form a X, or cross. Freud calls it "the royal road to the unconscious."[53]

Gospels share other features in common with unconscious discourse. Like dreams, Gospels pose special problems for interpretation. The concrete word-images of which they are composed—seed, water, bread, blood—are far richer

---

associations based on homonyms and verbal similarities treated as equal in value to the rest [i.e., to rational associations]" (Freud, *Interpretation of Dreams*, 5:596). According to Suzette Henke, the *Wake* "is written 'scotographically' . . . so that a photographic 'negative' inversion of Aristotelian logic evinces a feminine semiotic discourse" (*Politics of Desire*, 189; cf. Joyce, *Finnegans Wake*, 412.3).

50. Levin, *Opening of Vision*, 351, his emphasis.

51. Ibid.

52. Ibid., 351–52, his emphasis.

53. Freud, *Interpetation of Dreams*, 5:608.

in associations than conceptual terms (evangelism, baptism, communion, redemption).[54] When our abstract conceptual language or our commonsense everyday language is displaced by a concrete pictorial language, our understanding falters, because a Gospel or a dream, never, or almost never, tells us whether its elements are to be interpreted literally or figuratively—historically (as a recollection), for example, or symbolically.[55] Generally vivid, sometimes startling, a Gospel is a postcard, a pictogram, a picture script, a picture puzzle.

THE GOSPEL IN HIEROGLYPHICS

> . . . that strange exotic serpentine, since so properly banished
> from our scripture.
> —James Joyce, *Finnegans Wake*

A dream too is a picture puzzle (*Bilderrätsel*), according to Freud.[56] As such, it can be compared to hieroglyphic writing: "The interpretation of a dream is completely analogous to the decipherment of an ancient pictographic script such as Egyptian hieroglyphics."[57] To invent a "pictographic" script fitted to the wor(l)d of print, therefore, would be to compose in the manner of a dream—or a Gospel. It would be to reinvent a script as primitive as was Freud's ascription of meaning to the dream in the first place: "Freud appeared . . . to revert to the most archaic thinking—reading something in dreams."[58]

This is where Derrida comes into the picture. In texts such as *Glas* and *Signsponge,* he has "adopt[ed] hieroglyphic writing as a model, translating it into a discourse, producing thus in philosophy distortions similar to those achieved by those movements, labeled 'cubist' and 'primitivist,' which drew on the visual arts of non-Western cultures in order to deconstruct the look of logocentrism."[59] The task is that of miming, in an alphabetized, printed script, ideographic writing, thereby reinventing academic discourse.

Regressive? Unscientific? Not necessarily. Derrida reads the triumph of

---

54. Cf. ibid., 5:340. Needless to say, the opposition concrete/conceptual, which I employ for convenience, can be deconstructed. According to Nietzsche, for example, dead concrete images lie encrypted and forgotten within every conceptual term ("On Truth and Falsity," 2:180). In "White Mythology" Derrida unpacks Nietzsche's claim and seems to want to unburden Nietzsche of his attachment to the myth of an enlightened original language (Derrida, *Margins of Philosophy,* 217ff.).

55. Cf. Freud, *Interpretation of Dreams,* 5:341.

56. Ibid., 4:278.

57. Freud, *Totem and Taboo,* 177.

58. Lacan, *The Seminar, Book I,* 1.

59. Ulmer, *Applied Grammatology,* 18.

mathematical science in our culture as a return of the repressed pictogram. As he remarked in a 1968 interview: " 'The practice of science . . . has never ceased to protest the imperialism of the *Logos,* for example by calling upon, . . . more and more, nonphonetic writing.' Everything that has always linked *logos* to *phone* has been limited by mathematics, whose progress is in absolute solidarity with the practice of a nonphonetic inscription."[60] More recent is the pictographic intersection of the visual and the verbal everywhere in evidence in our culture—in advertisements and video games, newspapers and magazines, book and record jackets, cartoons and comic strips. More recent but also more ancient. And more biblical.

Speaking on behalf of every stylist worried about his figure(s), Somerset Maugham protests: "The Bible is an oriental book. Its alien imagery has nothing to do with us. Those hyperboles, those luscious metaphors, are foreign to our genius. . . . To write good prose is an affair of good manners . . . good prose should resemble the conversation of a well-bred man"[61]—or a well-read scholar. For me, however, the task would rather be that of replying to the Gospels in kind, speaking in a related dialect, responding to a pictographic text pictographically, to a narrative text narratively, writing a critical text that is no less visceral than the text it sets out to read.

It is not that there have not been graphic readings of Mark before; there have been many, beginning with Matthew and Luke. Some of them have been more graphic even than Mark itself. Take the *Book of Kells,* for example, an illuminated copy of the four Gospels, and the most spectacular of a family of manuscripts produced in Ireland and northern Britain between the seventh and tenth centuries. Umberto Eco has described it as a work of "erudite and whimsical composition, crazy and lucid, civilized and barbaric, . . . a continuous exercise in the decomposition and rearrangement of spoken language and figurative forms."[62] Erudite but not "earudite," it is a biblical commentary that enters through the eye:

> In a total refusal of realism, there was a flowering of *entrelacs,* of highly stylized and elegant animal forms in which small, monkey-like figures appear among an incredible geometrical foliage capable of enveloping whole pages. These are not repetitions like the themes of an ornamental carpet, for every line, each corymb represents an invention, a complexity of abstract, wandering spiral forms which deliberately ignore geometrical

60. Derrida, *Positions,* 34, quoting himself; see *Of Grammatology,* 3 (cf. 9–10).
61. Undocumented quotation in Hartman, "State of the Art," 94–95.
62. Eco, *The Middle Ages,* 78.

regularity. Delicate colors fan outward from red to yellow orange, from lemon to mauve. We find quadrupeds and birds, lions with bodies of other beasts, greyhounds with swans' beaks, unthinkable humanoid figures, contorted like the circus athlete who puts his head between his knees, thereby composing the initial of a letter. Beings as malleable and foldable as colored elastic are introduced into the maze of lacing; they peek out from behind abstract decorations, twist around the capital letters, and insinuate themselves between the lines. The page no longer stops before the gaze but assumes its own life. The reader no longer succeeds in choosing a reference point. There are no boundaries between animals, spirals, and *entrelacs*; everything mixes with everything. Nonetheless, figures or hints of figures emerge from the background, and the page tells a story, an inconceivable, unreal, abstract, and above all, fable-like story composed of protean characters whose identities are continuously disappearing.[63]

Hieroglyphic writing, therefore, is not the only model for a concrete criticism. The versions of Mark and Luke sketched in my own book bear the imprint of the Kells scriptorium. Like those of the Kells illuminators, my own arabesques are designed to "conceal, embellish, and reveal a page of gospel."[64] My desire is to be an inventive copyist, able to illuminate the Gospels without the benefit of color, to inscribe elaborate and extravagent designs in their margins, to write a critical page that "no longer stops before the gaze but assumes its own life," and to heap story upon surrealistic story—"inconceivable, unreal, abstract, and above all, fable-like . . . composed of protean characters whose identities are continuously disappearing." Hence a Jesus who is a bloodstained scrap of paper one minute and a common household item (a sponge, say, or an umbrella) the next.[65] I am willing, at least for a time, to deal

63. Ibid. 78–79. Similarly, in *Finnegans Wake* characters "are fluid and interchangeable, melting easily into their landscapes to become river and land, tree and stone" (Norris, *The Decentered Universe*, 4).

64. Tindall, *A Reader's Guide,* 239. Cf. Ulmer, *Applied Grammatology,* 50–51.

65. Hence a Jesus who is the subject of further parables? Jesus' own parables transgress "the bounds of realism. Scott, Crossan, Funk . . . speak for many when they . . . point to these anomalies as keys to understanding how the parables subvert the world, undermine conventional religion, and redefine the kingdom of God in terms of everydayness, vulnerability, indeterminacy, and the picaresque" (Blomberg, "Interpreting the Parables," 52). Blomberg is referring to Scott, *Hear Then the Parable*; Crossan, *In Parables*; and Funk, *Parables and Presence*. He also invokes the Ricoeur of "Biblical Hermeneutics," who defines parable in terms of "limit language" and "extravagance."

Figure 1.   The second beginning of Matthew (*XRI h generatio,* the abbreviated form
of *Christi autem generatio*) from
the *Book of Kells,* circa eighth
century.

only marginally (in the manner of a marginal illustrator) with what the Gospels
are said to be about.

The *chi* page from the *Book of Kells* (figure 1) epitomizes the technique that
interests me. A letter *chi,* huge and swollen, is sprawled across the page.

Surrounding the curved flowing lines of this initial of Christ are all sorts of
living things. Apart from tiny human figures on the left-hand side, we can
see an otter bending down with a fish [the symbol of Jesus] in its mouth at
the bottom of the page. Near the otter, to the left, two cats sit facing each
other, with their kittens. Two have climbed on to the backs of the mother-
cats. Two are sharing the little round white disc which they nibble. This
disc, marked with a cross, suggests the sacred communion bread of the
eucharist. A butterfly with spreading wings is tucked away near the top
right-hand corner of the page. . . .[66]

How do we get from there to here? Joyce slips into the breach, showing us
how to paint in print. A facsimile of selected plates from the *Book of Kells*

66. Simms, *Book of Kells,* 50.

followed him into exile. He would pore "over its workmanship for hours," searching for new ways to write.[67] And he picked his subject matter from whatever lay ready to hand, particularly as he composed *Finnegans Wake,* "the last word in stolentelling."[68] Not surprisingly, therefore, the *Wake* contains an elaborate pastiche of Edward Sullivan's scholarly introduction to the facsimile.[69] Here, for example, is Sullivan-Joyce on the *Book of Kells*'s technique: "The curt witty wotty dashes never quite just right at the trim trite truth letter; . . . a word as cunningly hidden in its maze of confused drapery as a fieldmouse in a nest of coloured ribbons: . . . and look at this prepronominal *funferal,* engraved and retouched and edgewiped and puddenpadded, very like a whale's egg farced with pemmican, as were it sentenced to be nuzzled over a full trillion times for ever and a night till his noddle sink or swim by that ideal reader suffering from an ideal insomnia. . . ."[70] And on the manuscript's *Sitz im Leben*:

> Every person, place and thing in the chaosmos of Alle anyway connected with the gobblydumped turkery was moving and changing every part of the time: the travelling inkhorn (possibly pot), the hare and turtle pen and paper, the continually more or less intermisunderstanding minds of the anticollaborators, the as time went on as it will variously inflected, differently pronounced, otherwise spelled, changeably meaning vocable scriptsigns. No, so holp me Petault, it is not a miseffectual whyacinthinous riot of blots and blurs and bars and balls and hoops and wriggles and juxtaposed jottings linked by spurts of speed: it only looks as like it as damn it; and, sure, we ought really to rest thankful that at this deleteful hour of dungflies dawning we have even a written on with dried ink scrap of paper at all to show for ourselves, tare it or leaf it . . . after all that we lost and plundered of it, . . . cling to it as with drowning hands, hoping against hope all the while that, by the light of philophosy, . . . things will begin to clear up a bit one way or another within the next quarrel of an hour. . . .[71]

In particular, "Joyce seems to have regarded the 'TUNC' page of [the *Book of Kells*], the incredibly involved illumination of Matthew xxvii. 38 (TUNC CRU— CIFIXERANT—XPI CUM EO DU—OS LATRONES), as having special affinity with his

---

67. Ellman, *James Joyce,* 545.
68. Joyce, *Finnegans Wake,* 424.35.
69. See ibid., 107–124; and Sullivan, *Book of Kells,* 1–48.
70. Joyce, *Finnegans Wake,* 120.2–14.
71. Ibid., 118.21–119.6.

own art."[72] My own earlier, *chi*-fixated reading of the Marcan crucifixion can be read as a less ambitious paraphrase of that same *Tunc* page (figure 2), itself a rendition of Matthew's reading of Mark's interpretation of Jesus' death. On that page, Matthew's description of the crucifixion is itself affixed to a cross. "The scribe seems to feel that he should not write in straight lines as he thinks about Jesus hanging on a cross between two thieves. The words 'Christ [XPI] and with him two robbers' are shaped like a diagonal or St. Andrew's Cross. . . . This way of writing with criss-cross words makes a great impression on the reader."[73] Crisscross words for the reinscription of a crucifixion: like concrete poetry, the *Book of Kells* shows us how to write with decorative designs instead of in straight lines. It shows us the contours of an alternative mimesis bound to the shapes of words. *In our own black-and-white wor(l)d of print, the closest analogue would be the pun,* a technique no less bound to the look (and the luck) of the word.[74]

And what of the initial page of Mark's Gospel in the *Book of Kells* (figures 3 and 4), which seems to depict a lion (Mark's symbol) attempting to swallow a man? Tickle the throat of this beast with your quill until the contents of its stomach are re(gurgit)a(te)d, and you will find several motifs that today would be termed "poststructuralist."

Who is this figure in the jaws of the beast? The commentators are themselves torn. Simms thinks the man is Mark himself, who "meets the attack of [this] hostile monster by calmly holding the beast's tongue to control him."[75] Is the author under threat of death from his text, then? If so, to grasp it by the tongue, reducing it to silence, would only intensify the danger. It is precisely the text's inability to function as a simple bearer of the author's voice that has him in this quandary. To paraphrase Barthes, the birth of the reader—whose job, like the illuminator's, it is to liberate the li(o)n(e)—must be at the cost of the death of the author.[76]

---

72. Litz, *Art of James Joyce,* 98. See esp. *Finnegans Wake,* 122.22–23. Campbell and Robinson claim: "The reader of *Finnegans Wake* will not fail to recognize in this [*Tunc*] page something like a mute indication that here is the key to the entire puzzle" (*A Skeleton Key,* 103).

73. Simms, *Book of Kells,* 53. Compare the instrument of execution in Kafka's "Penal Colony" that writes the sentences of the condemned upon their bodies: "the script itself runs round the body only in a narrow girdle; the rest of the body is reserved for the embellishments" (202–3).

74. Cf. Ulmer, *Applied Grammatology,* 51: "The new mimesis . . . is based on homophonic resemblance."

75. Simms, *Book of Kells,* 68. Sullivan, followed by Henry, identifies man and beast as the evangelist and his symbol (Sullivan, *Book of Kells,* 19; Henry, *Book of Kells,* 200). Brown, who also interprets the beast as the Marcan lion, is uncommitted on the identity of the man (*Book of Kells,* 87).

76. See Barthes, "Death of the Author," 148. "A text is not a line of words releasing a single 'theological' meaning (the 'message' of the Author-God) but a multi-dimensional space" (146).

Figure 2.   Matthew 27:38 (*Tunc crucifixerant XRI cum eo duos latrones*) from the *Book of Kells*.

Figure 3.   The beginning of Mark (*Initium evangelii IHU XRI*) from the *Book of Kells*.

Figure 4.   Detail from the beginning of Mark (figure 3).

But perhaps the imperiled figure is not, or is not only, the author; perhaps it is the reader as well. Mark is a text that swallows all who advance on it, whether to tame it or to unchain it, assigning each a place in its capacious belly, as we have seen time and again. This lion does not perform for its readers; it preforms them.

And could this figure also be Jesus? Note that the figure, covered with a curious body script, is being dragged into the text not only by the lion (itself a capital letter come to life) but also by his own beard, which has elongated so as to interlace with the design of the *Initium evangelii IHU XPI.* The beginning of the Gospel of Jesus Christ: Jesus becoming writing.

As the *Book of Kells* was for Joyce, so is *Finnegans Wake* for Derrida: a model. "You stay on the edge of reading Joyce," admits Derrida, "for me this has been going on for twenty-five or thirty years—and the endless plunge throws you back onto the river-bank, on the brink of another possible immersion, *ad infinitum.*"[77] In the womb of the *Wake,* a fetal deconstruction dreams and schemes. As one (predeconstructionist) commentator put it, "*Finnegans Wake* is about *Finnegans Wake* . . . : not only about everything, the book is about putting

77. Derrida, "Two Words for Joyce," 148. *Finnegans Wake* "ends," goes underground, in mid-sentence—"A way a lone a last a loved a long the"—resurfacing in the book's opening words: "riverrun, past Eve and Adam's. . . ."

everything down in records and interpreting them. Such records, their writing, and their reading compose the book or, at least, a great part of it."[78] And later: "Mainly about itself, this book is everywhere in this book. . . . Indeed the writing, method, nature, and reception of *Finnegans Wake* seem the principal concern of *Finnegans Wake*."[79] There is nothing outside this text.

All through Derrida's edifice, the ghost of Joyce rattles his homonymic chains. "Every time I write, and even in the most academic pieces of work, Joyce's ghost is always coming on board"[80]—although Derrida has never before "dared to write *on* Joyce."[81] Derrida recalls how in his very first book, "at the very centre of [that] book," he "compared the strategies of Husserl and of Joyce: two great models, two paradigms with respect to thought, but also with respect to a certain 'operation' of the relationship between language and history. . . . Husserl proposes to render language as transparent as possible, univocal, limited to that which, by being transmittable or able to be placed in tradition, thereby constitutes the only condition of possible historicity."[82] (Parallels with the project of traditional biblical scholarship hardly need spelling out.)

The other great paradigm, for Derrida, would be the Joyce of *Finnegans Wake,* the Joyce who declared "I'm at the end of English":[83]

> He repeats and mobilizes and babelizes the (asymptotic) totality of the equivocal, he makes this his theme and his operation, he tries to make outcrop, with the greatest possible synchrony, at great speed, the greatest power of the meanings buried in each syllabic fragment, subjecting each atom of writing to fission in order to overload the unconscious with the whole memory of man: mythologies, religion, philosophies, sciences, psychoanalysis, literatures. This generalized equivocality of writing does not translate one language into another on the basis of a common nuclei of meaning . . . ; it talks several languages at once.[84]

78. Tindall, *A Reader's Guide,* 237.

79. Ibid., 258.

80. Derrida, "Two Words for Joyce," 149.

81. Ibid., 148. He has since summoned up the courage to publish *Ulysse Gramophone,* a reprint of "Deux mots pour Joyce," coupled with an essay on *Ulysses* (translated as "Hear Say Yes in Joyce").

82. Derrida, "Two Words for Joyce," 149. The book in question is Derrida's *Edmund Husserl* (see 102–3).

83. Quoted in Ellmann, *James Joyce,* 546.

84. Derrida, "Two Words for Joyce," 149. *Finnegans Wake* crops up repeatedly in Derrida's writings, e.g., "Apocalyptic Tone," 85; *Dissemination,* 88n20; *Ear of the Other,* 98–99; *The Post Card,* 142, 165, 240–41; "Scribble," 9; and "Tours des Babel," 170–71. Lacan too was intrigued by the

In the multiverse of *Finnegans Wake* the printed pages silently explode like distant stars, although with laughter. Its lines *appear* to march in standard, parallel formation, *i*'s fixed straight ahead, but in reality each line of soldiers is not marching but doing a tap dance, is not in uniform but in drag. More than a wave of sound, each line is a weave of superimposed vocables,[85] an elaborate arabesque or grotesquerie, thanks to the intricacy of the *Wake*'s punning texture, its undecorous D(o)ublin' talk, so decorative that it demands to be seen.[86]

The pictography of the Gospels is not of this sort, needless to say. Here, by and large, it is not the look of the word that counts, but the concreteness of the concept (seed, water, road, bread, blood, wine, cross). Yet the Gospel of the Lion is, in my view, eminently capable of springing in either of two directions, as are its three companions, the ox, the eagle, and the man. It can immerse itself in standard academese, a vat of paint-stripper that swiftly relieves it of its residual hieroglyphic brilliance. But what of the other possibility? One option for a concrete criticism (the one I have pursued here) would be to plant Mark's pictographic seed in the furrow of one's own text and watch its shoots push up through one's page; to press the principle of pictorial writing through to its logical or graphical conclusion; to write a Marcan criticism that is yet more Marcan (more attentive to the graphic mark) than the Gospel of the Mark itself.

Joyce's technique of "stratification," evocative of the ancient or medieval palimpsest, would offer one model for such criticism: multiple layers of meaning are superimposed, thereby producing an effect of simultaneity or many-sidedness, analogous to the sculptural image or the cubist canvas.[87] The heart of the method would consist "in talking in a certain way."[88] The line of words would become "a miner's pick, a woodcarver's gouge, a surgeon's probe," or "a

---

Wake (see, e.g., Lacan et al., *Joyce avec Lacan*, 21–67 passim), as are Cixous, Kristeva, Sollers, and other masters and mistresses of French thought (see Lernout, *French Joyce*, 41–83, 119–68). In American a/theological circles, meanwhile, Mark Taylor has loosed Derrida's reading of the *Wake* on that of Thomas Altizer (Taylor, "p.s. fin again"; Altizer, *History as Apocalypse*, 209–54).

85. Joyce: "Yes. Some of the means I use are trivial—and some are quadrivial" (quoted in Ellmann, *James Joyce*, 546). Compare the *Book of Kells*: "The most distinguishing feature of the colouring . . . is the use of several colours painted one on top of another" (Brown, *Book of Kells*, 91).

86. Cf. Heath, "Ambiviolences," 58: "This 'soundscript' is not the reproduction of speech, but the ceaseless confrontation of writing and speech." What would Joyce have said? He was tormented with eye problems as he wrote the *Wake*. Yet "there was no possibility of dictating; he must write and see what he was writing, he said" (Ellmann, *James Joyce*, 573).

87. Cubism, and modernist painting generally, deconstructed the illusion of perspective. Homophonic writing deconstructs a parallel illusion, that in which writing is conceived as stored speech and nothing more.

88. Black, *Models and Metaphors*, 229, quoted in Ulmer, *Applied Grammatology*, 201.

fiber optic, flexible as wire . . . illumin[ating] the path just before its fragile tip."[89] Obligingly, language would think for you. Reasoning would be the careful unpacking of a metaphor, argumentation the delicate unfolding of an image. The word would take the idea by the hand.[90] And such a method would have no inherent boundaries, other than the skill of the scribe.

The task as I see it, finally, is not to *immerse* the Gospel in hieroglyphics (to watch it cleave the surface of the paint at the place reserved for it, the space between the *G* and the *L*). Should the Lion and the other Gospels only choose to shake themselves, drops of technicolored hieroglyphics would fly off in every direction. Taking my (curli)cue from the anagram yet again, I would say that the task is rather one of re(in)statement: to *rel(oc)ate* the Gospel in hieroglyphics.

Concluding pro-visionally, therefore,[91] we can say that Mark is at least as close to the dreamwork, the hieroglyph, the illuminated manuscript, or the Joycean experiment as to the scholarly commentary or monograph. In consequence, Mark can just as easily be approached through a postcritical writing that would attempt to match its concrete parabolic style by miming it, as through a critical reading that, in getting Mark right (in putting down the riot), would rewrite it altogether in colorless academese.

The question remains: How can scholarly writing on the Bible be put into communication with what is said in Genesis about a God who creates the names of the first man and woman through wordplay (2:7, 23, 3:20; compare 4:1);[92] or what is said in Exodus about a God who, in displaying himself to Moses, plays on his own name (3:14ff.); or "what is said in Numbers about the parched woman drinking the inky dust of the law [5:23–24]; or what is said in Exekiel [*sic*] about the son of man who fills his entrails with the scroll of the law which has become sweet as honey in his mouth [2:8–3:3; compare Rev 10:8–10]";[93] or what is said in Matthew about a Jesus who founds his church on a pun (16:18);[94] or

89. Dillard, *The Writing Life*, 3, 7.

90. Cf. Barthes, *Barthes by Barthes*, 152. And even Aristotle: "It is metaphor which most produces knowledge" (*Rhetoric* 3.1410; cf. *Poetics* 1459a).

91. Much more could be said on poststructuralism's relationship to precritical exegesis. Such discussion usually focuses on rabbinic exegesis, Gnosticism, or Kabbalah (e.g., Handelman, *Slayers of Moses*; Faur, *Golden Doves*; Hartman and Budick, *Midrash and Literature*; Smith, "Modern Relevance of Gnosticism"; Bloom, *Agon* and *Kabbalah and Criticism*). Certain of the techniques that I employ in this book do have analogues in rabbinic exegesis, and certain of the interpretations of Jesus that I venture do have parallels in Gnosticism. But that is another story.

92. "In the beginning was the pun" (Beckett, *Murphy*, 65).

93. Derrida, *Writing and Difference*, 231.

94. Joyce: "The Holy Roman Catholic Apostolic Church was built on a pun. It ought to be good enough for me" (quoted in Ellmann, *James Joyce*, 546).

what is said in Mark about a Jesus who is both a writer and a writing, and who, in a rite, bequeaths himself to his disciples to be (eaten as b)read: "Analyze the corpus that I tender to you, that I extend here on this bed of paper"?[95]

> And as they were writing, he took papyrus, and blessed, and
> tore it, and gave it to them, and said, "Take; this is my body."
> And he took ink, and when he had given thanks he gave it to
> them, and they all drank of it. And he said to them, "This is
> my blood of the new testament, which is poured out for
> many."
> —After Mark 14:22–24

95. Derrida, The Post Card, 99.

part two

The Gospel of the Look

For I did not suppose that things gained from books would profit me so much as things gained by means of a living, surviving voice.
—Papias, as quoted in Eusebius, *Hist. Eccl.* 3.39.4

Everything we believe, we believe either through sight or through hearing. Sight is often deceived, hearing serves as guarantee.
—Ambrose of Milan, *Commentary on St. Luke* (4.5)

444

The So(u)n(d) of God

"Everything began with history and eschatology," explains François Bovon. "Luke was caught between the anvil of *redaktionsgeschichtlich* exegesis and the hammer of Bultmannian theology."[1] *Redaktionsgeschichte* was first applied to the Gospels in Germany in the 1950s. Under its influence, the evangelists ceased to be seen as mere compilers of traditional material and came instead to be seen as creative reshapers of tradition with consistent theological viewpoints of their own.[2] It spread swiftly through the international community of gospel scholars, leavening the entire lump. And although the gospel scholar's diet is now more varied than at any time in the past, redaction criticism remains the staple for most.

The Bultmannian hammer beating on Luke was wielded by Phillipp Vielhauer, Ernst Käsemann, Hans Conzelmann, and Ernst Haenchen.[3] The message it hammered out in a Pauline staccato—one for which Luke was said to have no ear—was that "the meaning of history lies always in the present," in the encounter with the kerygmatic word.[4] Bultmann himself had struck Luke a passing blow in his *Theology of the New Testament* (1948–53), accusing him of having "surrendered the original kerygmatic sense of the Jesus-tradition."[5]

1. Bovon, *Luke the Theologian,* 9.

2. See further Perrin, *What Is Redaction Criticism?* (*Redaktionsgeschichte,* lit. "redaction history," is rendered as "redaction criticism" in English.)

3. Vielhauer, " 'Paulinism' of Acts" (1950–51); Käsemann, "The Historical Jesus" (1953); Conzelmann, "Zur Lukas-Analyse" (1952), and *Theology of St. Luke* (1954); Haenchen, *Acts of the Apostles* (1955). Martin Dibelius's essays on Acts (1923–47) anticipated the approach adopted in several of these works (see his *Studies in the Acts*).

4. Bultmann, *History and Eschatology,* 155.

5. Bultmann, *Theology,* 2:117; cf. 2:116–18, 126.

An uncritical privileging of voice and presence thus attended the birth of *Redaktionsgeschichte* in Germany in the 1950s.[6] A critical interrogation of voice and presence attended the birth in France in the 1960s of what would later be called deconstruction. Heidegger was godfather at both births. He was related to redaction criticism through Bultmann, who was attempting to reinterpret the gospel message in light of early Heideggerian categories. But Heidegger was also related to deconstruction, being the father that Derrida had to slay.[7] What did the birth of deconstruction—an ill omen, as even it acknowledged, darkly styling itself a "formless, mute, infant, and terrifying form of monstrosity"[8]— portend for the future of redaction criticism? No one thought to ask at the time.

By 1961 C. K. Barrett was able to announce that "the focus of New Testament studies is now moving to the Lucan writings."[9] Prompting that move was the troubling question that Bultmann and his progeny had raised: Had Luke "spoiled" the primitive Christian kerygma—God's urgent address to humanity in the person of Jesus Christ—by de-eschatologizing it? By writing a sequel to his Gospel (the Acts of the Apostles), had Luke caused the kerygma to recede into the historical past? Had he undercut its ever-present word of salvation, its crisis-inducing call to conversion? Had he deprived it of its existential immediacy? Eschatology in Luke-Acts "no longer has the immediate effect of a summons," wrote Conzelmann in his *Theology of St. Luke*.[10] "The Eschaton no longer signifies present, but exclusively future circumstances."[11] Even the "today" of Luke 4:21—"today [*sēmeron*] this scripture has been fulfilled in your hearing"—"belongs to the past and is now described as a historical phenomenon."[12] In Luke-Acts, "instead of the nearness of [the saving] events," there is only "the Church with its permanent function."[13]

6. Preeminently in the Lucan field; yet even Willi Marxsen, putative father of Marcan redaction criticism, gives Paul—the Paul of Luther, Barth, and Bultmann—the last word: "It is important to see that Mark takes up the Pauline fundamentals" (*Mark the Evangelist,* 214–15).

7. "What I have attempted to do would not have been possible without the opening of Heidegger's questions" (Derrida, *Positions,* 9). Debt and death intermesh in *Of Spirit,* Derrida's most important study of Heidegger, which touches on the latter's relationship to Nazism.

8. Derrida, *Writing and Difference,* 293. A similarly worded "warning" occurs in *Of Grammatology,* 5. Both statements date from 1966.

9. Barrett, *Luke the Historian,* 50. Soon afterwards W. C. van Unnik declared Luke-Acts "one of the great storm centers of New Testament scholarship, second only to that of the historical Jesus" ("Storm Center," 16).

10. Conzelmann, *Theology of St. Luke,* 232.

11. Ibid., 230; cf. 97, 186. Similar complaints occur in Käsemann, "The Historical Jesus," 28, and Haenchen, *Acts of the Apostles,* 96.

12. Conzelmann, *Theology of St. Luke,* 168; cf. 170, 195.

13. Ibid., 208. Conzelmann's Luke is un-Bultmannian (and un-Barthian). For Bultmann, "the

Luke did not lack defenders, especially outside of Germany. But by the late 1970s the controversy had grown cold.[14] In 1981, Joseph A. Fitzmyer opened his magisterial commentary on Luke with an indignant defense of him against the accusations of the post-Bultmannians, but by then the jury had dispersed.[15] Lucan scholarship has since heard evidence on other important cases, such as Luke's treatment of the Jews. Its flank is still vulnerable to deconstruction, although it no longer presents its rear to the beast, red rags streaming from its pockets. But let us turn back the clock a little. It may still be possible to avert a truce.

The critical erosion of Conzelmann's landmark *Die Mitte der Zeit* (The Middle of Time), unremitting since it first appeared,[16] has yet to touch the logocentrism at its core.[17] Indeed, certain of Conzelmann's critics, far from demolishing his logocentric premises, have simply extended them instead. For me, the most interesting of these extensions or outhouses is Richard J. Dillon's *From Eye-Witnesses to Ministers of the Word,* a well-regarded study in Lucan redaction criticism, although not one that towers above the field. It is a book built over a stream, however, one in which the logocentric undertow of the post-Bultmannian current in Lucan studies finds unusually clear expression—an expression all the more striking for the fact that its author is attempting to swim against that current.

Derrida's signal gesture has been to read certain texts as symptomatic of a certain repression—"the repression of that which threatens presence and the mastering of absence."[18] Its symptom is "the metaphor of writing which haunts European discourse."[19] Later he elaborates: "One can follow the treatment accorded to writing as a particularly revelatory symptom, from Plato to Rousseau, Saussure, Husserl, occasionally Heidegger himself, and *a fortiori* in all

---

eschatological event which is Jesus Christ happens here and now as the Word is being proclaimed" (*Jesus Christ and Mythology,* 81).

14. For a blast of it at its hottest, see Kümmel, "Accusations against Luke."

15. See "The Current State of Lucan Studies" in Fitzmyer, *Luke I–IX,* 3–34.

16. Published in 1954, and translated as *The Theology of St. Luke,* it set a new agenda for Lucan scholarship, although by 1976 C. H. Talbert could write: "At present, widespread agreement [on Luke-Acts] is difficult to find, except on the point that Conzelmann's synthesis is inadequate" ("Shifting Sands," 395).

17. The term *logocentrism,* as used by Derrida, connotes "any signifying system governed by the notion of the self-presence of meaning"—for example, the "valorization of speech over writing, immediacy over distance, identity over difference, and (self-) presence over all forms of absence" (translator's note in Derrida, *Dissemination,* 4).

18. Derrida, *Writing and Difference,* 197.

19. Ibid.

the modern discourses . . . that remain within Husserl's and Heidegger's questions"—especially Heidegger's "determination of the meaning of Being as presence."[20] Do the Conzelmann tradition and its discontents[21] constitute one of these "discourses"? Poised on the threshold of a more comprehensive survey, one I shall not undertake here, this chapter will read Dillon (reading Conzelmann) reading Luke and will listen as Luke (with Derrida at his elbow) reads Dillon and Conzelmann in return.

FEAR OF WRITING

> No doubt the corpse is a signifier, but Moses's tomb is as
> empty for Freud as that of Christ was for Hegel.
> —Jacques Lacan, *Ecrits*

> . . . a crypt within . . . , partitions, hidden passages, . . . an
> internal labyrinth endlessly echoing, . . . and yet somewhere
> inside all that noise, a deathly silence, a blackout.
> —Jacques Derrida, "Fors"

> . . . *the dead time* within the presence of the living present. . . .
> The dead time is at work.
> —Jacques Derrida, *Of Grammatology*

Here is Conzelmann's reading of Luke, as Dillon reads it: "In that he allegedly stresses Jesus' deeds as objective historical verification of the divine action in him, Lk is judged to depart from the vital center of NT thought and deprive the Christian gospel of its *skandalon*."[22] Dillon disagrees. His reading of Luke's resurrection accounts precludes "attributing to the evangelist any conviction of the transparency of historical facts and deeds."[23] First, the discovery of the empty tomb (24:1–12) serves no evidential purpose. Rather, the tomb depicts the tension "between *Easter phenomena and Easter faith*."[24] It rounds off "an

20. Derrida, *Positions,* 7.

21. Dillon is not the most discontented of these—compare Gasque, *Criticism of Acts,* 291–305; cf. 246–50, 283–91.

22. Dillon, *Ministers of the Word,* 127n171; cf. viii–ix, 269–70. See Conzelmann, *Theology of St. Luke,* 202–6, and compare Bultmann's indictment of liberal Christianity: "The attempt is made to provide a basis for faith, and by this very attempt the essence of faith is destroyed" (*Glauben und Verstehen,* 1:13).

23. Dillon, *Ministers of the Word,* 127.

24. Ibid., 26, his emphasis.

observation of all the material *facta paschalia,* but after it faith is yet to be born."[25] The dialectic is one of completed observation coupled with complete misrecognition. "Peter's wonderment . . . is the 'last word' of the tomb story. . . . Standing up front at the breach between human experience and the transcendent reality of Easter . . . Peter will be the first summoned to cross it . . . (v. 34)."[26]

How can that breach be crossed? Not by sight, according to Dillon. Compare Walter J. Ong, who assigns a similar role to vision: "Vision . . . of itself manifests only surfaces, superficies, outsides."[27] For Luke, as Dillon reads him, the breach can be crossed "only under the self-disclosing word of the risen Lord."[28] And for Ong the word in general, paradigmatic of sound for the human being, "*is a special sensory key to interiority.* Sound has to do with interiors . . . which means with interiors as manifesting themselves."[29]

At issue here is the ear, the "organ that produces the effect of proximity."[30] Acclamations of sound and hearing have always echoed loudly in the "earopean" intellectual tradition.[31] The bigger the book, the greater the volume. ("Loud, hear us! Loud graciously hear us!" cries *Finnegans Wake.*)[32] The hierarchy of the senses thus established is nowhere more evident than in Hegel. Here is Derrida's précis of Hegel's exquisite thesis: "Ideal objectivity maintains its . . . integrity . . . in [not] depending on an empirical sensuous exteriority. Here, the combination of . . . two criteria [objectivity and interiority] permits the elimination of touch (which is concerned only with a material exteriority . . .), taste (a consummation which dissolves the object in the interiority), and smell (which permits the object to dissociate itself into evaporation). . . . Sight is imperfectly . . . ideal (it lets the objectivity of the object be, but cannot interiorize its sensuous and spatial opaqueness)." Derrida concludes: "Accord-

25. Ibid., 18; cf. 55–56, 58, 91, 103, 110, 114, 134–35, 197ff., 216, 217, 270, 272, 288, 292–93. Dillon takes his lead from Helmut Flender's *Heil und Geschichte* (64, 149), as he acknowledges (*Ministers of the Word,* 114n131).

26. Dillon, *Ministers of the Word,* 66.

27. Ong, *Presence of the Word,* 146.

28. Dillon, *Ministers of the Word,* 32. Cf. ibid., ix: "What Luke is not supposed to stand for: Easter revelation as the *pure gift* of God, conveyed only through the personal presence and conclusive *word of the risen Christ*" (his emphasis). Unlike Conzelmann, Dillon tends to eulogize the word (67, 127, 135, 144, 155, 197, 200, 213, 288, 292, etc.).

29. Ong, *Presence of the Word,* 117, his emphasis.

30. Derrida, *Margins of Philosophy,* xvii.

31. Joyce, *Finnegans Wake,* 598.15.

32. Ibid., 258.25–25.

ing to a metaphor well coordinated with the entire system of metaphysics, only hearing, which preserves both objectivity *and* interiority, can be called fully ideal. . . ."[33]

And what of writing? "Though serviceable and enriching beyond all measure, nevertheless, by comparison with the oral medium, writing and print are permanently decadent," writes Ong,[34] echoing Plato, Rousseau, Hegel, and a host of other writers unsettled by writing because it is external, material, and mute—but so is Luke's empty tomb. To the breathless silence of the tomb as a sign of absence, Dillon opposes "the word of the risen Lord, alive and fully present."[35]

Jesus as God's own So(u)n(d): throughout most of Western history the Son of God has been sound ("and the *logos* became flesh and lived among us"—John 1:14). What of Luke-Acts? Is it too an echosystem in which the Son reverberates as sound?[36] Does it have us by one ear, and Plato and Hegel by the other?

Two philosophies of language meet at the empty tomb. According to the first, whose emblem is the word of the risen Lord, alive and fully present, the acoustic or visual material of language, its *signifier,* is (ideally) like a transparent film over its inner meaning, over what is being *signified*. This philosophy says: "My words are 'alive' because they seem not to leave me: not to fall outside me, outside my breath, at a visible distance; not to cease to belong to me."[37] According to the second philosophy, whose emblem is the empty tomb itself, but also writing, the relationship between the signifier (here, lifeless stone) and the signified (Jesus restored to life) is arbitrary. No analogical, mimetic, necessary, or natural relationship obtains between the tomb and what it is taken to signify, between signifier and signified.[38] The transparent signifier shatters on the opacity of writing.

The fear of writing is the fear of language's otherness. It is symptomatic of another fear, loss of individual selfhood. Language, overflowing the gorges and defiles of my unconscious, has its untraceable wellsprings outside of me; my

---

33. Derrida, *Margins of Philosophy,* 93n21; cf. Hegel, *Lectures on Aesthetics,* 2:622. A similar hierarchy of the senses can be found in Kant (Derrida again provides a précis; see his "Economimesis," 19–20, 24–25). Ong ventures a less elaborate hierarchy (*Presence of the Word,* 117–18).

34. Ong, *Presence of the Word,* 138; cf. 321–22.

35. Dillon, *Ministers of the Word,* 67.

36. The French for "sound" happens to be *son*. "It has you by the ear," as Derrida might say (*Ear of the Other,* 35).

37. Derrida, *Speech and Phenomena,* 76.

38. Cf. Derrida, *Margins of Philosophy,* 84.

mother tongue is always an other's tongue. Language's alterity, ever threatening to dispossess me of my self, has its emblem in the exteriority of writing. My writing is always unmoored from me, even when it bears my signature. It begins outside me, is funneled through me, and goes on talking without me. I fade behind it and slip beneath it.[39]

The alterity of language is suppressed in Dillon's reading, at least as I read it. Cold stone offers cold comfort. The tomb, like writing, is read as a dead letter. Moreover, it is a cryptic letter, a hieroglyph etched in stone: "The women's experience at the tomb will await the . . . interpretive word of the risen Lord, without which it remains productive only of confusion."[40] Breathlessly the crypt awaits its advent. More than a dead letter, the crypt, unless spoken for, is a dead-letter office or mortuary, the cold repository of an undelivered message that might remain forever lifeless.

Then the stony silence of the tomb *is* shattered by speech—not, however, a "self-disclosing word" that is "alive and fully present" but a memo borne by two (mail)men (*andres duo*), which reads: "Why do you look for the living among the dead? . . . Remember [*mnēsthēte*] how he told you, while he was still in Galilee, that the Son of man must be handed over to sinners, and be crucified, and on the third day rise again" (24:5–7).

Mo(u)rning at the tomb ("at early dawn, they came to the tomb, taking the spices that they had prepared"—24:1). The tomb (*to mnēma*) is a place of remembrance (*mnēsthēte*), but also a place of forgetting, of repression, an unconscious vault. The women come in remembrance to the tomb only because they have forgotten (buried) what was told to them earlier: "Why do you look for the living among the dead?[41] Remember how he told you. . . ."

But what they have buried is itself a crypt, or cryptic saying (see 9:45, 18:34—"this saying was hid [*kryptō*] from them").[42] This crypt is hermetically sealed ("let us set aside the name *hermetics* to designate the science of cryptologi-

---

39. Derrida and Lacan merge in this paragraph, which they are not supposed to do, being rivals. But perhaps they were rivals because each threatened to fade into the other. A case can certainly be made for Lacan's claim that he had already said everything that Derrida set out to say (see MacCannell, *Figuring Lacan,* 20–21, 47–48, 152, 174; cf. Roudinesco, *Jacques Lacan & Co.,* 409–11).

40. Dillon, *Ministers of the Word,* 27; cf. 19–20. Interestingly for my reading of the empty tomb as writing, Dillon states that the scriptures, like the *facta paschalia,* "are not transparent to the human observer either. They too require the illuminating word of him who is their goal, the risen Saviour" (144).

41. "The inhabitant of a crypt is always a living dead" (Derrida, "Fors," xxi).

42. "Messianic *krypsis*" is Dillon's term for Jesus' unreadable passion predictions (*Ministers of the Word,* 105).

cal interpretation").[43] And it contains (the promise of) a corpse that will revive: "They will kill him, and . . . he will rise." The women are standing in an open tomb, then ("they found the stone rolled away . . . [and] they went in"). But there is a sealed crypt within *them*. In this second vault a Jesus *revenant* slumbers, waiting for the crypt to be unlocked: "Why do you look for the living . . . dead?"

The open tomb is also a mouth. The mouth that swallowed Jesus was unable to keep him down; he has risen from the belly of the earth (compare 11:29–30). The rock-hewn tomb would speak of its nausea, but its jaws are locked: rigor mortis has set in. Instead, once its stone gag is rolled away, it offers a mute sign, its own emptiness, to signify that Jesus has burst out of its body. The women, however, cannot decrypt its sign language ("they did not find his body . . . [and] were perplexed about this"—24:3–4), and so a team of interpreters is called in: "Suddenly two men . . . stood beside them" (24:4).

An empty mouth, the tomb is a void that will now be filled with words[44]— others' words, echoing words, which arouse memories of earlier words ("remember how he told you"), which themselves gestured away toward the written: "See, we are going up to Jerusalem, and everything that is written [*gegrammena*] about the Son of man . . . will be accomplished" (18:31). A place of remembrance, the tomb is an echo chamber. But recall Dillon's reading of it. If the alterity of language is indeed suppressed in his reading, then the tomb for him, as for the women, is a place of repression, of "purposeful forgetting." Freud's other term for such forgetting, as it so happens, is *cryptomnesia*.[45]

A 1986 article by Dillon, "The Prophecy of Christ and His Witnesses according to the Discourses in Acts," attempts to extend the reach of *From Eye-Witnesses to Ministers of the Word* by showing that the kerygma of Acts, "being the call to final repentence by the apostles and Paul, is really the personal prophecy of the risen Christ. This, and not some absentee Christology is authentic Lucan theory of salvation."[46] By the same token, Dillon describes the ecclesiology of Acts as "a *Christus-praesens* ecclesiology."[47] But does this *Christus-praesens* hypoth-

43. Derrida, "Fors," viv–xv.

44. Cf. ibid., xxxvii: "The mouth's empty cavity begins as a place for shouts, sobs, . . . then, gradually, . . . it tends toward 'phonic self-filling, through the . . . exploration of its own void' " (quoting Abraham and Torok, "Introjection—Incorporation," 5–6).

45. The term appears, for example, in a letter from Freud to Israel Doryon written in 1938 (quoted in Gay, *Freud,* 637n). Freud himself never forgot the crypt—he lived in one: "Look at photographs of Freud's office and note . . . the staggering number of funerary objects. . . . He hoarded them . . . to such an extent that his offices almost resemble a tomb" (Schneiderman, *Jacques Lacan,* 7).

46. Dillon, "Prophecy of Christ," 549. The "absentee Christology" goes back to Conzelmann and Haenchen.

47. Ibid., 551.

esis have a sound basis in Acts? It assuredly does, and a sentence from an earlier article by Dillon lets that sound slip out. In "Previewing Luke's Project from His Prologue" Dillon wrote: "Obviously, a story which fully told how Jesus' own words of instruction were committed to appointed witnesses (Luke 24:44–48) could effectively instill a catechumen's *asphaleia logōn* ["certainty of instruction"—Luke 1:4]. But a story which went on to document how those witnesses actually *echoed* the Master's speech in founding the churches could instill it incomparably better."[48] Yet what is an echo if not a sound that, in self-dividing, severs and distances itself from its origin? An echo is sound in flight from itself, an earwitness to that irreducible self-differing that hollows out every speech act, however immediate-seeming, the Speech Acts of the Apostles being no exception. Thus, we find ourselves in "a labyrinth which is, of course, the labyrinth of the ear. Proceed, then, by seeking out the edges, the inner walls, the passages."[49]

In Luke-Acts, the burial chamber is the engine room. It is attended by two angelic engineers assigned to explain its workings to the nonmechanically minded women. But it is also Luke-Acts' most resonant echo chamber. All its echoes lead back to scripture, as we have heard, which means that they resound with(in a) massive volume. "Hush! Caution! Echoland!" warns the *Wake*.[50] And Derrida adds: "Tympanum, . . . labyrinth, Ariadne's thread. We are now traveling through (upright, walking, dancing), included and enveloped within it, never to emerge, the form of an ear, . . . going around its inner walls."[51]

Like the linguistic signifier of which it is a token, the sepulcher in and of itself is empty, shrouded in silence, unable to speak. Its capacity to signify is solely the effect of its position in a differential weave of signifiers—which is to say, a text. And every text rewrites the epitaph of the full, simple present. "The linguistic signifier . . . is . . . incorporeal—constituted not by its material substance but by the differences that separate its sound-image from all others."[52] In any text, then (but especially in this one, a "hard text of stones covered with inscription"),[53] presence is incorporeal, a (g)host, the inhabitant of a tomb or tome, a "Real Absence."[54] In Luke's lithograph of the rock-hewn tomb (see 23:53), tomb and tome devour each other unnaturally and interminably, the *b* of tomb and the *e* of tome refusing to conjugate reproductively, refusing to form the

48. Dillon, "Previewing Luke's Project," 225, emphasis added.
49. Derrida, *Ear of the Other,* 11.
50. James Joyce, *Finnegans Wake,* 13.5.
51. Derrida, *Margins of Philosophy,* xviiin9.
52. Saussure, *Course in General Linguistics,* 164; cf. 120.
53. Derrida, *Margins of Philosophy,* 83.
54. Joyce, *Finnegans Wake,* 536.5–6.

copula. Nothing is left over that could nourish and sustain a self-disclosing, self-present word. "Why do you seek the living among the dead?"

Resisting full penetration and possession, the crypt keeps the necessity of interpretation(s) intact. Not surprisingly, this unmasterable sign of a tomb (womb), borne by women ("returning from the tomb, they told all this to the eleven and to all the rest"—24:9), is greeted as so much *lēros* (nonsense, idle talk, women's chatter) by the eleven apostles—although the disputed verse 12 does have Peter rising and rushing at the tomb in an effort to uncover and penetrate its mysteries. But all that is offered him is cloth, weave, text—the grave cloths of an already absent signified: "Stooping and looking in, he saw the linen cloths [or grave cloths—*ta othōnia*] by themselves; and he went home wondering at what had happened." What he finds is not a living word, but writing.

Dillon's reading of the risen Jesus' encounter with Cleopas and his companion on the road to Emmaus (24:13–35) is of the same weave as his reading of the empty tomb. He writes: "In the recital of empirical paschal events by Cleopas ['some of those who were with us went to the tomb and found it just as the women had said; but him they did not see'—24:24] . . . the totality of empirical observation by the travelers acts as a foil to the actual inception of their Easter faith *in verbo Domini*."[55] There is a problem, however. Although the travelers' hearts do "burn" as the stranger "opens" the scriptures to them (24:32), he is "made known to them" only "in the breaking of the bread" (24:35). Dillon counters with a detailed argument to the effect that the breaking of bread in Luke-Acts is "the normal and necessary accompaniment of . . . passion instruction, so that the two are really a *single act*."[56] Hence, as

> risen Lord, present in word and sacrament, he . . . imparts to his followers that ministry of the word which continues to unlock the secret otherwise hidden away in the sacred pages. *His voice* is what continues to be heard in that ministry of the word . . . for it is only *in personal encounter with him* . . . that the whole mystery of God's plan of salvation is opened to the eye of faith. That is . . . the teaching of the Emmaus story. *It precisely forbids any ironclad separation of the time of Jesus from the time of the Church,* as if the latter saw only an institutionalizing of what could no longer be a real presence or a living word![57]

55. Dillon, *Ministers of the Word,* 47.
56. Ibid., 154, his emphasis; cf. 105–8.
57. Ibid., 155, his emphasis. The last sentence is aimed at the Conzelmann-Haenchen stance (cf. Conzelmann, *Theology of St. Luke,* 12–17, and Haenchen, *Acts of the Apostles,* 96).

But if the breaking of bread and the passion instruction are really a single act, why does the passion instruction not occur at table in the Emmaus story? And doesn't voice appear to be subordinated to gesture in this story? "He took bread, blessed and broke it, and gave it to them. Then their eyes were opened, and they recognized him" (24:31). True, he does bless the bread. All the more telling, then, is the selective retelling, which omits the blessing, giving gesture the last word: "Then they told what had happened on the road, and how he had been made known to them in the breaking of the bread [*hōs egnōsthē autois en tē klasei tou artou*]" (24:35). How is gesture read? "Gesture is apprehended visually," observes Ong, "with a large admixture of tactile and kinesthetic awareness."[58] In the breaking of bread in our scene, hearing plays an auxiliary role ("he . . . blessed . . . it"), while taste is at least implied, as at the Last Supper (Luke 22:19; compare 9:16–17; Acts 27:35–36).

Dillon's reading of the Emmaus episode suppresses another structural feature of language—its *iterability,* which also finds its emblem in writing: "For the written to be the written, it must continue to 'act' and to be legible even if what is called the author of the writing no longer answers for what he has written, for what he seems to have signed, whether he is provisionally absent, or if he is dead, or if in general he does not support, with his absolutely current and present intention or attention, the plenitude of his meaning, of that very thing which seems to be written 'in his name.'"[59] Promiscuously capable of performing textual acts for anyone and everyone, writing belongs to no one.

Now, to read the rite of the eucharist as "an institutionalizing of what could no longer be a real presence or a living word" (à la Conzelmann)[60] is to read it as an iterable act, as an instance of *gestural writing.*[61] Dillon resists such a reading, but it slips through his defenses nonetheless. On the one hand, he subordinates the breaking of bread to the categories of voice, personal encounter, and presence ("his voice is what continues to be heard . . . it is only in personal encounter with him . . . a real presence or a living word"). At the same time, he styles the breaking of bread in Luke-Acts "the sacramental *signature* of Jesus' bequest of his . . . mission and destiny to his followers."[62]

The gestural writing that Jesus bequeaths is undoubtedly a signature. But does a signature mark a presence or an absence? "By definition, a written

58. Ong, *Presence of the Word,* 147.
59. Derrida, *Margins of Philosophy,* 316.
60. Dillon, *Ministers of the Word,* 155.
61. Cf. Derrida, *Of Grammatology,* 9: "We say 'writing' for all that gives rise to an inscription in general, . . . even if what it distributes in space is alien to the order of the voice. . . ."
62. Dillon, *Ministers of the Word,* 154, emphasis added.

signature implies the actual or empirical nonpresence of the signer. . . . In order to function, that is, in order to be legible, a signature must have a repeatable, iterable, imitable form; it must be able to detach itself from the present . . . of its production."[63] Luke's Jesus is recognized ("they recognized him"—24:31) in his signature, although only as an absent presence. With impeccable logic, the text has him "vanish out of their sight" (*aphantos egeneto ap' autōn*) in the very act of signing, before the ink has even had time to dry.

HOW (W)RITUAL ACTS:
THE LAST SUPPER AS SUPPLEMENT

> No one will ever have asked the dead person how he would
> have preferred to be eaten.
> —Jacques Derrida, "Fors"

Of course, Jesus has already signed everything over to his disciples in Jerusalem. Over the bread and wine of the Last Supper Paul has Jesus say, "Do this in remembrance of me [*touto poieite eis tēn emēn anamnēsin*]" (1 Cor 11:24–25). In Mark or Matthew, Jesus says nothing of the sort (Mark 14:22–25; Matt 26:26–29). What of Luke? "The text-critical problem involved . . . is probably the most notorious one in the entire Gospel," groans Fitzmyer, who sides with most modern authorities in allowing the words to Luke's Jesus (who utters them over the bread only).[64]

Jesus' words prompt Derrida (who seems to have come upon them neither in Luke nor in Paul but in Hegel) to ask: "What then is Jesus doing when he says while breaking the bread: take this, this is my body given for you, do this in memory of me? Why already memory in the present feeling? Why does he present himself, in the present, before the hour, as cut off from his very own body . . . ? What is he doing when he says in picking up the cup: drink all of you, this is my blood, the blood of the New Testament, . . . do this in memory of me? Think me, Jesus says to his friends while burdening their arms, in advance, with a bloody corpse. Prepare the shrouds, the bandages, the oily substance."[65]

At issue here is that duplicitous structure that Derrida elsewhere names *the supplement*. Among its ordinary senses, the term *supplement* includes two "whose

63. Derrida, *Margins of Philosophy*, 328.

64. Fitzmyer, *Luke X–XXIV*, 1387–88. He appends a bibliography of some two dozen works on the problem.

65. Derrida, *Glas*, 65a–66a. For a similar reading of the Last Supper, one that also takes its lead from Hegel, see Hamacher, "The Reader's Supper."

cohabitation is as strange as it is necessary." On the one hand, the supplement "is a surplus, a plenitude enriching another plenitude." The sum of this two-plus-two should therefore amount to "the *fullest measure* of presence."[66] "I am present to you now," says Jesus, "and thanks to this sacrament that I bequeath to you, I shall be present to you always and forever, presence heaped upon presence." But this gift has traces of poison in it, for the supplement is also an addition that replaces. It "insinuates itself *in-the-place-of*; if it fills, it is as if one fills a void," or a hole in presence. The supplement is "the mark of an emptiness."[67] Thus can Jesus present himself, in the present, before the hour, as cut off from his own body. "I am present to you now," says Jesus as he spreads himself out, a corpse, upon the table, a gesture he will repeat to infinity. For the Last Supper scene is not the last Supper seen: Last Supper, first Christian eucharist. The eucharist takes the form of a supp(l)e(menta)r(ity). And there can be no *Last* Supplement, because supplementarity, as a (w)hole, never ends. "An indefinitely multiplied structure, . . . supplementarity has always already *infiltrated* presence, always already inscribed there the space of repetition and the splitting of the self."[68] "This is my body," says Jesus (if he did), and the echo has never stopped sounding. The So(u)n(d) of God has issued from a trillion consecrated mouths, Jesus splitting and resplitting himself to infinity, an amoeba at the end of a food chain. "In certain respects, the theme of supplementarity is certainly no more than one theme among others," adds Derrida. "It is in a chain, carried by it. . . . *But it happens that this theme describes the chain itself, the being-chain of a textual chain, the structure of substitution.* . . . It tells us in a text what a text is."[69] Or it tells us in a rite what writing is.

SOUND SCHOLARSHIP

The unity of sound and of sense is indeed . . . the reassuring
closing of play.
—Jacques Derrida, *Of Grammatology*

"We shall have to approach our subject-matter systematically and methodically," cautions Dillon in his prologue to *Ministers of the Word*, "*hearing* it out

---

66. Derrida, *Of Grammatology,* 144, his emphasis.
67. Ibid., 145, his emphasis.
68. Ibid., 163, his emphasis. The supplement "*is nothing,* neither a presence nor an absence. . . . It is precisely the play of presence and absence, the opening of this play that no metaphysical or ontological concept can comprehend" (ibid., 244, his emphasis). And later: "Writing will appear to us more and more as another name for this structure of supplementarity" (ibid., 245).
69. Ibid., 163, his emphasis.

patiently on its own terms and applying to it *sound* norms of both tradition- and redaction criticism."[70] As we might expect, therefore, his reading of Jesus' resurrection appearance to the disciples cloistered in Jerusalem (24:36–53) also subordinates sight and taste to hearing:

> The invitation to physical verification in v. 39 ["touch me"]—especially if the actual display in v. 40 is genuine ["he showed them his hands and his feet"]—amounts to only a frustrated momentum in the narrative, put in check by the witnesses' reaction: *epi de apistountōn autōn ktl.* ["and while they still disbelieved," etc.] (v. 41). Nor is it correct to say that v. 41 makes the doubt persist only as a heightened threshhold for the risen One's *manducatio* ["Have you anything here to eat? They gave him a piece of broiled fish, and he . . . ate it"—v. 43], intended to be the conclusive *Identitätsbeweis.* . . . [71]

In a footnote Dillon adds: "The widespread assumption that the eating is intended as apologetic proof *ne plus ultra* . . . causes many to overlook the absence of an explicit affirmation that the disbelieving disciples were finally convinced by it. . . . Inevitably we are told that the moment of faith can be assumed after 24, 43, although Lk leaves it unspoken."[72] Here, as at the tomb and on the road to Emmaus, the dialectic of material fact versus revealed truth unfolds, "dividing [the] exhaustive but fruitless demonstration of the Master's physical reality" from "the decisive utterance of the *revealing word*."[73]

Yet the revealing word ("he opened [*diēnoixen*] their minds to understand the scriptures"—24:45) is not accompanied by an explicit affirmation that the disbelieving disciples are finally convinced. Why suppose that *this* penetration of the disciples' minds has induced climactic recognition of the risen One, given that the earlier opening of minds on the road to Emmaus ("he opened [*diēnoigen*] to us the scriptures"—24:32) induced no such recognition, which had to wait instead for the eucharistic signature (24:30–31)?

All in all, the word of the risen Lord plays a surprisingly modest role in Luke's epistemology. "Were not our hearts burning . . . while he talked to us . . . ?" say the travelers, but our author remains oddly lukewarm. Consider what the verbal

---

70. Dillon, *Ministers of the Word,* x, emphasis redistributed. Earlier he complains: "Lk 24 will not be heard out on its own terms!" (viii).

71. Ibid., 166.

72. Ibid., n28.

73. Ibid., 197, his emphasis; cf. 103.

self-disclosure of the risen Jesus amounts to. Jesus' word remains unintelligible (9:45, 18:34) until it assumes a position in a text: "These are my words that I spoke to you while I was still with you—that everything written about me in the law of Moses, the prophets, and the psalms must be fulfilled. Then he opened their minds to understand the scriptures" (24:44–45; compare 24:25–27). Jesus opens his disciples' minds not to the self-sufficiency of his word but to its intertextuality. Far from being self-evident or self-disclosing, his word signifies only in so far as it circulates through the arteries and veins of a written corpus, a body in which it constantly runs the risk of death. Acts ends with a Jesus-in-the-text once again rejected by a nation of poor readers: "From morning until evening, he explained the matter to them, . . . trying to convince them about Jesus both from the law of Moses and from the prophets" (28:23; compare 25–28).

Moreover, Jesus's eating of the broiled fish does appear to function as "the apologetic proof *ne plus ultra*" (compare Acts 1:3). As the leftovers from the disciples' supper vanish down the gullet of the risen Lord, all remaining doubt is swallowed up. The tactile ("touch me") and the gustatory ("he . . . ate before them") achieve what the visual ("terrified, [they] thought that they were seeing a ghost") and the auditory ("he said . . . 'Why are you frightened . . . ?'") could not (compare John 20:20, 27–28). Yet Dillon still has doubts: "The determining factor is *not* what human sense could perceive, but the . . . *complete self-disclosure* of the risen One: *living presence, illuminating word!*"[74] Why then do we read in Acts 10:40–41: "God raised him on the third day and made him manifest, not to all the people but to us who were chosen by God as witnesses, who *ate and drank with him* [*hoitines sunephagomen kai sunepiomen autō*] after he rose from the dead"?

Paradoxically, it may well be that the Barthian, Bultmannian legacy in Lucan studies is nowhere better attested to than in *From Eye-Witnesses to Ministers of the Word,* written although it is by a Roman Catholic priest and published by the Pontifical Biblical Institute.[75] *Ministers of the Word,* like *Die Mitte der Zeit,* is a voice recording. But where the Conzelmann tradition hears only noise and interference, Dillon hears a clear affirmation of the kerygmatic word. This suggests that he has hit *play* instead of *rewind,* but he is locked into the same recording nonetheless. He too has attempted to measure against a Western metaphysics of

74. Ibid., 200, his emphasis.

75. The institute's coat of arms, reproduced on Dillon's title page, bears the motto *Verbum Domini manet in aeternum*—a fitting motto for a book that argues "the inception of Easter faith *in verbo Domini*" (47).

voice and presence a text that, subtly or utterly, is other to such categories. The post-Bultmannian and counter-Bultmannian readings are equally earsighted.[76] Each fails to read Luke's body language. Two conflicting verdicts are delivered, but from within the confines of a single courtroom. Each exhibits sound judgment, each being the echo of the other. Each is equally the result of sound scholarship.

EAROTIC EXEGESIS:
"TO EXPOSE THIS AUTHOR'S MIND"

What can't be coded can be decorded if an ear aye seize what
no eye ere grieved for.
—James Joyce, *Finnegans Wake*

What of Lucan scholarship in general? Does it pronounce its decisions from any other bench? Luke-Acts is no longer the polemical storm center of New Testament studies. But has the preoccupation with voice and presence as the privileged loci of truth, the (blind) eye of that storm, also receded with the controversy? No, because the quest for the evangelists' intentions continues to be the linchpin of gospel studies, whether overtly, as in redaction criticism, or covertly, as in the newer literary criticism that appears to center on the text or the reader.[77] And this quest is itself motivated by a fixation with voice and presence. To search for an author's intentions is to search for an absent author, but only in order to return his textual property to him in the mint condition in which it emerged from his head ("here is your pound, which I kept laid away in a piece of cloth"—Luke 19:20–21). Derrida mimics this anxiety in *Glas*: "The work must *remain present* to the artist, without falling from him like a thing truncated in space, like some wonderful excrement on top of which the master sits enthroned."[78]

The critic, then, would be that well-meaning soul who, gingerly scooping up the masterpiece he or she has come upon, gives chase to the dead (mortified) author in order to tap him on the shoulder and say: "I think this belongs to you!" The title of Quentin Quesnell's well-known monograph, *The Mind of Mark*, would be symptomatic of this general compulsion. So too would be the

---

76. My hypothesis, one that needs further testing, is that many other vocalists are locked into this sound studio with Conzelmann and Dillon, producing ever more subtle variations on the same antiphonal refrains.

77. While still centering on the author; see my *Literary Criticism*, esp. 12, 103–4.

78. Derrida, *Glas*, 258a.

assertion of Dillon that the "cooperative responsibility" of the "international enterprise" of Lucan studies is that of "exposing this author's mind."[79] The task for these, as for the majority of biblical scholars, is to return the material text to an immaterial intentionality. But to be successful it must reduce writing to the voice.

Is the author dead or is he buried alive? Do his living words, borne by his breath, still resonate from within his tome, his tomb, his script, his crypt? The intentionality sought in the text is a ghostly or ideal quantity. And the ideality of any object "can only be expressed in an element whose phenomenality does not have worldly form. *The name of this element is the voice,*" writes Derrida. "My words are 'alive' because they seem not to leave me: not to fall outside me, outside my breath, at a visible distance, not to cease to belong to me."[80] Ulmer adds: "The special status of the voice-ear circuit . . . is that every other form of auto-affection must pass through what is outside the sphere of 'ownness' . . .— they must risk death in the body of the signifier given over to the world."[81] In other words, they must risk death in the written.

Every effort, every trial at intention-centred scholarship is held within the circuit(-court) of the voice and ear. Its decisions rest on the authority of this court. Its examinations are most often attempts to lead the material witness, the text, back to a time when it was but a thought in the mind of (an Author-)God, a time prior to the separation of its sound and its sense, the one being formed from the side of the other, condemned to live as two instead of as one, and to multiply meanings upon the surface of the text. The assumption is that the voice of the Author at the moment of creation is the unity of sound and sense in his intention. And the echoes of that now dismembered voice must be (re)collected and re-membered, and be restored to their mutilated parent. In the field(-hospital) of gospel studies, a vast team of restorative surgeons is at work.

79. Dillon, "Prophecy of Christ," 552n1. Cf. Dillon, *Ministers of the Word,* x, which outlines "the primary procedure for any student of Luke's mind to follow" and "the adequate means of access to his mind."

80. Derrida, *Speech and Phenomena,* 76, his emphasis.

81. Ulmer, *Applied Grammatology,* 52.

55

The Flavor of the Lord

O taste and see that the Lord is good!
—Psalm 34:8

The narrative line of Luke-Acts is knotted in such a way that it cannot be threaded through the ear. What does this mean for Christian theology? What does it mean, for example, that Jesus' bequest to his followers is inscribed in a *gustatory* medium—"I have eagerly desired to eat [*phagein*] this passover with you before I suffer. . . . Do this in remembrance of me" (22:15, 19)—and not only in Luke (compare Mark 14:22–25; Matt 26:26–29; 1 Cor 11:23–26; John 6:35, 48–58)?

In certain traditions (Roman Catholicism, for example), the privileged site of encounter between Jesus and the believer has been not the ear (as in most Reformed traditions) but the palate: "His body is sensually present, handled, broken, chewed."[1] Through the ages, a great mass of legendary and speculative material—mystical, arcane, alchemical—has coagulated around the ingestion and digestion of the host. As Piero Camporesi notes:

> Believers, particularly in earlier centuries, confusedly understood God's sacrifice as a prodigy of abominable grandeur, and were quite conscious of the bloody fragments of divine flesh that descended into their stomachs in the guise of the Host. . . . Both the sensibility of believers and ecclesiastic doctrine (*incruente immolatur*, according to the Tridentine canon) have over time nearly obliterated this bloody offering, anesthetizing and reducing it to little more than a symbolic act. They have edulcorated and disincarnated it, reinterpreted it merely as a trope. In other words, they have unconsciously rejected the awesome notion of transubstantiation, and have refused its intolerable weight. But the image and feeling of a bloody

1. Brown, *Love's Body*, 172; cf. 162–75 passim.

totemic rite . . . weighed on the conscience, at least until the eighteenth century, of all those who received Communion.[2]

Even as the Lord's Supper was being civilized by eighteenth-century table manners, Christian theology, Roman Catholic and Protestant, was clearing a space for itself in post-Enlightenment thought by quietly distancing itself from the crude proximity senses. The modern theologian is distinguished from his or her forebears by an increase in the propensity to think in abstractions. And "for abstract thinking," as Ong observes, "the proximity senses . . . must be minimized in favor of the more abstract hearing and sight."[3] But the more we privilege abstract thinking, the more we privilege presence along with it. For Ong, as for innumerable others, "sound and hearing have a special relationship to our sense of presence."[4]

A BOOK WITH BITE

> I would not work too hard composing the thing, it is a scrap
> copy of scrapped paths that I will leave in their hands. Certain
> people will take it into their mouths, in order to recognize the
> taste, occasionally in order to reject it immediately with a
> grimace, or in order to bite, or to swallow, in order to
> conceive, even, I mean a child.
> —Jacques Derrida, *The Post Card*

Not surprisingly, Derrida's interrogation of the metaphysics of presence is coupled with an interrogation of the abstracting senses. This is most of all evident in *Glas,* a Promethean attempt to reshuffle the sensorium so as to effect a new equilibrium in which the ordinarily excluded chemical senses of taste, touch, and smell, posed as alternative models for thinking, reading, and writing, are no longer eclipsed or drowned out by the abstracting senses of sight and hearing.[5]

2. Camporesi, "The Consecrated Host," 233–34. It was not only the ignorant who trembled. "With concern and anxiety, [medieval] theologians follow the descent of Christ's body into the *antrum,* the damp and smelly bowels" (228). Choice morsels of this often bizarre discourse are lovingly assembled by Camporesi.

3. Ong, *Presence of the Word,* 6. Cf. Freud, *Civilization and Its Discontents,* 99–100, 106, which links the privileging of the eye to the devaluation of the nose.

4. Ong, *Presence of the Word,* 130.

5. Ulmer, *Applied Grammatology,* pt. 1 ("Beyond Deconstruction"), reads *Glas,* and Derrida's oeuvre generally, in this way. Cf. Hartman, *Saving the Text,* 28: "Deconstruction may lead to a new construction, of which we are here [in *Glas*] seeing a first installment or prelude." *Saving the Text* is mainly about *Glas.* Leavey, *Glassary,* glosses *Glas* at still greater length.

Two vertical columns, each of which begins and ends in mid-sentence, split *Glas* from "beginning" to "end."[6] Each column is itself a collage of insets and contrasting typefaces. The effect is similar to a page of Talmud. The left-hand column is a "commentary" on Hegel, the philosopher of sublation, as he expostulates on such themes as Christianity, the eucharist, Judaism, and the family, all the while playing unwitting straight man to the antihero of the right-hand column, Jean Genet—novelist, thief, homosexual—whose texts provide the pretexts for *Glas*'s tasteful, often touching, sometimes smelly footnote to Western philosophy and theology.[7]

Take taste, for example. "A logical place to begin the deconstruction of the logocentric privilege of speech," observes Ulmer, "is to take note of the other function performed by the same organs that make speech possible."[8] *Glas*'s logic is impeccable in this regard. "To think being as life in the mouth, that is the *logos,*" says *Glas.*[9] But only if we approach the logos from the side of the stream of air, the invisible breath (*pneuma*), the immaterial Idea, the Spirit (also *pneuma*). *Glas* will instead think the logos from the side of the stream of saliva, approaching it not from the side of Spirit but from the side of spit, that amniotic fluid that has always sustained the logos.

And so we exit the lair of the ear to slip between the teeth: "The membranous partition that is called the soft palate, fixed by its upper edge to the limit of the vault, freely *floats,* at its lower edge, over the base of the tongue. Its two lateral edges (it has four sides) are called 'pillars.' In the middle of the floating edge, at the entrance to the throat, hangs the fleshy appendix of the uvula, like a small grape. The text is spit out. It is like a discourse whose unities are molded in the manner of an excrement, a secretion . . . saliva is the element that . . . glues the unities to one another."[10] The secret (of) sense is the secretion that makes sense—saliva, the alkaline fluid secreted by (the) gla(n)(d)s discharging into the mouth, the glue that courses through the body of the logos. But the logos also risks decapitation in the mouth that puts it together, as it negotiates the perilous passage between the teeth. The logos's compulsive movement to

6. Derrida also employs double vertical columns in "Tympan," and double horizontal columns in "Living On."

7. "What is *Glas* but the *Finnegans Wake* of philosophy?" asks Megill (*Prophets of Extremity,* 290). *Glas* can mean "death knell" (see *Glas,* 89b); thus it is but a short step from a funeral and a wake, as Derrida himself acknowledges ("Two Words for Joyce," 150).

8. Ulmer, *Applied Grammatology,* 55.

9. Derrida, *Glas,* 72a.

10. Ibid., 142b, his emphasis. Derrida's ruminations on taste continue in "Economimesis," 13–25.

the transcendental plane can always be cut off by a convulsive movement of the dental plate. Upward-thrusting logos can have its head bitten off.[11]

Fittingly, the crucifixion of the logos in John's Gospel becomes a decapitation in Jean's *Glaspel*—Genet's *Our Lady of the Flowers*:

> When Our-Lady-of-the-Flowers was given back to the guards, he seemed to them invested with a sacred character, like the kind that expiatory victims, whether goat, ox, or child, had in olden times and which kings and Jews still have today. The guards spoke to him and served him as if, knowing he was laden with the weight of the sins of the world, they had wanted to bring down upon themselves the benediction of the Redeemer. Forty days later, on a spring evening, the machine was set up in the prison yard. At dawn, it was ready to cut. Our-Lady-of-the-Flowers had his head cut off with a real knife. And nothing happened. What would be the point? There is no need for the veil of the temple to be ripped from top to bottom because a god gives up the ghost. All that this can prove is the bad quality of the cloth and its deterioration.[12]

Glas's own dental guillotine is a fitting emblem of the French revolution of the 1960s and 1970s. Derrida will later refer to *Glas* as "my apocalypse."[13] But whereas the Apocalypse of John told of an ever-living logos (see Rev 19:13), the apocalypse of Jacques tolls its death knell (*glas*). In *Glas* "there is no sign, . . . no name, and above all no 'primitive word' in the Cratylean sense."[14] In *Glas*, however, there *is*—literally—a *gl*, the headless trunk or dismembered remains of a logos.[15] "It is not a word—gl hoists the tongue but does not hold it and always lets the tongue fall back, does not belong to it. . . ."[16] Gl ascends from the g(u)l(let), but only in order to stick in the throat. It is a g(u)l(p), a "sublingual slaver,"[17] the most that *Glas*, with its salivation problem, can get out in terms of a master term. If the logos descends into the wor(l)d, it is only in order to reason, to reascend. It mediates between signifiers and signifieds. Its essence is to manifest the signified in the body of the signifier. But gl is stuck in the

---

11. "I do not cease to decapitate metalanguage, or rather to replunge its head into the text" (Derrida, *Glas*, 115b).

12. Genet, *Our Lady*, 225–26, quoted in Derrida, *Glas*, 10b.

13. Derrida, "Living On," 164; also 123, 125, 128.

14. Derrida, *Glas*, 235b.

15. Or not even that. See Derrida's comments on gl in *Truth in Painting*, 159–60, 174, and *The Post Card*, 516.

16. Derrida, *Glas*, 236b.

17. Ibid., 235b.

(under)wor(l)d. A gl(ue), a g(e)l, it gl(ut)s itself on signifiers, gl(id)ing from one to the other. It is not Homoousian but homonymic: it works by (ag)gl(utin)a-tion, (ag)gl(omer)ation, association. Its "progress is rhythmed by *little jerks, gripping and suction*,"[18] not by smooth ascent. "The glue [*colle*] of chance makes sense."[19]

The pen that writes *Glas* is dipped in heavy white ink, then—"a clot of milk in the throat, the tickled laughter or the glairy vomit of a baby glutton, . . . the gluing, frozen [*glace*], pissing cold name of an impassive Teutonic philosopher, with a notorious stammer, sometimes liquid and sometimes gutturo-tetanic, a swollen or cooing goiter, all that rings in the tympanic channel or fossa, the spit or plaster on the soft palate, the orgasm of the glottis or the uvula, the clitoral glue, the cloaca of the abortion, the gasp of sperm."[20] Gl "flows from every-where" in *Glas,* "overflows through every orifice."[21] Its polyglottal org(l)asm "tears the 'body,' 'sex,' 'voice,' and 'writing' from the logic of consciousness and representation."[22] *Glas* itself seems stuck for words in gl's none-too-solid presence: "I do not say either the signifier GL," it gulps, "or the phoneme GL, or the grapheme GL. Mark would be better, if that word were well understood, or if one's ears were open to it; not even mark then."[23]

A NEW TASTE-AMENT

> I took the little scroll from the hand of the angel and ate it.
> —Rev 10:10

> What if knowledge itself were *delicious?*
> —Roland Barthes, *The Pleasure of the Text*

Gl *could* be a mark, however—that much is admitted. And what of (a) Mark, if it were well understood ("do you not yet understand?"—8:21), if one's ears were open to it (gl must "overflow through every orifice") along with one's eyes—opened with spittle, needless to say ("he put his fingers into his ears, and he spat [*ptuō*] and touched his tongue. . . . And his ears were opened and his tongue released . . . he spat on his eyes . . . and he saw everything clearly"—7:33–35, 8:23–25; compare John 9:6)? Perhaps we should then speak not of the Gospel of

18. Ibid., 142b.

19. Ibid., 140b, repeated in 142b (and cf. Derrida, "Living On," 76). Quite by chance, *colle* is a gl word in English.

20. Ibid., 120b–21b.

21. Ibid., 145b.

22. Ibid.

23. Ibid., 119b.

Mark but of the mark of the G(ospe)l—the warm wet imprint left on our G(l)os(s)pel by the evangelist's glossal organ. The lick acts also in Luke-Acts, giving it unity. We would gloss these texts differently. We would no longer look for immaterial signifieds but would immerse ourselves in the signifying paste. We would cease to comment on Mark's sandwich technique, for example;[24] instead, we would sample his sandwiches. New meanings would be thrown up as a result. We would examine such neglected issues as (the) Spi(ir)t in Mark, in expect(or)ation of finding a solution. We would look for examples, or specimens, and run, with Jesus, the risk of acquiring them ("they . . . spat upon him"—15:19).[25] We would allow ourselves to be interrogated by Palate. We would begin the ascent—or descent—to G(o)l(gotha).

According to John D. Caputo, texts such as *Glas* represent

> in part at least the latest installment in the debate between Athens and Jerusalem, the latest and most subtle version of de-Hellenization. Deconstruction in my view is *not* the latest version of the death of God theology, a more ruthlessly atheistic theology, an atheism with a Saussurian twist, as Mark Taylor holds. It is more feasibly put to work, I suggest, in a low christology, to take but one example, a very low christology which is ruthless about the limiting, textualizing conditions from which the logos of christology tries to ascend. . . . Every time we think we are breathing the air of the living logos and are filled with the spirit, Derrida clogs our throat with the thick mucus of textuality, chokes us with the glue of glas.[26]

If text is tissue, *Glas* is fatty tissue—a text that overreads, becoming so obese that it cannot leap up to the level of the Idea. *Glas* answers Hegel with its mouth full; "Glas *ist was* Glas *isst,*" it mumbles. "*Edo ergo sum,*" it adds, and belches in Descartes' face.

---

24. A common expression for one of Mark's stylistic trademarks, that of splitting a pericope and inserting another pericope between the two halves. See, e.g., 5:21–43, 11:12–25, 14:53–72; cf. 3:19b–35, 6:7–30.

25. Spittle was highly regarded in the ancient world. See, e.g., Pliny, *Nat. Hist.* 28.4.7, Tacitus, *Hist.* 6.18, and Suetonius, *Vesp.* 7 (list from Guelich, *Mark 1–8:26,* 395). For its status in Judaism, see Strack and Billerbeck, *Kommentar zum Neuen Testament,* 2:15–17.

26. Caputo, "Derrida and Religion," 25. The issue Caputo raises with Taylor is a sticky one. In 1968 Derrida wrote: "The detours, locutions, and syntax in which I will often have to take recourse will resemble those of negative theology, occasionally to the point of being indistinguishable from negative theology" (*Margins of Philosophy,* 6; cf. Derrida, *Writing and Difference,* 297). Recently he has issued what amounts to a sixty-seven-page qualification of that statement ("How to Avoid Speaking").

It is not the only one that does. although its table manners are somewhat better than *Glas*'s, Barthes's *Pleasure of the Text* wants equally to stick in the gullet. It ends with an apocalips, saying in effect: "One who is more corpulent is coming after me." And there will be heard in its carnal style, when it appears, "the grain of the throat, the patina of consonants, the voluptuousness of vowels, a whole carnal stereophony: the articulation of the body, of the tongue."[27] Made up of "language lined with flesh," the effect of this lubricious text will be "to make us hear in their materiality, their sensuality, the breath, the gutturals, the fleshiness of the lips, a whole presence of the human muzzle."[28]

True, Barthes and Derrida mouth off in a way that the evangelists do not (as do I—people in *Glas*-houses shouldn't throw stones). But although Luke, specifically, is no *Glas*(pel), it does seem to me that the subtle body (of) knowledge *Glas* feels for, its tongue extended,[29] is somehow more in touch with Luke's epistemic accommodation of taste and touch than with the idealization of hearing, which, booming forth from Bultmann and echoing from his followers, has reverberated, sometimes deafeningly, in Lucan studies of the last half-century.

But Luke likes the look even better.

27. Barthes, *Pleasure of the Text,* 66–67.
28. Ibid. Cf. Barthes, "Grain of the Voice."
29. Its nose and its fingers also, as we shall see later.

Look-Acts:

Seeing Is Believing

On Lucan theology, Christology, soteriology, pneumatology, and ecclesiology much has been written. Lucan epistemology, by comparison, is a virginal sheet. Is this an "-ology" of which Luke is innocent? Or does Luke-Acts also contain a discourse on knowledge about knowledge—an epistemology, or theory of knowledge?

Knowledge *is* a theoretical matter in Luke-Acts. Theory stems from the verb *theōreō,* as Heidegger reminds us, in which *thea* and *horaō* have fused. "*Thea* (cf. Theatre) is the outward look, the aspect, in which something shows itself. . . . To have seen this aspect, *eidenai,* is to know." *Horaō,* the second root, means "to look at something attentively, to look it over, to view it closely."[1] Theory is looking (so as) to know, then. Let theory denote a certain look that is also (a) certain knowledge, and we are ready to look at Luke-Acts.

(RE)COGNITION/(IN)SIGHT

Caught in the act of looking: knowing glances are exchanged in Luke-Acts as the shutter slides back and the critic's eye fills the aperture. For what the critic has seen, everywhere, is people in the act of looking. Let me list some examples.

In the nativity scene, following the angelic epiphany, the shepherds say to each other: " 'Let us go . . . and see [*horaō*] this thing that has taken place. . . .' When they saw [*horaō*] it, they made known the saying which had been told them" (Luke 2:15, 17).

---

1. Heidegger, *Question Concerning Technology,* 164.

It is not the only one that does. Although its table manners are somewhat seen [*horaō*] the Lord's Christ. On seeing Jesus he declares: "Master, now you are dismissing your servant in peace . . . ; for my eyes have seen [*horaō*] your salvation . . . , a light for revelation to the Gentiles" (2:26, 29–30; compare Isa 42:6, 49:6).

Salvation is again something to see in 3:6: "And all flesh shall see [*horaō*] the salvation of God" (compare Isa 40:3–5; contrast Mark 1:2–3; Matt 3:3).

The quotation of Isaiah 61:1–2, which Luke 4:18 applies to the work of Jesus (compare 7:22; Isa 29:18, 35:6, LXX), puts sight at the center by means of a chiasmus:[2]

A   And he *stood up* to read.
  B   And there *was given* to him the book of the prophet Isaiah.
    C   He *opened the book* and found the place where it was written
      D   "The Spirit of *the Lord* is upon me, because he has anointed me
        E   *to proclaim good news* to the poor.
          F   He *has sent* me to proclaim release *to captives*
            G   and recovering of sight to the blind [*kai tuphlois anablepsin*],
          F'   to *set at liberty* those who are oppressed,
        E'   *to proclaim*
      D'   the acceptable year of *the Lord*."
    C'   And he *closed the book*,
  B'   and *gave it back* to the attendant,
A'   and *sat down*.

The call of the first disciples turns on Peter's moment of (in)sight: "But when Simon Peter saw [*horaō*] it, he fell down at Jesus' knees, saying, 'Go away from me, Lord, for I am a sinful man!' " (5:8).

John sends two disciples to Jesus with the question, "Are you the one who is to come . . . ?" Jesus replies with a spectacle—"in that hour he cured many . . . and on many that were blind he bestowed sight [*charizomai blepein*]"—and the command: "Go and tell John what you have seen [*horaō*] and heard:[3] the blind receive their sight [*anablepō*]" (7:19–23). Healing of blindness is the foremost

---

2. Here I am following Hamm, "Sight to the Blind," 458–59, who is drawing on Roland Meynet, who builds on the work of Niels Lund.

3. Cf. Matt 11:4, which has the reverse order—"what you hear and see." Verbs of seeing usually precede verbs of hearing in Luke-Acts, the principal exceptions being Luke 2:20 and Acts 8:6. Precisely because either order can be used, it is tempting to ascribe significance to the order that predominates. Note, too, Luke 5:26: "We have seen [*horaō*] strange things today"; sight displaces hearing altogether, even though Jesus has been teaching as well as healing.

clue to Jesus' identity offered here, since it is "named last in the summary of v. 21, and . . . is immediately repeated as first in the cluster of v. 22."[4]

Many of the parables peculiar to Luke pivot on a moment of recognition.[5] The parable of the two debtors, for example, coupled with Jesus' question, "Do you see [blepō] this woman?" shows the Pharisee that he has not really seen "who and what kind of woman this is" (7:36–50).

In the parable of the good Samaritan (10:30–36), the blindness of those who "pass by" ("a priest was going down . . . and when he saw [horaō] him, he passed by. . . . Likewise a Levite, when he . . . saw [horaō] him, passed by") contrasts with the (in)sight of the Samaritan, who sees the victim for the neighbor that he is: "And when he saw [horaō] him, he had compassion [splagchnizomai]" (compare 7:13).

In the parable of the prodigal son (15:11–32), the exile "comes to himself [eis heauton elthōn]" in the far country, achieves the insight that induces repentence (compare 16:23–28). As he returns home, his father sees (horaō) him and has compassion (splagchnizomai), like the Samaritan.

In 8:10 Jesus says to his disciples, "To you it has been given to know [ginōskō] the secrets of the kingdom . . . but for others they are in parables, so that 'seeing [blepō] they may not see, and hearing they may not understand' " (compare Acts 28:26–27).

On the return of the seventy (or seventy-two), Jesus again declares: "Blessed are the eyes that see [blepō] what you see [blepō]! For I tell you that many prophets and kings desired to see [horaō] what you see [blepō], but did not see [horaō] it, and to hear what you hear but did not hear it" (10:23–24). Jesus himself has seen something remarkable while they have been away: "I saw [theōreō] Satan fall like lightning from heaven" (10:18).

"Your eye is the lamp of your body," says Jesus, and elaborates at greater length than his Matthean cousin (Luke 11:34–36; compare Matt 6:22–23).[6]

The disciples' response to Jesus' second passion prediction—a prediction aimed at the ear ("let these words sink into your ears")—is couched in visual terms: "This saying . . . was concealed [parakalyptomai] from them, so that they could not perceive [aisthanomai] it" (9:44–45).

Sound is similarly rendered as sight in their response to the third passion prediction: "This saying was hid [kryptō] from them" (18:34). The healing of a

---

4. Hamm, "Sight to the Blind," 461.

5. See Nuttall, *Moment of Recognition,* 10ff.

6. A recent article begins: "For many interpreters, the several sayings about 'light' in Luke 11:33–36 are themselves a fount of darkness" (Garrett, "Lest the Light," 93).

blind man immediately follows: "Jesus said to him, 'Receive your sight [*anablepson*, only in Luke]. . . .' And immediately he received his sight and followed him, glorifying God" (18:42–43). Restored sight contrasts with the renewed blindness of the Twelve.[7]

The next pericope has Zacchaeus seeking not simply to see Jesus but to "see who Jesus is [*ezētei idein ton Iēsoun tis estin*]" (19:3). To *see* Jesus is to *know* who he is and to understand his demands. Repentance again follows (in)sight: "Look [*idou*], half of my possessions, Lord, I will give to the poor" (19:8).

As Jesus drew near to Jerusalem, "the whole multitude of the disciples began to praise God joyfully with a loud voice for all the deeds of power that they had seen [*horaō*]" (19:37).

In 19:41–44 Jesus laments the blindness of the unrepentant city: "The things that make for peace . . . are hid from your eyes [*ekrubē apo ophthalmōn sou*]." Blindness is again the privileged metaphor for ignorance: "You did not know [*ginōskō*] the time of your visitation."

In Luke, unlike Mark, it is Jesus' *look* that induces remembrance and repentance in Peter following his third denial: "The Lord turned and looked [*emblepō*] at Peter" (22:61; compare Mark 14:72).

Later, Pilate sends Jesus over to Herod. "When Herod saw [*horaō*] Jesus, he was very glad, for he had long desired to see [*horaō*] him [compare 9:9, 13:31] . . . and was hoping to see [*horaō*] him perform some sign" (23:7–8). Here, however, seeing induces no recognition, only a blindly ironic response: "They arrayed him in a splendid robe [*esthēta lampran*]."[8]

Juxtaposed with Herod's blindness is the insight of the centurion: "When the centurion saw [*horaō*] what had taken place, he praised God, and said, 'Certainly this man was innocent!' " (23:47).

"The people stood by, watching [*theōreō*]; but the leaders scoffed at him" (23:35). At Jesus' expiration, "all the crowds who had gathered there for this spectacle [*theōria*], when they saw [*theōreō*] what had taken place, returned home beating their breasts"—repentance (or its inception)[9] once again following (in)sight (23:48; compare 18:13; Acts 2:36–38). Meanwhile, "all his acquaintances, including the women who had followed him from Galilee, . . . saw [*horaō*] these things" (23:49).

Recognition on the road to Emmaus is rendered with a visual metaphor, as

7. See Fitzmyer, *Luke X–XXIV,* 1214.
8. Generally taken to mock either Jesus' kingship or his innocence.
9. So Grundmann, *Evangelium nach Lukas,* 435–36.

we have seen: "And their eyes were opened [*diēnoichthēsan hoi ophthalmoi*] and they knew [*ginōskō*] him" (24:31).[10]

Similarly, the moment some scholars would see as the climactic moment of Jesus' self-disclosure in Luke[11]—a verbal disclosure—is relayed with a visual metaphor: "Then he opened their minds [*diēnoixen autōn to noun*] to understand the scriptures" (24:45; compare 24:32). The image is that of the mind as an eye that has been blind (compare 11:34; Acts 26:18). Understanding is seen as vision.

Acts also contains some notable scenes of seeing/knowing—4:13–14, for example: "Now when they saw [*theōreō*] the boldness of Peter and John . . . they recognized [*epiginōskō*] that they had been with Jesus. But when they saw [*blepō*] the man who had been cured standing beside them, they had nothing to say in opposition." Interrogated, the pair reply: "We cannot but speak of what we have seen [*horaō*] and heard" (4:20). (Compare 2:33, in which Peter says: "Being therefore exalted at the right hand of God . . . he has poured out this which you see [*blepō*] and hear.")

The healing that got Peter and John into trouble was itself a sight to behold: "Seeing [*horaō*] Peter and John . . . he asked for alms. Peter looked intently [*atenizō*] at him, as did John, and said, 'Look [*blepō*] at us.' And he fixed his attention on them."[12] The healing ensued after which "all the people saw [*horaō*] him walking . . . and they recognized [*epiginōskō*] him as the one who used to sit and ask for alms . . . and they were filled with wonder" (3:3–10).

Stephen has a vision that proves unbearable, although not for him: "He gazed [*atenizō*] into heaven and saw [*horaō*] the glory of God and Jesus standing at the right hand of God. 'Look [*idou*],' he said, 'I see [*theōreō*] the heavens opened and the Son of Man standing at the right hand of God!' " His audience "covers their ears" to block out the vision (7:55–57).

10. Wojcik, *Road to Emmaus,* is studded with interesting observations on the visual dynamics of this episode.

11. E.g., Schubert, "Structure and Significance," 177; Lohfink, *Die Himmelfahrt Jesu,* 113–14; and Dillon, *Ministers of the Word,* 200.

12. Acts 14:9–10 may shed some light on this odd exchange of glances. There Paul heals another man "crippled from birth" after "looking intently [*atenizō*] at him and seeing [*horaō*] that he had faith to be made well." Is this why Peter and John need a better look ("look at us")? The intent gaze that is twice the prelude to healing has its counterpart in the gaze that is the prelude to punishment: "Saul . . . looked intently [*atenizō*] at him and said, 'You son of the devil' " (see Pesch, *Die Apostelgeschichte,* 1:138). Saul's perspicacity results in the benighted Elymas becoming blind: "You shall be blind and unable to see [*blepō*] the sun" (13:11).

Saul's conversion is accompanied by a symbolic passage from blindness to (in)sight: "Though his eyes were open, he could see [*blepō*] nothing. . . . For three days he was without sight"—until Ananias comes to him: "'The Lord Jesus . . . has sent me so that you may see again [*anablepō*] and be filled with the Holy Spirit.' And immediately something like scales fell from his eyes, and he saw again [*anablepō*]" (9:8–9, 17–18).

Following Elymas's symbolic blinding, "the proconsul believed when he saw [*horaō*] what had occurred" (13:11–12). (Compare 8:13: "And seeing [*theōreō*] signs and great miracles performed, he [Simon Magus] was amazed.")

In 14:11, "when the crowds saw [*horaō*] what Paul had done, they shouted in the Lycaonian language, 'The gods have come down to us in human form!'"

In 22:14–15 Paul reports that Ananias had said to him, "The God of our ancestors has chosen you to know his will, to see [*horaō*] the Righteous One and to hear his own voice; for you will be his witness to all the world of what you have seen [*horaō*] and heard."

Later Paul reports Jesus' words to him: "I have appeared to you for this purpose, to appoint you to serve and testify to the things in which you have seen [*horaō*] me and to those in which I will appear [*horaō*] to you. I will rescue you from your people and from the Gentiles—to whom I am sending you to open their eyes [*anoixai ophthalmous autōn*] so that they may turn from darkness to light" (26:16–18). We are returned to the birth stories and the salvation that will shine in the darkness (Luke 1:79, 2:30–32).

This list could, of course, be extended. But perhaps enough has been shown to enable us to see that Luke is fascinated by the "dialectic of men's ignorance and knowledge, of their blindness and the moment of recognition."[13] Let us peer more closely at some of these scenes.

GOD'S WORD-THING

Do you hear what I'm seeing . . . ?
—James Joyce, *Finnegans Wake*

The shepherds set out to "see [*horaō*] this thing that has taken place" (2:15). What they see seems unspectacular, a "child lying in a manger" (2:16), but it is a sight that has already been read for them ("this will be a sign [*sēmeion*] for you:

---

13. Nuttall, *Moment of Recognition*, 13. Hamm, "Sight to the Blind," is also very helpful on Lucan in/sight. He provides a short bibliography on the topic (457n3), to which can be added Minear, *To Heal*, esp. 40–45, and Karris, *Artist and Theologian*, 87–88, 91, 109–13, as well as the books by Nuttall and Wojcik.

you will find a child"), and with spectacular brilliance at that ("the glory of the Lord shone around them"—2:12, 9).

"Meaning is only ever erected," observes Jacqueline Rose.[14] What makes meaning erect is an act of authority, here a decree by Authority itself: the divine Author in the person of his reliable spokesman. And what the angel decrees is that the sign—the *sēmeion*—in the manger be read for what it manifestly is not (see 2:18: "And all who heard it were amazed [*ethaumasan*] at what the shepherds told them").

How does the seminar gathered around the *sēmeion* read it after the shepherds' presentation? Is Luke's sign theory, his semiology, similar to that of Plato? Recall that *thea* "is the outward look, the aspect, in which something shows itself."[15] Now, "Plato names this aspect in which what presences shows what it is, *eidos*. To have seen this aspect, *eidenai,* is to know."[16] "We, late born, are no longer in a position to appreciate the significance of Plato's daring. . . . For *eidos,* in the common speech, meant the outward aspect that a visible thing offers to the physical eye. Plato exacts of this word, however, something utterly extraordinary: that it name what precisely is not and never will be perceivable with physical eyes. For *idea* names . . . the nonsensuous aspect of what is physically visible."[17] Can Luke's *sēmeion* then be read as an allegory of Plato's boldest gesture—*eidos* as outward appearance transparent on *eidos* as idea (whatever it is the shepherds have seen that those who are amazed have not)? God's messianic power (see 1:32–33, 35, 43, 2:11) present in the powerless infant? The senses displaced by the sense? The *sēmeion* would then be a metaphysical ideogram, *eidos* as outward aspect (*physikos*) pointing beyond (*meta*) to *eidos* as idea.

But Luke's Semitic *sēmeion* (compare Exod 3:12; 1 Sam 2:34, 14:10; 2 Kgs 19:29, 20:9; Isa 37:30, 38:7) would hardly be content with this Platonic relationship to meaning. In the Septuagint, the Greek translation of the Hebrew scriptures, whose style Luke's birth stories emulate, *sēmeion* usually translates '*ôth,* the Hebrew word for "sign." K. H. Rengstorf notes: "From a whole series of sayings which contain '*ôth* it may be gathered with certainty that what is denoted thereby can be perceived with the senses and is often meant to be so. As a rule the reference is to visual perception."[18] Should Luke's *sēmeion* be seen as an '*ôth,* then?

To see is indeed to know in the nativity scene—but only if one has first heard

14. Introducing Lacan, *Feminine Sexuality,* 43.

15. Heidegger, *Question Concerning Technology,* 164.

16. Ibid.

17. Ibid., 20.

18. Rengstorf, "*Sēmeion,*" 211.

a word that doubles as a *thing,* a word one sees as well as hears: "Let us go over to Bethlehem and see this *rhēma* that has happened, which the Lord has made known to us" (2:15). *Rhēma* usually means "word" (compare 1:38, 2:17). But in the Septuagint (where it often translates *dābār*), *rhēma* can also mean "thing," "matter," or "deed."[19] Like the word (*logos*) of logocentric metaphysics, the *rhēma* to be heard at Bethlehem is a word that lives and breathes. It is a "child lying in a manger" (2:16). But unlike that aerated logos, the *rhēma* is something to see: "Let us go and see this word-thing."

Luke's ideology finds its natural support in this logos capable of being seen (*idein*). "What we call ideology is precisely the confusion of linguistic and natural reality," writes de Man.[20] The effect of the *rhēma* is rhetorical, then: to (con)fuse "the materiality of the signifier with the materiality of what it signifies."[21]

The confusing logic of this uncommonly sensible *logos* is further glossed by Jean-Joseph Goux: "If the signifier *stands for* the thing, in simple equivalence, it is because it *is* the thing itself. Here the signifier appears to refer neither to an ideal signified nor even, beyond the signified, to the absent thing: it is a *double* of the thing, with the same properties, powers, faculties."[22] Goux is speaking here of a primitive mode of signifying that shades over into magic. And the fusion characteristic of this mode of signifying is also characteristic of the unconscious.

Israel's Messiah is indeed a dream child. "Words are often treated as things in dreams," observes Freud.[23] Into the hole that gapes between words and things, a word-thing is inserted by divine fiat. The shepherds see it clearly. Can they also hear, touch, and smell it? Later, others will taste it: "This is my body." Possibly it dreams of what it already is: "Even the . . . simplest dreams of the child . . . show miraculous or forbidden objects."[24]

This *rhēma* will not be mute for long. It is ripe with the promise of speech. The flesh of the signifier undulates to the breath of the signified. Contrast this ripening word with the husk of the empty tomb: "When they went in, they did not find the body" (24:3). Alien to a metaphysics of the voice (sense present to

19. "This is a deed that speaks," says Brown (*Birth of the Messiah,* 405). According to Plummer, *logos* in classical Greek can also denote "deed" or "thing," although he lists only one example, Hdt. 1.21.2 (*St. Luke,* 59).

20. De Man, *Resistance to Theory,* 11.

21. Ibid.

22. Goux, *Symbolic Economies,* 173, his emphasis.

23. Freud, *Interpretation of Dreams,* 5:603. Cf. Abraham and Torok, *Wolf Man's Magic Word,* 46: "It is a word that operates only from the Unconscious, that is, as a *word-thing.*"

24. Lacan, *Ecrits,* 263.

sound in speech), the empty tomb signifies absence as the condition of life. It is a hieroglyph etched in stone. Goux's remarks are again apposite: "The *glyph* is sacred, the signifier of a mystery that it manifests but does not elucidate or articulate; it is the indecipherable, *enigmatic* sign of a hierarchically superior, overwhelming meaning; like an intercessor, it bears eternal witness to the impenetrability of a transcendent generative mystery, which it signifies in a cryptophoric rather than a metaphoric way, since it cannot reflect this mystery."[25] The tomb is such a cryptophor.

The crib is the reliquary of a phantasmic word-thing. It is attended by interpreters who are custodians of the authoritative reading: "They made known what had been told them about this child" (2:17). The crypt, in contrast, contains no-thing: the absent object of desire ("he is not here"—24:5). It is attended by garden-variety interpreters who have no choice but to read. The women and Peter are presented with a text more cryptic than swaddling clothes (compare 2:12), the grave cloths empty of their expected contents ("looking in, he saw the linen cloths by themselves"—24:12). One *sēmeion* has been displaced by another (compare 11:30). Each is material, each maternal. The first was phantasmic, barely conceivable: " 'You will conceive in your womb and bear a son. . . .' Mary said . . . , 'How can this be, since I do not know man?' The angel said to her, ' . . . nothing will be impossible with God.' Then Mary said, ' . . . let it be done unto me according to your *rhēma*' " (1:30–38). The second is the sign of an open crypt that keeps the necessity of reading alive, precisely because it resists penetration and possession. It is the emblem of writing, as we have seen. Sarah Kofman observes: "Writing, that form of disruption of presence, is, like the woman, always put down and reduced to the lowest rung ['these (women's) words seemed to them an idle tale, and they did not believe them'—24:11]. Like the feminine genitalia, it is troubling, petrifying—it has a Medusa effect."[26] An open script, itself made of stone, the crypt petrifies all the apostles except Peter: "But Peter rose and ran to the tomb. . . ." He comes to violate a sepulcher, but is brought up short by an inscription in stone. Even he will turn back troubled, his tail (limp) between his legs: "He went home wondering at what had happened" (24:12).

So Peter goes away hungry. He has come to feast with his eyes, but his teeth have shattered on the stone. He can be compared to the lost explorer who strays into Derrida's "Fors": "I am thinking (detached illustration) of the paleontologist standing motionless, suddenly, in the sun, bewitched by the delicate stay of

25. Goux, *Symbolic Economies,* 171, his emphasis.
26. Kofman, "Un philosophe 'unheimlich,' " 125–26.

a word-thing, an abandoned stone instrument, like a tombstone burning in the grass, the double-edged stare of a two-faced Medusa.

"And then I can feel, on the tip of my tongue, the angular cut of a shattered word."[27]

LUKE, LOOK, LACK, LACAN

> . . . the gaping chasm of castration.
> —Jacques Lacan, "Names-of-the-Father"

Let us turn to another of the birth stories, the presentation of Jesus in the temple. It has been revealed to Simeon "by the Holy Spirit that he should not see [horaō] death before he [has] seen [horaō] the Lord's Christ" (2:26). Immediately upon seeing and handling the Christ, however ("he took him in his arms"), Simeon *is* ready to see death: "Now you may release [apolyō] your slave, Master . . . ; for my eyes have seen [horaō] your salvation" (2:29–30).[28]

(Simeon's desire for Jesus: "All of a sudden . . . the small volume was there, on the table, I didn't dare touch it . . . for a long time I believed that I would not be given the thing, that I would be forever separated from it. . . . I wound up spreading the pages while holding the bound cover in both hands. I didn't know where to start reading, looking, opening. . . . It would be good if I died tonight . . . after having seen the thing at the end of the race.")[29]

But what exactly has Simeon seen that so spectacularly effects his release?

Let Lacan take Simeon aside for a moment. Meanwhile, a partial recital of the Lacanian myth of origins will be in order. Lacan himself shied away from such recitals. "My discourse proceeds in the following way," he said; "each term is sustained only in its topological relation with the others."[30] Each circles the others like the elements of a mobile. Attempts at a Lacanian summa abound, nonetheless.[31] "Their interest will be that they transmit what I have said literally," he said, "like the amber which holds the fly so as to know nothing of

27. Derrida, "Fors," xlviii.

28. In the Septuagint, *apolyō* is a euphemism for the release of death, e.g., Gen 15:2; Num 20:29; Tobit 3:6, 13 (see Brown, *Birth of the Messiah,* 439; Fitzmyer, *Luke I–IX,* 428). Salvation is also "seen" in Ps 97 [98]:3; Isa 40:5, 52:10; Bar 4:24.

29. Derrida, *The Post Card,* 208–10. Of course, Simeon is not the speaker in Derrida's text.

30. Lacan, *Four Fundamental Concepts,* 89.

31. Lemaire's *Jacques Lacan* was the first, although Ragland-Sullivan's *Jacques Lacan* is the most exhaustive to date.

its flight."[32] Discarding our flyswatter if not our amber, let us hazard a few remarks on this firefly.

For Lacan, cutting into the Freudian corpus with instruments forged in a bewildering variety of workshops—philosophy and anthropology, linguistics and semiotics, psychiatry and psychology, mathematics and theology, literature, painting, sculpture—the human subject is irremediably split, barred from symbiotic union with the mother through being inserted into a symbolic order (sociocultural, linguistic), whose first "thou shalt not" is the prohibition of such (con)fusion. To refuse to tie this symbolic (k)not is to risk psychosis. Henceforth the subject's primordial desire—to be the sole desire of the (M)Other—will be deflected through an interminable chain of substitutions, none of which can ever stop up that hole in being, that lack, or want-to-be (manque-à-être). Lacan terms this lack castration, after Freud. It is not, however, a threatening sword of Damocles hovering over the male subject only, but the constitutive condition of *every* subject, male or female, who accedes to the symbolic order. And Lacan terms the agent of castration the Name-of-the-Father, the symbolic locus of the Law's emphatic No (non/nom du père).[33]

How does Lacan's myth of human origins relate to the Lucan myth of Jesus' origins? Jesus' subjection to his Father (see 2:49) is inaugurated by a symbolic castration ("at the end of eight days . . . he was circumcised"—2:21) and completed by his consecration in the temple. Moreover, it is to the *Law* of the Father that Jesus is made subject; note the insistent repetition of the term *nomos* ("law") in the passage—an insistence all the more striking for the fact that "there was . . . no Mosaic or customary requirement that parents present their first-born in the Temple."[34]

When the time came for their purification according to the law [kata ton nomon] of Moses, they brought him up to Jerusalem to present him to the Lord (as it is written in the law of the Lord [kathōs gegraptai en nomō kyriou],

---

32. Lacan, "Preface," xv. Attempts to capture Lacan in flight include Felman, *Jacques Lacan;* Gallop, *Reading Lacan;* and MacCannell, *Figuring Lacan.* The most readable (i.e., anecdotal) books on Lacan are Clément, *Lives and Legends,* and Schneiderman, *Jacques Lacan,* but for the official court history see Roudinesco, *Jacques Lacan & Co.* On Lacan and literary theory, see Davis, *Lacan and Narration.* On Lacan and religion, see Wyschogrod et al., *Lacan and Theological Discourse*; Taylor, *Altarity,* 83–113; and "Applying Lacan: Religion," pt. 5 of Hogan and Pandit, *Criticism and Lacan.*

33. "It is in the *name of the father* that we must recognize the support of the symbolic function which, from the dawn of history, has identified his person with the figure of the law" (Lacan, *Ecrits,* 67, his emphasis; cf. 199, 310–11).

34. Esler, *Community and Gospel,* 112.

"Every firstborn male shall be designated as holy to the Lord"), and they offered a sacrifice according what is stated in the law of the Lord [*kata to eirēmenon en tō nomō kyriou*], "a pair of turtledoves or two young pigeons" . . . and when the parents brought in the child Jesus, to do for him what was customary under the law [*kata to eithismenon tou nomou*], Simeon took him in his arms. . . . When they had finished everything required by the law of the Lord [*kata ton nomon kyriou*], they returned into Galilee . . . [2:22–24, 27–28, 39].

It is to the "so shall you do" that the social is due. Jesus is a subject, then,[35] but is he more? His accession to the Law of the Father coincides with Simeon's release: "Now you may release your slave [*doulos*], Master" (2:29). How is this release to be read? As a release from desire, Simeon's desire regaining in a glance the lost object for which it has always looked ("my eyes have seen your salvation"—2:30)?[36] Can the look in Luke repair the lack, Lac(k)an notwithstanding? What if the object of the look were himself to lack being (*manque-à-être*, the Lacanian lacuna), were himself a Son of Man(que) who required regular injections of meaning from some outside supplier (God, the Holy Spirit, angelic interpreters, scripture)? What if he were himself subject to the desire of the Other ("I came to bring fire to the earth, and how I wish [*ti thelō*] it were already kindled! I have a baptism with which to be baptized; and how I am constrained [*synechomai*] until it is accomplished!"—12:49), the desire of the Other displacing his own desire ("Father, if you are willing [*ei boulei*] . . . ; yet, not my will [*to thelēma mou*] but yours be done"—22:42; compare 23:46)?[37]

Jesus' hole in being, however, does not prevent him from filling a phallic position in Luke-Acts, from being erected by acts of authority (see 4:32, 36, 5:24, 6:5, 19, 7:7–8, 8:25, 10:17–19, 19:37, 20:2ff., 21:27, 22:69) and by order of the Father (see 3:22, 4:43, 9:35, 10:22, 11:20, 20:13, 22:29) to the position of master of the house and overseer of the Father's business ("Did you not know

35. It has been suggested that the title Son of God, as used in the New Testament, "essentially implies [Jesus'] obedience to the Father" (Cullmann, *Christology*, 270). Fitzmyer adds that this is especially true of Luke, for it is as Son that Jesus is tempted in that Gospel (4:3, 9; see Fitzmyer, *Luke I–IX*, 208).

36. Cf. Nolland, *Luke 1–9:20*, 119: "This patient slave . . . is now being released by his Master . . . from his duty as watchman . . . , because the goal of his watching is now accomplished."

37. Here, the desire of the Other bespeaks a lack in the Other also. What is specific to the Judeo-Christian tradition, in Lacan's view, is that unlike most Eastern religious traditions it turns not on God's "bliss" but on his desire ("Names-of-the-Father," 89–90; cf. *Le Séminaire, livre III*, 323ff.).

that I must be in my Father's house / about my Father's business [*en tois tou patrou mou*]?"—2:49).[38] Significantly, it is Luke's leading female character, Jesus' mother, who is the main beneficiary of this lesson in home management (2:48, 51). The Father has handed Jesus a blade on the assumption that he knows what to do with it (" 'Your mother and your brothers are standing outside, desiring [*thelontes*] to see you.' But he said . . . , 'My mother and my brothers are those who hear the word [*logos*] of God and do it' "—8:20–21; compare 2:35).

Simeon's "cure" contrasts interestingly with that of Simon. Lacan remarks: "When I speak to you of the unconscious . . . you may picture it to yourselves as a *hoop net* . . . at the bottom of which the catch of fish will be found."[39] The scene of (self-)recognition centered on the marvelous catch of fish (5:1–11) is the scene of analysis. On Jesus' advice, Simon "put[s] out into the deep [*epanagō eis to bathos*] and let[s] down [his] nets for a catch." The result is traumatic, dreamlike: "When they had done this, they caught so many fish that their nets were beginning to break. So they signaled their partners in the other boat to come and help them. And they came and filled both boats, so that they began to sink." Ordinarily the unconscious announces itself in the *lapsus,* the slip. So this slithering morass must have been all but screaming at Simon. But it is a silent scream, a written communiqué: it presents itself as something to be read ("when Simon Peter saw [*horaō*] it"). Faced with the subaqueous representatives of his own unconscious writ(h)ing grotesquely in the analytic net (compare 2:35: "the inner thoughts of many will be revealed"), Simon yields his own soft underbelly to the analyst's knife, lets himself be cleaned like a fish, spills his guts at the analyst's feet ("he fell down at Jesus' knees, saying, 'Go away from me, Lord, for I am a sinful man!' "). Filleted, Simon is forced to acknowledge that he too is a split subject. But only that he might better serve as bait. "From now on you will be taking human beings alive [*anthrōpous esē zōgrōn*]," Jesus reassures him.

In Acts the therapy continues. Simon Peter must decipher yet another manifestation of his own unconscious writ(h)ing: "He fell into a trance [*ekstasis*]. He saw the heaven opened and something like a large sheet coming down. . . . In it were all kinds of four-footed creatures and reptiles and birds of the air" (10:11–12). His cure is effected only as he accepts the "unclean thing" ("I heard a voice saying to me, 'Get up, Peter; kill and eat.' But I replied, 'By no means,

---

38. Or "I must be among those who belong to my Father," a less frequent translation. Some scholars (de Jonge, Weinert) are driven to opt for polyvalence here (see Brown, *Birth of the Messiah,* 475–77, or Nolland, *Luke 1–9:20,* 131–32, for a résumé).

39. Lacan, *Four Fundamental Concepts,* 143–44, his emphasis.

Lord; for nothing profane [*koinon*] or unclean [*akatharton*] has ever entered my mouth' "—11:7–8). The "unclean thing" is uncircumcision (see 11:3), the obverse of that arbitrary cut which forms the precarious basis of his own self-identity. This is the "bloody scrap" that Lacan speaks of, become, impossibly, "the signifier of signifiers."[40] For Peter to accept that the other is *not* cut, or rather, that he or she is cut differently, is to accept the contingent character of his own cut. Only then can he be in a position to "take [the other] alive," to let him or her be in his or her difference.

Let us return to Simeon's phantasmic scene of recognition and to Jesus' parents, who listen in amazement, lacking the (in)sight able to penetrate the body of the sign ("this child is destined . . . to be a sign [*sēmeion*]," says Simeon, and she who is unable to pierce the phallic signifier will herself be run through with it—2:34–35). In contrast, Anna, herself a devotee of desire ("she never left the temple but worshiped there with fasting and prayer night and day"), "coming up at that very hour," sees whatever it is that Simeon has seen: "She began to praise God and to speak about the child to all who were looking for the redemption of Jerusalem" (2:36–38).[41]

Two kinds of reader are contrasted in this reading lesson. The parents of Jesus, although eager for what "is written in the law of the Lord" (2:23), are unable to decipher the script that is their son. Literal readers, they skid on the surface of the text. They are foils for Simeon and Anna, ironic readers for whom the surface of the *sēmeion* is in any case immaterial, since it is transparent on a signified that lights it up from within ("a light [*phōs*] for revelation to the Gentiles"—2:32; compare 11:36). To see (*idein*) and to know (*eidenai/gnōnai*) is to read (*anagnōnai*) as pre-scribed. Such is Luke's reading theory (*theōrein*). But there is more.

THE SUN OF GOD

> And ceaselessly Thou didst hit the weakness of my sight with
> the violence of Thy light-rays upon me, and I trembled with
> love and horror.
> —St. Augustine, *Confessions* L.VII, C.X., 16

40. Lacan, *Ecrits,* 265. Furthermore, what Peter's *ekstasis* has exposed him to is that dangerously pleasurable threat to selfhood that Lacan terms *jouissance*—a hard-to-translate term whose nearest English equivalent is "ecstasy."

41. Exactly what all these observers, here and in the crucifixion scene (23:47–49), are seeing is not altogether clear. Cf. Tiede, *Prophecy and History,* 115.

I could not see because of the brightness of that light.
—Acts 22:11

. . . the greatest light is also, is it not, the source of all
obscurity.
—Jacques Lacan, *The Seminar, Book I*

To read Luke-Acts is to exegete a sequence of entextualized events. The reader's performance interlocks with that of the participants in the story, including those who "know how to interpret [*dokimazein*] the appearance of earth and sky" but "not . . . how to interpret the present time" (12:56). Interpretation of this crucial time (the time of the cross) is the critical role that character and reader share and that links them across the chasm (compare 16:26) that otherwise divides them, joining the time of crisis to the time of criticism, transferring a crucial urgency to the critical task ("everyone who does not listen to that prophet shall be destroyed"—Acts 3:23; compare Luke 13:1–5). Luke's privileged signifier, the "sign that is spoken against," or violently misread, "is destined for the fall and the rising of many" (2:34). Indeed, he himself is set to fall *upon* many. Like the "rock-hewn tomb" (23:53) that crushes the hopes of his followers (see 24:31), Jesus is himself a shattering-stone: "Everyone who falls on that stone [*lithos*] will be broken to pieces; but it will crush anyone on whom it falls" (20:18; compare Isa 8:14–15).

Now, if the Lucan disciples are not readers in the literal sense but metaphorical readers only, then so is the "real" reader, who tails Jesus from his conception to the grave and beyond, a metaphorical follower only and not a follower in the literal sense. A chiasma emerges of readers required to be followers and followers required to be readers. Its purpose is to make the reader a true follower by making the disciples true (competent) readers. A chiasma, or X, thus marks the spot in Luke-Acts, actually a changing area, where reader and disciple cross-dress, reader becoming disciple, disciple becoming reader. This chiasma is in fact the cross to which the submissive reader is nailed in Luke-Acts, and under which he or she is liable to be crushed as by a shattering-stone ("that a cross may crush me if I refuse to believe in it").[42] Moreover, as a cross erected for an unspecifiable reading-body, X is also the sign of an unknown quantity, the sign of multiplication, and the signature that anybody can appropriate.

From his first appearances in Luke, Jesus is the object of blindness or insight, reading or misreading (2:18, 33, 47–50, and so forth). Small wonder, then, that he inaugurates his ministry with a self-reading. In the Nazareth synagogue

42. Joyce, *Finnegans Wake*, 193.24–26.

(4:16ff.) he assumes not just the role of a reader ("he stood up to read [*anagnōnai*]") but that of an *ideal* reader, and in a double sense. First, his performance is quite simply that of an ideal, or model, reader of scripture (his ministry will end with him reassuming that role—24:27, 32, 45). Second, by an act of reading he gestures to that immaterial *eidos* that "is not and never will be perceivable with physical eyes"[43]—his own identity as the near-illegible sign (see 9:45, 18:34) said to effect release from blindness, misery, and oppression (4:18). The congregation's initial response is to "gaze [*atenizō*]" at him, mouthing blind words of approval.[44] Now, Jesus' ideal reading of scripture consists in letting scripture read *him* ("today this scripture has been fulfilled in your hearing"—4:21). But his pre-scribed role is precisely what his audience cannot, or will not, read. And in refusing the ideal reading it assumes its own part in the script (4:24–27; compare Acts 13:27).

What makes seeing and reading possible in Luke-Acts? On the mount of transfiguration, Peter, John, and James are permitted a glimpse behind the veil: "They saw [*horaō*] his glory [*doxa*]" (9:32). It is a dazzling sight: "the appearance of his face changed, and his clothes became dazzling white / white as lightning [*leukos exastraptōn*]" (9:29; compare 17:24). Jesus as Sun of God (compare Acts 9:3, 22:6, 9, 11, 26:13)?[45] Certainly without light there can be neither sight nor reading. "The metaphor of darkness and light (of . . . revelation and concealment) [is] the founding metaphor of Western philosophy as metaphysics," writes Derrida. "In this respect the entire history of our philosophy is a photology, a name given to a history of, or treatise on, light."[46] And elsewhere: "Everything . . . that passes through . . . *eidos* . . . is articulated with the analogy between . . . the intelligible . . . and the visible sun."[47]

Whereas the transfiguration is implicitly articulated with the analogy between the intelligible and the visible *sun,* it is explicitly articulated with the analogy between the intelligible and the visible *Son:* "This is my Son, . . . listen to him!" (9:35). But the light is too bright for Peter to see or read by (see 9:33); he might as well be reading in the dark. "Christ and the saints in glory," exclaims

43. Heidegger, *Question Concerning Technology,* 20 (see above).

44. Cf. Acts 3:12, where *atenizō* similarly connotes misrecognition.

45. Cf. Derrida, *Dissemination,* 82ff., and "Shibboleth," 343: "Ra, the Rabbi cut in two, is perhaps the Egyptian God as well, the sun or light."

46. Derrida, *Writing and Difference,* 27. For the role of light in early Christianity, see Malmede, *Lichtsymbolik im Neuen Testament,* esp. 61–75.

47. Derrida, *Margins of Philosophy,* 253–54. Cf. Heidegger, *Question Concerning Technology,* 106–7.

Plummer; "the chosen three blinded by the light; the remaining nine baffled by the powers of darkness [9:40]."[48] A phosphorescent Jesus makes a poor reading lamp.

Elisabeth Roudinesco's *Jacques Lacan & Co.* recounts a similar epiphany: "What was striking was the kind of *radiant influence* emanating from both [his] physical person and from his diction, his gestures. I have seen quite a few shamans functioning in exotic societies, and I rediscovered there a kind of equivalent of the shaman's power. I confess that, as far as what I heard went, I didn't understand. And I found myself in the middle of an audience that seemed to understand." The speaker is not Peter but Claude Lévi-Strauss. And the venue is not the mount of transfiguration but the seminar of Jacques Lacan.[49] Perhaps Lacan can shed some light on Luke's irradiated Jesus—or at least provide some Songlasses through which to read him.

Teetering on the edge of sleep in a dreamscape (they "were drowsy with sleep"), Peter and his daz(zl)ed companions are able to gaze at the master signifier ("Master, it is good for us to be here"), now unveiled in all its naked glory, only by diffusing its brightness through a misreading: " 'Let us make three dwellings, one for you, one for Moses, and one for Elijah'—not knowing what he said," adds the Beloved Physician, also an adept Analyst (9:32–33). Lacan may well be right: the phallus "can play its role only when veiled."[50] But our text already knows that. It says: "This *rhēma* was veiled [*ēn parakekalummenon*] from them" (9:45; compare 18:34, 24:16)—veiled, that is, by the Father.[51]

The *rhēma* stipulated that "the Son of Man must [*dei*] suffer many things, and be rejected . . . and be killed, and . . . be raised" (9:22; compare 22:37, 24:26, 44). Now, *dei* ("it ought," "it must") is used seven times in Luke-Acts to

48. Plummer, *St. Luke*, 254.

49. Interview with Lévi-Strauss, quoted in Roudinesco, *Jacques Lacan & Co.*, 362, my emphasis.

50. Lacan, *Ecrits*, 288. The Lacanian phallus is not the penis; rather, it is the signifier of that (unconscious) lack in every subject that feeds desire while keeping it insatiable. It is "the signifier which has no signified" (Lacan, *Feminine Sexuality*, 152). More controversially, it is "the privileged signifier" (*Ecrits*, 287). Debate still rages among feminists as to whether the Lacanian phallus connotes complicity with, or a critique of, the phallocratic social order (see Irigaray, "Così Fan Tutti"; Gallop, *Reading Lacan*, 133–56; Grosz, *Jacques Lacan*, 147–87; Ragland-Sullivan, *Jacques Lacan*, 267–308). Whatever the case with Lacan, no such critique can be ascribed to Luke-Acts, where Jesus' authority ("who . . . gave you this authority?"—Luke 20:2) comes directly from the Father ("this is my Son, my Chosen, listen to him!"—9:35). Lacan's phallus (the patriarchal version) is prominent in the Lucan corpus.

51. See Ernst, *Evangelium nach Lukas*, 310; Marshall, *Gospel of Luke*, 394; and Schürmann, *Das Lukasevangelium*, 1:573.

designate the Law of the Father that binds and obligates his Son (9:22, 13:33, 17:25, 22:37, 24:7, 26, 44).[52] But the Law that binds also blinds; demanding that the Son suffer, it demands as well that the disciples not see why until the Sun has risen ("at early dawn, they went to the tomb"—24:1; compare 24:45–46, 26–27). Luke, look, lack, Lacan. . . . In the Lucan text, as in Lacan's, the paternal *dei* bars the desiring subject from ever completely possessing the phallus. The *dei* in Luke-Acts is inerasably inscribed in its deity, and so the *lack* in Luke-Acts is literally irremovable.

Thus "the phallus . . . always slips through your fingers"[53] whenever you try to seize it ("passing through the midst of them he went away"—Luke 4:30). It *can* erupt "in sudden manifestations, . . . in a flash,"[54] as here on the mount of transfiguration, also a mount of phallophany.[55] But it permits these titillating glimpses of itself only to disappear again, thereby luring you on ("they recognized him; and he vanished from their sight"—24:31; compare Acts 1:9). It always slips away, and sometimes you can't even be sure that it has come ("are you he who is to come, or shall we look for another?"—Luke 7:18). And although it attempts to persuade you of its solidity ("touch me, and see"—24:39), "the phallus, even the real phallus, is a *ghost*."[56]

By a stroke of luck—or is it Luke?—the term commonly translated as "appearance" in the phrase "the appearance of his countenance was altered" (9:29) is *eidos,* whose tracks we detected earlier in the nativity scene but which we now come upon in broad daylight—the enhanced daylight of the transfiguration.[57] More than any other term, *eidos* connotes the subsumption of visibility in intelligibility, signifier in signified, body in mind, and mat(t)er in the paternal Law. Everything in Look-Acts that is refracted through *eidos-idein-eidenai* is articulated with the analogy between Son and sun, enlightenment and light, insight and sight, and never more brilliantly than here.

52. Elsewhere in Luke-Acts, *dei* is used more innocuously. See Cosgrove, "The Divine *Dei,*" for a breakdown.

53. Lacan, "Desire in *Hamlet,*" 52.

54. Ibid., 48.

55. Cf. ibid., 39.

56. Ibid., 50, his emphasis. And what of Lacan himself, whose garments glowed while Lévi-Strauss looked on? The reader is invited to turn to Jane Gallop, *The Daughter's Seduction,* specifically the chapter entitled "Of Phallic Proportions: Lacanian Conceit."

57. Or Sonlight, at any rate. The detail "drowsy with sleep" (9:32) "may be Luke's way of indicating that it was night" (Fitzmyer, *Luke I–IX,* 801–2; cf. Luke 9:37).

Look-Ax:

Luke's Cutting Glance

> . . . knowledge . . . is made for cutting.
> —Michel Foucault, "Nietzsche, Genealogy, History"

> . . . the master of that slave will . . . cut him in pieces.
> —Luke 12:46

The longer we stare at the Son, however, the less we are likely to see. Earlier I argued for a criticism that would be graphic, pictorial, and visual, countering a tendency in biblical exegesis to mystify the spoken word. But sight need not be mystified in turn. There is a dark side to seeing that should not be overlooked. "Sight registers surfaces," observes Ong, "which means that of itself it encourages one to consider even persons not as interiors but from the outside. Thus persons, too, tend to be thought of somehow as objects."[1] Freud associated the act of seeing with anal activity, with control and the desire for mastery.[2] Lacan, as always, goes further: "In this matter of the visible, everything is a trap,"[3] a verdict that is echoed by Foucault.[4]

It is women, however, who have expressed the strongest discomfort with (under) the (male) gaze. "The *gaze* enacts the voyeur's desire for sadistic power," writes Toril Moi, "in which the object of the gaze is cast as its passive,

---

1. Ong, *Presence of the Word,* 228.

2. See, e.g., Freud, "Instincts and Their Vicissitudes," 127ff., and *Three Essays,* 157.

3. Lacan, *Four Fundamental Concepts,* 93. Part 2 of this volume is entitled "Of the Gaze." Lacan's famous "Seminar on 'The Purloined Letter'" is also structured around the glance—or three glances, to be precise (32).

4. "Visibility is a trap," declares Foucault in the "Panopticism" chapter of *Discipline and Punish,* 200. Cf. Foucault, "The Eye of Power," an addendum to this chapter; also "Seeing and Knowing" in Foucault, *Birth of the Clinic,* 107–23. Increasingly commentators have stressed the importance of vision for Foucault's work as a whole (e.g., Deleuze, *Foucault,* 32ff., 47–69; Jay, "Empire of the Gaze"; Rajchman, "Art of Seeing"). Unique perspectives on vision have also been provided by Heidegger, Sartre, Merleau-Ponty, Levinas, Bataille, Derrida, and Irigaray, to name but a few.

masochistic, feminine victim."[5] And Luce Irigaray writes: "*Seeing remains the special prerogative of the Father*. It is in his gaze that everything comes into being."[6] "As for the mother, let there be no mistake about it, *she has no eyes,* or so they say, no gaze. . . . And if one were to turn back toward her, in order to re-enter, one would not have to be concerned about her point of view. The danger would rather be of losing one's bearings (or perhaps finding them?). Of falling into a dark hole where lucidity may founder."[7]

Within the optical economy of Luke's epistemology, the primary focus of the look, Jesus, is not an object of the gaze in Ong's sense. The look commended in Luke is the one that does *not* glance off the surface (the look of the shepherds, Simeon, or Anna, for example, or that of the centurion at the foot of the cross). Moreover, even when the gaze directed at Jesus is superficial, he can hardly be said to be its victim. Rather, those who do the gazing (such as the *atenizontes* in Luke 4:20) are themselves cast as victims of blindness.[8] Luke's scopic economy has one fundamental law of exchange: sight's superficies must be ever capable of being converted into deep insight.

But this is not to say that Luke is innocent of the imperial eye.

INTRODUCTION TO THE PUNOPTICON

In the elegant antechamber that forms the entrance to this Gospel, the narrator, Look, introduces himself: "Inasmuch as many have undertaken to compile a narrative of the things which have been accomplished among us, just as they were delivered to us by those who from the beginning were eyewitnesses and ministers of the word"—with a gracious bow, he invites you to accompany him—"it seemed good to me also, having followed all things closely for some time past, to write an orderly account for you, most excellent Theophilus"— this is not your name, but you let it pass—"that you may know the truth concerning the things of which you have been informed" (1:1–4).

He leads and you follow. Together you ascend the tower that looms above this written wor(l)d. Gradually you realize that you have just entered a pen-itentiary.

5. Moi, *Sexual/Textual Politics,* 180n8. The gaze is further examined in Owens, "Discourse of Others," 70–77, and Rose, *Field of Vision,* esp. 165ff.

6. Irigaray, *Speculum,* 323, her emphasis.

7. Ibid., 340, her emphasis.

8. Similar reversals occur in Luke 6:7–11, 14:1–6, and 20:20–26. In each case, Jesus is the object of the verb *paratēreō* ("watch," "scrutinize," etc.; cf. Acts 9:24). According to Hamm, *paratēreō* connotes "a special kind of non-seeing," "a manipulative scrutiny of surfaces which cannot perceive . . . his true identity" ("Sight to the Blind," 467, 476).

Foucault might put it thus: "An uninterrupted work of writing links the center and the periphery . . . power is exercised . . . according to a . . . hierarchical figure, in which each individual is constantly located, examined and distributed."[9] Foucault is describing the Panopticon, Jeremy Bentham's late eighteenth-century design for the perfect disciplinary institution. "At the periphery, an annular building; at the center, a tower; this tower is pierced with wide windows that open onto the inner side of the ring; the peripheric building is divided into cells. . . . All that is needed, then, is to place a supervisor in a central tower and to shut up in each cell a madman, a patient, a condemned man, a worker or a schoolboy."[10] However, "the arrangement of this machine is such that its enclosed nature does not preclude a permanent presence from the outside: . . . anyone may come and exercise in the central tower the functions of surveillance"[11]—enter the reader.

Luke's written wor(l)d is a panoptic disciplinary mechanism designed to monitor the discipline of its inmates—its condemned men ("two others . . . were led away to be put to death with him"—23:32), its workers ("henceforth you will be catching human beings"—5:10), its madmen ("demons came out of many"—4:41), its patients ("all those . . . who were sick"—4:40). It is also designed to transform readers into disciples. The reader is enlisted to help the author discipline and punish the inmates of his work(house). Strict discipline is maintained by means of a sharp, cutting glance, exchanged between Luke and the reader, that is used unsparingly on the inmates. But the reader too is subjected to a regimen of model discipleship even as he or she exercises his or her functions of surveillance in this prison, asylum, workhouse, and hospital whose director is "the beloved physician" (Col 4:14).

Of course, there are twists and turns in this labyrinthine mechanism that my own Punopticon, undisciplined and punnish as it is, will be unable to monitor. The trickiest twist of all concerns my own place in the design. It arises from the fact that while I am attempting to read against the restraints, the straitjacket, of an institution(alized discipline), I am also reading by means of them.

LOOK—A PANOPTIC GOSPEL

Since the 18th century the first three Gospels have been referred to as "synoptic," because they . . . should be "viewed together."
—Conzelmann and Lindemann, *Interpreting the New Testament*

9. Foucault, *Discipline and Punish,* 197.
10. Ibid., 200.
11. Ibid., 207.

Look—we are in the "transparent, circular cage, with its high tower, powerful and knowing."[12] This multistoried watchtower is what makes Look's story possible. One ascends it by means of stares. The tower's design is such that the character-inmates are always visible from within it but are themselves unable to see into it: "In the peripheric ring, one is totally seen, without ever seeing; in the central tower, one sees everything without ever being seen."[13] The characters have a name for this invisible overseer, who speaks to them sometimes through a megaphone ("this is my Son, my Chosen; listen to him!"—9:35; compare 3:22). They call him God.

The secret of Look's power is his tower: it enables him to be omnipresent in his wor(l)d.[14] That is how Look, who admits that he himself was not an eyewitness of the events he recounts (Luke 1:2), can nevertheless conjure up in his reader the illusion of unmediated reference. The out-of-body experience that gets the Gospel of Look off the ground is not the least of its many miracles. Look's spatial relationship to his written wor(l)d is a special one: it is that of a disembodied observer.

Look has a press card that permits him to move freely in his wor(l)d, bringing live coverage to the reader. Legend has it that Luke was a painter;[15] more likely he was a photographer. In Luke-Acts the narrating "I" (see Luke 1:3; Acts 1:1) turns out to be an Eye: that of a roving-eye or at-the-scene reporter. It is also the eye of a detective fitted out with the latest surveillance equipment. "Taking photographs sets up a chronic voyeuristic relation to the world," observes Susan Sontag.[16] Look is a private eye for whom no scene is too private, whether it be Zechariah's or Mary's troubled encounters with the angel (Luke 1:8–23, 26–38), or Jesus' struggles with temptation (4:1–13; 22:41–45). These and other such scenes are narrated not as having been told to a narrator-researcher

12. Ibid., 208.

13. Ibid., 202.

14. Seymour Chatman's term (*Story and Discourse,* 212).

15. It seems that Luke painted a portrait of the Virgin, which later fell into the hands of Empress Eudoxia of Constantinople and eventually made its way to Venice (Plummer, *St. Luke,* xxi–xxii). If so, Luke might also have painted himself into Luke-Acts, in the manner of Velázquez in *Las Meninas*. Foucault's comments on Velázquez's technique would then apply to Luke. "The painter is turning his eyes towards us only in so far as we happen to occupy the same position as his subject"—the inscribed reader whose role he is sketching. His "gaze, addressed to the void confronting him outside the picture, accepts as many models as there are spectators"—or readers. "As soon as they place the spectator in the field of their gaze, the painter's eyes seize hold of him, force him to enter the picture, assign him a place at once privileged and inescapable"—a predetermined role of reading (*The Order of Things,* 4–5). Touch the canvas or the page, and the work snaps shut behind you.

16. Sontag, *On Photography,* 11.

(compare 1:2–3) but as directly witnessed by an on-the-spot narrator-observer.

Luke-Acts is replete with what Käte Hamburger would call *situation verbs,* verbs that designate the experiential "here and now" of a character. Take Luke's nativity account (2:1–7), for example. Up to and including the description of Jesus' birth ("and she gave birth to her firstborn son"), the narrative is general and summary in accordance with the temporal perspective, which is one of distance: "And it came to pass in those days *[egeneto de en tais hēmerais ekeinais].* . . ." Verse 7b, however ("and she wrapped him in bands of cloth, and laid him in a manger"), marks a significant shift in presentational mode. Abruptly, we are no longer in the past of a narrator but in the present of a character. We are invisible spectators of the minutiae of her life, courtesy of the omnipresent narrator.

Today, live coverage is no longer the province of the historian. Situation verbs ("wrapped him in bands of cloth, . . . laid him in a manger") are not normally used "to make statements about points of time that are either indefinite or that lie far back within the distant past. We can say: yesterday, or a week ago, Peter cycled to the city, but we do not usually say something like: ten years ago, or at the start of this century, Peter cycled to the city, or got up from a chair."[17] Luke, however, while purporting to present events long past relative to the time of writing, has Peter, Jesus, and every other major character cycling to the city or getting up from chairs at every turn—"he rolled up the scroll, and gave it back to the attendant, and sat down" (4:20); "they beckoned to their partners in the other boat to come and help them" (5:7); "his disciples plucked some heads of grain, rubbed them in their hands, and ate them" (6:1); "he lifted up his eyes on his disciples" (6:20); and so on.

Here we touch on what Foucault has called "the infinitely small of political power." Complete supervision seeks "ideally to reach the most elementary particle, the most passing phenomenon." Such supervision, to be successful, requires an "instrument of permanent, exhaustive, omnipresent surveillance, capable of making all visible," while itself remaining invisible. It has "to be like a faceless gaze that transform[s] the whole social body into a field of perception: thousands of eyes posted everywhere."[18]

---

17. Hamburger, *Logic of Literature,* 96. Bennison Gray terms this presentational mode *moment-by-moment narration:* "An event can be stated in two different ways. It can be presented moment-by-moment, with or without transitional summaries, and thus constitute a statement *of* an event. Or it can be narrated in summary, with little or no moment-by-moment presentation, and thus constitute a statement *referring* to an event. The first way is characteristic of literature. The second way is characteristic of history" (*Phenomenon of Literature,* 100, his emphasis).

18. Foucault, *Discipline and Punish,* 214.

Seeing all is not enough, however; Luke must also hear all, as we are about to learn. Luke's Panopticon (he sees without being seen) is also a confessional (he hears without being seen)—his is a Gospel of repentance, after all.[19] Luke is "the one who listens and says nothing."[20] Of course, Luke's many penitents are deaf to the fact that he is listening. And blind to the fact that the confessional encaging them is also a television set.

Arguably, Luke-Acts concerns a conflict between light and darkness (see Luke 22:53b; Acts 26:18).[21] Luke turns it into a living-room war. He transmits live audio as well as video; direct speech proliferates in Luke-Acts.[22] Now, if the situation verb permits moment-by-moment presentation, the direct-speech reporting epitomizes it, "the temporal sequence of words occurring one after another as they are uttered."[23] There is a corresponding dearth of indirect-speech reporting in Luke-Acts.[24] In short, Luke puts Jesus and his interlocutors on television: "At its best, television delivers a palpable sense of urgency and excitement. The huge advances in technology mean that networks are able to transport their viewers directly to the scene of the story, reporting on events live and in real time. Good television news grabs viewers by the throat with visceral, immediate imagery, and forces them to confront events far outside the realm of the familiar."[25]

Conventional historiography cannot compete with television, needless to say, nor even with televangelists such as Luke. In a modern history or biography, direct speech implies "that the words recorded between quotation marks have a documented source, and that they are reproduced word for word, [whereas] represented [or indirect] speech does not. . . . 'He would be going to Saint Moritz again in August—could Marcel come too?' implies only that Robert de Montesquiou said something *like that* to Marcel Proust, that this sentence captures the 'gist' of the conversation."[26] Contrast the speech of Lucan charac-

---

19. See Fitzmyer, *Luke I–IX*, 237–39. It may also be an example of "early Catholicism," as Vielhauer, Käsemann, and others claimed.

20. Foucault, *History of Sexuality*, 1:62, commenting on the penitential rite.

21. See Garrett, "Lest the Light," 95–96, 100–105.

22. *Legō* ("say") is far and away the most common verb of speech in Luke-Acts, occurring either alone (Luke 1:13, 18, 24, etc.) or in participial phrases (1:19, 67, 3:10, etc.). Other verbs used to introduce direct speech (of which there are few) include *anakrazō* ("cry out"—4:33), *apaggelō* ("report"—8:20), and *blasphēmeō* ("blaspheme"—23:39).

23. Gray, *Phenomenon of Literature*, 114. Cf. Hamburger, *Logic of Literature*, 83–84.

24. The principal examples in Luke are 6:11, 7:18, 9:10, 31, 11:53, 22:4–5, and 23:9. These are all of a rudimentary kind; the topic of the speech event is indicated, but no attempt is made to paraphrase its content.

25. White, "Inside CNN," 8.

26. Banfield, *Unspeakable Sentences*, 260, her emphasis.

ters, which is seldom transmitted indirectly as something that was said in the past, the gist of which is now repeated. The actors in Luke's docudrama are instead foregrounded as figures that can be directly experienced in the act of speech.

Luke-Acts brings audiovisual technology to Bentham's eighteenth-century Panopticon. The Panopticon was dreamed up by Bentham as a more "enlightened" penal institution: "No more bars, no more chains, no more heavy locks."[27] Acts 12:7 speaks of this reform: "An angel of the Lord appeared and a *light* shone in the cell. . . . And the chains fell off [Peter's] wrists." But a panoptic mechanism *is* light, dispensing with the "heaviness of the old 'houses of security,' with their fortress-like architecture."[28] Peter does not know that it is Look, his enlightened supervisor, who has arranged his escape. "Full lighting and the eye of a supervisor capture better than darkness, which ultimately protected."[29] Thanks to panopticism, power "throw[s] off its physical weight; it tends to the non-corporal." In the case of written narrative, it becomes (as) light as paper. And "the more it approaches this limit, the more constant, profound and permanent are its effects."[30] Panopticism thus "makes it possible to perfect the exercise of power. It does this in several ways: because it can reduce the number of those who exercise it"—in the case of narrative, it reduces the number to one—"while increasing the number of those on whom it is exercised"[31]—in the case of a Gospel, it increases it to infinity.

In Look-Acts, supervision is pen-al. It derives from a certain style of writing. Text, fabric, fabrication, fiction. "A real subjection is born mechanically from a fictitious relation."[32] Look-Acts is a penoptic mechanism, then, a prison house of language. Its theology is a technology of power. "Inspection functions ceaselessly. The gaze is alert everywhere."[33]

To a remarkable extent, therefore, Foucault's reflections on the panoptic mechanism apply mutatis mutandis to the device of omnipresence in fictional narrative.[34] "We are much less Greeks than we believe," said Foucault. "We are

27. Foucault, *Discipline and Punish,* 202.
28. Ibid.
29. Ibid., 200.
30. Ibid., 203.
31. Ibid., 206.
32. Ibid., 202.
33. Ibid., 195.
34. Certain observations in Spanos, *Repetitions* (156ff.), coupled with Foucault's "Behind the Fable," got me started on this line of thinking. Foucault himself does not think (does not wish?) to make this connection, although he does write such sentences as: "Right next to the principal characters, speaks a shadow that shares their privacy, knows their faces, their habits, their vital

neither in the amphitheatre, nor on the stage, but in the panoptic machine."[35] But the technique of omnipresence in fiction prefigures Foucault's "disciplinary society," one whose emblem is the Panopticon, one less of spectacle than of surveillance. (Today Jesus' claims would lead him not to the cross but to the psychiatric ward. Having been examined by Dr. Pilate, he would be led away for further observation.)

Luke's historiographic assumptions allow him the use of an omnipresent narrator. This enables his own assumption, or ascension, his translation to a sphere free of spatial limitation: his apotheosis. The author of Luke-Acts is dead. Enter his tome, however, and you will not find his body ("he is not here"— Luke 24:5). Reborn as an omnipresent narrator, he has exited the tomb (womb) of mat(t)er, like the hero of his tale (for the risen Jesus too is not bound by material constraints: "He vanished out of their sight. . . . As they were saying this, Jesus himself stood among them"—24:31, 36; compare 24:51; Acts 1:9; 9:3ff.). But unlike Jesus, who, still in a body, is subject to touch ("handle me"— 24:39), Look is wholly spirit. Aptly, therefore, this Gospel of Look is also known as the Gospel of the Holy Spirit.[36]

But even if Look *is* God in his wor(l)d, Third Person of the Blessed Trinity— Author, Jesus, Narrator—he nevertheless works a nine-to-five job. Thanks to the device of omnipresence, the Lucan Author can assume a secret identity in his written wor(l)d, can be transformed from a mere earwitness ("I have heard from some who were told by others who were there"—see Luke 1:2) into an eyewitness, can present the Good News as the Six O'Clock News. And the reader is made an eye-and-ear-witness by extension, thanks to the roving camcorder and floating mike Luke has become.

To be an eyewitness in Luke-Acts is to qualify not only for the rank of reporter but also for a seat on the board of directors of the Good News Network itself. It is to qualify for the position of apostle. Acts 1:21–22 states the hiring policy: "One of the men who have accompanied us during all the time that the Lord Jesus went in and out among us, beginning from the baptism of John until the day when he was taken up from us—one of these must become a witness with us to his resurrection" (compare 10:39–41; Luke 24:48). Afterward, the job is offered to the successful candidate: "The lot fell on Matthias; and he was added to the eleven apostles" (Acts 1:26). And although the ideal reader whose

statistics, and also their thoughts and the secret folds of their character; it listens to their dialogues, but it also registers their feelings as if from within" ("Behind the Fable," 2).

35. Foucault, *Discipline and Punish*, 217.

36. Whereas Mark has only six mentions of the Holy Spirit and Matthew twelve, Luke has seventeen (possibly eighteen) in his Gospel alone, with a further fifty-seven in Acts. For the full list, see Fitzmyer, *Luke I–IX*, 227.

career we are about to follow has been so well trained by Look that she succeeds in outperforming the entire managerial corps of Jesus' corporate economy (Jesus' body being its main investment), she is passed over for the position advertised in Acts 1.[37]

Of course, Luke's training school itself demands an investigation. To read this Panoptic Gospel is to be submitted to a battery of tests. "The Panopticon was also a laboratory," explains Foucault; "it could be used as a machine to . . . alter behaviour, to train or correct individuals."[38] The model reader is (s)trapped in(to) the text, made to swallow the role of reading pre-scribed for her by the Beloved Physician. Luke is guilty of mal(e)practice.

But what if our author were a woman,[39] and the reader a man, like the Theophilus to whom "Luke" ostensibly addresses herself (Luke 1:3; Acts 1:1)? Would the implied author of Luke-Acts be any less phallic on that account? Would her implied reader be any less pliable? "The phallic personality needs a receptive audience or womb," as Norman O. Brown has suggested, or perhaps admitted.[40] And the owner of the phallus might well be a woman, just as the owner of the womb might be a man.

Look's superpowers are not limited to omnipresence. This panoptic overseer is but one of a pantheon of narrators who seem to "have complete control [over their narrative worlds] owing to [their] godlike privileges of unhampered vision, penetration to the innermost recesses of [their] agents' minds, free movement in time and space, and knowledge of past and future."[41] This divine stance is, to put it mildly, hardly "amenable to the usual canons of probability."[42] Traditionally it has been termed the narrator's *privilege,* and its telepathic trajectory (the power to read characters' minds) has been termed his *omniscience*.

"Come, let us build ourselves . . . a tower with its top in the heavens" (Gen 11:4). God might be permitted a moment of anxiety as the elevator doors open and the omniscient and omnipresent narrator steps forth. Irigaray writes of

> the gaze of God which, ever on high, sees everything at one and the same
> time, looming over the whole universe. . . . From that perspective one

---

37. As are the women who have followed Jesus from Galilee (8:2–3), who have also outperformed the apostles (23:49, 55), and who have been the first witnesses of the resurrection (24:1–11, 22–24).

38. Foucault, *Discipline and Punish,* 203.

39. As Jane Via has suggested ("Women in Luke," 49–50nn37–40), undeterred by Luke 1:3, which applies the masculine form of the participle (*parēkolouthēkoti*) to the narrator.

40. Brown, *Love's Body,* 125.

41. Sternberg, *Expositional Modes and Temporal Ordering,* 257.

42. Ibid., 295.

cannot glimpse, calculate, or even imagine what the vanishing point might be. . . . Supreme erection that exceeds every horizon; even the sharpest, the most piercing gaze will be incapable of calculating its angles of incidence, for the eye remains captive in the world of the visible. . . . Light that nothing resists . . . alien to all shadow, outshining the Sun itself. . . . Gaze that no bodily organ . . . can limit. Without any blind spot, even one that might represent something forgotten.[43]

But is Luke really in this league?

Luke's narrator can "know" any of his characters at will (in the biblical sense, needless to say). His (g)lance is able to penetrate every body in his written wor(l)d. Wayne C. Booth writes of a narrator's "most important privilege" being "that of obtaining an inside view of [a] character,"[44] and of narrators who provide inside views differing "in the depth and the axis of their plunge."[45]

Again, we are in the dark recess of the confessional, a place designed for (self-)disclosure.[46] The power of the Father Confessor, like that of the omniscient narrator, "cannot be exercised without knowing the inside of people's minds, without exploring their souls, without making them reveal their innermost secrets."[47] "Nothing is covered up that will not be uncovered," says Look, "and nothing is secret that will not become known" (12:2; compare 8:17).

However, "Knowing All need not mean Telling All."[48] Luke is a photographer, and the confessional is his darkroom. Too much light would spoil the plot he is developing (although a modicum of light is essential). Does Luke respect the confidentiality of the confessional, then? Not entirely. He confides his characters' inner states to Theophilus, forgetting that others are listening. From Luke's Gos(si)p(el) we learn that Mary "was much perplexed [dietarachthē]" by the angel's words "and considered in her mind [dielogizeto] what sort of greeting this might be" (1:29); that the congregation "wondered [ethaumazon]" at Jesus' words (4:22); that Jesus "was moved with pity [esplagchnisthē]" for the bereaved mother (7:13); that the Pharisee "said to himself [eipen en heautō], 'If this man were a prophet'" (7:39); that Herod "was perplexed [dieporei]" by reports of Jesus (9:7); that Peter "remembered [hypemnēsthē]" Jesus' prediction (22:61); and so on.[49]

43. Irigaray, Speculum, 328–29.

44. Booth, Rhetoric of Fiction, 160.

45. Ibid., 77.

46. Sexual self-disclosure, in particular. Cf. Foucault, History of Sexuality, 1:61.

47. Foucault, "The Subject and Power," 214. His topic is "pastoral power."

48. Chatman, Story and Discourse, 212.

49. Limiting ourselves to the Gospel we find that Luke uses inner-action verbs to disclose his

Most of these plunges into the inner lives of characters are relatively shallow. This is particularly true of the emotional states they reveal (astonishment, fear, joy, anger, anxiety, sorrow), which barely qualify as data that could not be inferred by strictly "natural" means—the ordinary glance of an observer as distinct from the extraordinary glance of a narrator. The border between external and internal observation is in any case an uncertain one. "Purely 'external' vision," notes Todorov, "the one that confines itself to describing perceptible actions without accompanying them with any interpretation, any incursion into the protagonist's mind, never exists in the pure state: it would lead into the unintelligible."[50] What Dorrit Cohn says of the earliest novelists can also be said of Luke—that he dwells mainly on "manifest behaviour, with the characters' inner selves revealed only indirectly through spoken language and telling gesture."[51] In short, Luke makes video recordings.

(Jesus: "What determines me . . . is the gaze that is outside. It is through the gaze that I enter light. . . . Hence it comes about that the gaze is the instrument

---

characters' astonishment (1:63, 2:18, 33, 47, 48, 4:22, 32, 36, 5:9, 26, 8:25, 56, 9:43, 11:14, 38, 20:26, 24:41); fear (1:65, 2:9, 7:16, 8:25, 35, 37, 9:34, 45, 20:19, 22:2, 24:5, 37); joy (1:58, 10:17, 13:17, 19:6, 22:5, 23:8, 24:52); anger (4:28, 6:11, 13:14); anxiety (1:12, 29); sorrow (18:23, 22:45); reflections (1:66, 2:19, 51, 3:15); suppositions (2:44, 19:11, 24:37); knowledge or ignorance (1:22, 2:50, 8:53, 9:33, 9:45, 18:34); disbelief (24:11, 41); perplexity (9:7); recognition (24:31); recollection (22:61); thoughts (7:39); and hopes (23:51; cf. 2:26). Sometimes a phrase is used instead of a single verb; e.g., "they were filled with fear [*ephobēthēsan phobon megan*]" (2:9). At other times, two or three inner-action verbs or phrases are used in a single sentence; e.g., "they were afraid and they marveled [*phobēthentes de ethaumasan*]" (8:25); "he was very glad [*echarē lian*], for he had long desired to see him [*thelōn idein auton*] . . . and he was hoping [*ēlpizen*] to see some sign" (23:8).

50. Todorov, *Introduction to Poetics*, 34.

51. Cohn, *Transparent Minds*, 21. This is not without significance for historical scholarship. Culpepper suggests that the inside views in John preserve a measure of verisimilitude by reason of their limited depth (*Anatomy*, 22–23). Hamburger anticipated a similar objection, namely, that verbs such as *to believe, to intend*, or *to think* can be used in a modern history. It can be stated, for example, that Napoleon believed he would conquer Russia. However, "the use of 'believe' here is only a derived one. . . . From those documents transmitted to us it is . . . concluded, that Napoleon was of the belief that he would conquer Russia. In a historical . . . account, however, Napoleon cannot be portrayed as someone in the act of believing 'here and now.' That is, he cannot be portrayed in the subjectivity . . . of his inner, mental processes. . . . Should this occur, we would find ourselves in a novel about Napoleon, in a work of fiction" (*Logic of Literature*, 82–83). Cohn adds: "Narrative fiction is the only . . . kind of narrative, in which the unspoken thoughts, feelings, perceptions of a person other than the speaker can be portrayed" (*Transparent Minds*, 7). Such pronouncements beg questions of another sort. But it is beyond my reach for now to test the various "cans" and "cannots" in these quotations, to see whether and under what circumstances they would bend, or to ask, with Foucault, when and why they became necessary.

through which . . .—if you will allow me to use a word, as I often do, in a fragmented form—I am *photo-graphed*.")[52]

Photography too can be phallic, as Sontag has pointed out,[53] but its penetration is relatively shallow. Shallow penetration is all that Look needs, however, in order to impregnate his text with meaning—meaning that the reader will be expected to adopt. To put it another way, it is not necessary that (the) Look probe deeply, for it is cosmetic surgery that is being performed, not on the characters but on the reader. Henceforth the reader will *look* better: he or she will see more clearly.

EYES ONLY:
A CLASSIFIED GOSPEL

This speaking eye would be . . . the master of truth.
—Michel Foucault, *The Birth of the Clinic*

"To photograph . . . means putting oneself into a certain relation to the world that feels like knowledge—and, therefore, like power," says Sontag.[54] This knowledge-power equation is especially associated with Foucault. In *The Will to Knowledge,* the introduction to his *History of Sexuality,* Foucault insists that power should not be thought of as emanating from some central, sovereign, or exterior site. Neither is it to be thought of as a group of institutions or a system of regulations. "These are only the terminal forms power takes."[55] Instead, power is a "moving substrate" of relationships that are ubiquitous, unequal, and unstable—economic relationships, sexual relationships, knowledge relationships.[56] But if power cannot be sited, can it at least be sighted? Yes and no, Foucault would seem to say. Certainly, there is no uncompromised high ground from which to observe the workings of power, to take an "instant photograph of multiple struggles continuously in transformation."[57] Luke is a keen photographer; what would he say to Foucault?

52. Lacan, *Four Fundamental Concepts,* 106. Etymologically, photography is a writing (*graphē*) with light (*phōs*).

53. Sontag, *On Photography,* 13–14. Cf. Barthes, *La Chambre claire,* 48: "A word exists in Latin to designate that wound, that prick, that mark made by a pointed instrument. . . . I will thus call it *punctum.* . . . The *punctum* of a photo, it's that accident which, in it, stings me."

54. Sontag, *On Photography,* 4.

55. Foucault, *History of Sexuality,* 1:92.

56. Ibid., 93–94. Cf. Foucault, *Discipline and Punish,* 26ff.

57. Foucault, "Clarifications," 188.

Like Foucault, Luke has a thing about power. His Gospel "uses the term 'power' (*dynamis*) more frequently than either Matthew or Mark," as Susan R. Garrett notes, "introducing it into several accounts where it was not present in his source (Luke 4:36, 5:17, 6:19, 9:1; see also 10:19, 24:49). On occasion the evangelist's narration indicates that he conceived of 'power' in material terms: it is like a substance that flows forth from someone (Luke 6:19; 8:46; cf. Acts 5:15; 19:12)," or through someone—although Garrett rejects John Hull's suggestion that power in Luke-Acts is "impersonal and free-floating."[58] For Garrett, all power in Luke-Acts is centered in God, Satan, and their respective agents. But what of the power of that other Lucan deity, its omniscient and omnipresent narrator?

In Luke-Acts, the textual technique of the inside view works less to foster the reader's intimate identification with the characters, Jesus included,[59] than to effect a certain distribution of knowledge, and hence of power, among narrator, characters, and audience. This distribution involves a cumulative apportioning to the reader of certain classified (eyes-only) information, which, in its entirety, is unavailable to anyone in the story world except Jesus and his Father. Wedded to Jesus at penpoint, the reader is inducted into the family business. It is not as if the reader is privately taken aside and coerced by the God/Father of this influential family. Power here "has its principle not so much in a person as in a certain concerted distribution of bodies, surfaces, lights, gazes; in an arrangement whose internal mechanisms produce the relation in which individuals are caught up."[60]

The reader is given access to privileged information that is withheld from most of the participants in the story. Here are some examples from the Gospel:

1:59–61: The reader knows why Elizabeth and Zechariah must name their son John (see 1:13), whereas their neighbors and kinsfolk do not.

---

58. Garrett, *Demise of the Devil,* 65–66; cf. Hull, *Hellenistic Magic,* 105–14. Foucault's decentered notion of power is in some respects a very ancient one. See Castelli, *Imitating Paul* and "Interpretations of Power," for analyses of power in 1 Cor that take their lead from Foucault.

59. Exposure of Jesus' inner life is sporadic and depthless: "He was hungry" (4:2), "he was amazed" (7:9), "he was moved with pity" (7:13), "he rejoiced" (10:21). The most exposing inside view of Jesus (or of any other Lucan character) is 22:44. (The verse is omitted from many MSS; see Ehrman and Plunkett, "Angel and Agony," for a discussion.) But here too disclosure depends mainly on external data—the words of Jesus' prayer and the detail of his sweat. The appearance of the strengthening angel would also seem to be an externally observable event, like Satan's temptations earlier (4:1–13). Similarly, the revelation at Jesus' baptism, although intended primarily for him (3:22; contrast Matt 3:17), is presented as an observable occurrence ("in bodily form [*sōmatikō eidei*]"; contrast Mark 1:10; Matt 3:16).

60. Foucault, *Discipline and Punish,* 202.

1:66, 4:36, 8:25, 9:9: Groomed by the narrator, the reader knows the answers to all these unanswered questions.

2:48–50: The reader is better equipped than Jesus' parents to make sense of their son's explanation.

3:15: The reader knows better (see 2:11, 26) than to subscribe to the popular opinion of John.

4:22: The congregation's question "Is not this Joseph's son?" has the reader positively smirking (compare 5:21).

11:14–54: The performance of the characters (crowds, religious authorities) is especially inept in this sequence, giving the reader a chance to shine.

16:30–31: The reader knows that the Pharisees are unaware that Jesus is referring to himself.

Without having to sign for it, every Lucan reader is extended a dossier of highly classified information concerning Jesus ("tell this to no one"—Luke 9:21; compare 4:41, 5:14, 8:56). Among the human characters, the disciples alone have access to this file. Reader response becomes reader responsibility. Luke's wor(l)d is carefully drafted so as to underscore the solemn character of the disciples' contract with its Central Intelligence, mediated through the agency of his Son. The contract begins: "To you it has been given to know the secrets [*ta mystēria*] of the kingdom of God; but for others [*tois de loipois*] they are in parables, so that 'looking they may not perceive and listening they may not understand' " (8:10; compare Isa 6:9–10). But the reader, under the narrator's adept supervision, will soon outmaneuver Jesus' inept trainees.

The reader's infiltration of Jesus' core group is made possible not so much by Look's omniscience (which he shares with Jesus)[61] as his omnipresence (which he withholds from Jesus until the latter has accomplished his mission). From the moment that the adult Jesus makes his entrance in Luke-Acts as God's special agent (Luke 3:21), the narrator, Look, is expected to tail Jesus throughout Judea and Galilee as the author's private investigator in the story world (see 1:3: "after investigating [*parēkolouthēkoti*] everything carefully"). Omnipresent, Look can

---

61. Jesus displays his omniscience in Luke 5:22, 6:8, 9:47, 11:17, 20:23, and 24:38, although it fails him mysteriously in 8:45–46 (and possibly in 9:18, depending on whether or not we take his question to be rhetorical). Joy Lawrence remarks of 8:45–46: "A woman has a hidden flow of blood which Luke manages to disclose to the reader, but not to Jesus. And the woman herself manages to avoid Jesus' gaze—leaving him in the dark. For at least once in the text, Jesus is unenlightened. . . . The woman, for her part, sees that she is 'not hidden,' and reveals herself to Jesus. . . . She is irresistibly drawn into the light of the Son, yet at the very moment in which he is discovered not as light but as darkness" ("Response," 3).

also bilocate so as to photograph Judas, for example, on his errand of betrayal (22:3–6), or Peter in the act of breaking his contract (22:54b–62). Look will only look, however; being a voyeur he will not intervene. "Photographing is essentially an act of non-intervention," says Sontag.[62]

Where Look leads, the reader must follow. Unable to escape except by suicide (that is, by ceasing to read), the reader is stuck in a gumshoe role. But it is a role in which she is made to excel. For example, on reaching Jairus's house, Jesus will allow no one to enter with him "except Peter, John, and James, and the child's father and mother" (8:51). But the reader-in-the-text is already between the covers; she is already an undercover disciple. And so she slips in unnoticed to witness a spectacle that Jesus wants covered up: "He ordered them to tell no one" (8:56). Jesus' position is swiftly becoming impossible.

(Jesus to Look: "What you will never know, what I have hidden from you and will hide from you, barring collapse and madness, until my death, you already know it, instantly and almost before me. I know that you know it.")[63]

By the time of Jesus' second passion prediction (9:44), the disciples are struggling to survive his brutal training program (see 8:25a; 9:33, 40), and things will only get tougher (see 9:46, 49–50, 54–55, and so on). Their predicament is highlighted in 9:45—"they did not understand . . . and it was concealed from them . . . and they were afraid to ask"—which suggests that their ignorance is due to a decision at the top: the passive verbal form "it was concealed [ēn parakekalummenon]" implies the agency of a Central Intelligence (compare 18:34, 24:16), as we noted earlier. Jesus' secret instructions constantly vanish into the shredder before the disciples have had time to decipher them. But first they must cross the desk of the reader, who is being trained to crack their code.

Reading Luke-Acts is no desk job, however. The reader is in the trenches with Jesus, clad in the trench coat of a fictional follower. And to be assigned the role of a tail in this way is to make one's way through this tale as a model disciple. In the confusion attending Jesus' arrest, for example, the disciples are finally shaken off his tail. Peter does try to follow "at a distance" (22:54), but he breaks under interrogation (22:53–62). The reader follows Jesus with ease, however, never letting him out of her sight—until he gives even her the slip by descending into the tomb (23:53). Here at last is a lead-lined vault that Look's super vision cannot penetrate.[64] The reader is made to turn and walk away with him, as he follows some women home (23:56).

62. Sontag, *On Photography*, 11.
63. Derrida, "Telepathy," 15.
64. The tomb would remain secure until 1522, when Hans Holbein the Younger painted *The Body of the Dead Christ in the Tomb*. Julia Kristeva describes the effect: "Holbein's Christ is alone. Who sees him? . . . There is, of course, the painter. And ourselves. . . . The viewer's gaze penetrates this closed-in coffin from below" ("Holbein's Dead Christ," 242, 265).

POSTSTRIPTUM

Our narrator's traditional name, Luke, alerts us to his scopophilia by sounding so like *look*—such is the luck of the homonym. Complicity of the look and the book: Luke's narrator is omniscient and omnipresent, his Gospel panoptic as well as synoptic. Luke's sharp glance, his pointed look, is able to penetrate every body in his written wor(l)d.

If Luke acts superior to Jesus, however, presuming to penetrate even him, it is not because he is in fact superior. The Son is at the center of Luke's photological economy, his Sunoptic Gospel. In the light of the Son there is only (in)sight or blindness, brightness or deep shadow. Luke too is subject to the Son, for he writes by the Son's light. Luke-Acts is not light reading, but it is light writing: photo-graphy. Jesus is a model in Luke-Acts, a model for Paul, Peter, and Stephen, as has often been noted,[65] but a photographic model also. Luke, as photographer, circles endlessly around Jesus. So does everybody and everything else in the Lucan cosmos. Luke's system of knowledge is a solar system. The centrality of the Son is its first law of (meta)physics.

Luke's probing look is fashioned from a voice, that of Luke's narrator. And this voice is pitched so as to penetrate the reader also. "Sound . . . *penetrates us,*" writ(h)es Derrida. "Its reception is obligatory. . . . I can close my eyes, I can avoid being touched by that which I see. . . . [But v]oice penetrates into me violently, it is the privileged route for forced entry."[66] Even the reader does not escape the Beloved Physican without a rubber-glove examination, then ("the doctor will see you now"). Of course, even if we cannot close our ears, we can always close the book. We can cease reading, commit readerly suicide. Or we can counterread, as here.

65. See the research survey in Radl, *Paulus und Jesus,* 44–59.
66. Derrida, *Of Grammatology,* 240, his emphasis. Cf. Derrida, *Ear of the Other,* 33: "The ear is the most tendered and most open organ, the one that, as Freud reminds us, the infant cannot close."

88

Reading the Largest Body of

Writing in the New Testament

Luke's system is not an echonomic system, as we have seen. But it is a capitalist system. Capitalism's basic token of exchange, the dollar bill, depicts a decapitated pyramid, or tomb, surmounted by an eye in a triangle radiating sunlight. "The image of the eye within a triangle surrounded by rays of the sun is a common symbol for the all-seeing, panoptical, penal, eagle eye of God," notes Taylor.[1]

The dazzling light of the Son in Luke-Acts, at noonday strength in Jesus' transfiguration (Luke 9:29; compare 17:24; Acts 9:3, 22:6, 9, 11, 26:13),[2] is but a dim reflection of a still brighter light, that of God. (The irradiated Son can be looked at without glasses, but a protective filter, an overshadowing cloud, is necessary in order to face his Father—Luke 9:34–35.) Similarly, the luminous gaze of the Lucan narrator is but a dim reflection of the dazzling intelligence that oversees this written wor(l)d, namely, the Implied Author, the Prime Mover of the plot, whose divine role mirrors that of his character, God.

The following homology emerges. God is the internal overseer of Luke's story-world. His inscrutable will has been inscribed in a body of writing that Jesus alone can decipher (Luke 18:31–34, 22:37, 24:25–27, 44–47). The Implied Author is the external overseer of Luke's story world. His cryptic intentions are similarly inscribed in a body of writing, Luke-Acts, which the scholar alone can decipher. The scholar is Jesus' double, just as the Implied

1. Taylor, *Altarity,* 257.
2. Note that Paul's blinding exposure to the full light of the Son occurs at noon: "About noon [*peri mesēmbrian*] a great light from heaven suddenly shone about me" (Acts 22:6); "at midday [*hēmeras mesēs*] . . . I saw a light from heaven, brighter than the sun, shining around me" (26:13).

Author is God's double. Just as Jesus claims authority to unveil God's hidden purpose for those in Israel who grope for it, so too does the scholar claim authority to unveil Luke's hidden purpose for those in the church or the academy who grope for it. The critic and the Christ must both discriminate (*krinō*) between those who hear or read correctly and those who do not. To the elite audiences of each is it "given to know the secrets" (*ta mystēria*), but "for the rest" (*tois de loipois*) the secrets are "in parables, so that 'looking they may not perceive, and listening they may not understand'" (Luke 8:10; compare Acts 28:26–27, Isa 6:9–10).

Luke is a speaking eye, as we have seen. But in that eye there is a (de)Manic glint.[3] Should the scholar only peer into it, he or she would see himself or herself mirrored in its depths. The economy of Lucan studies, like the economy of Luke-Acts itself, is predicated on the controlled exchange of deciphered meanings. This exchange is conducted in paper currency. And since it is the Author who is thought to regulate this exchange, the currency bears his paternal profile: "father . . . chief, capital, and good(s). . . . *Pater* in Greek means all that at once."[4]

SOLID SCHOLARSHIP—THE ANAL(YTIC) STAGE

> . . . there is very little question of the pleasure that may
> accrue from the relation to "fluids." The anal stage is already
> given over to the pleasure of the "solid."
> —Luce Irigaray, "The 'Mechanics' of Fluids"

> . . . the solid and fundamental unit of the author and the
> work. . . . The author is the principle of thrift in the
> proliferation of meaning.
> —Michel Foucault, "What Is an Author?"

How did the Evangelist of the Poor ever amass such wealth?[5] Today every author is the owner of a text rich in meaning, but it was not always so. "The author is a modern figure," notes Barthes, "a product of our society insofar as, emerging from the Middle Ages with English empiricism, French rationalism and the personal faith of the Reformation, it discovered the prestige of the individual. . . . It is . . . this positivism, the epitome and culmination of capitalist

---

3. "Any narrative is primarily the allegory of its own reading" (de Man, *Allegories of Reading,* 76). Cf. de Man, ibid., 205, *Blindness and Insight,* 136, and *Critical Writings,* 223.

4. Derrida, *Dissemination,* 81.

5. So called because of his radical attitude toward material possessions (e.g., Acts 2:44–45, 4:32–37, 5:1–11). See Degenhardt, *Lukas—Evangelist der Armen.*

ideology, which has attached the greatest importance to the 'person' of the author."[6] And Foucault recalls that it was not until the end of the eighteenth and the beginning of the nineteenth centuries that "a system of ownership for texts came into being, [that] strict rules concerning author's rights, author-publisher relations, right of reproduction, and related matters were enacted."[7] Authors whose texts predated this legislation, however, could benefit retroactively from it. Ably represented by the firm of Cadbury, Dibelius, Conzelmann, and Haenchen, Luke was eventually declared the owner of Luke-Acts.[8] By then he was old and penurious.

Foucault writes: "We are accustomed . . . to saying that the author is the genial creator of a work in which he deposits, with infinite wealth and generosity, an inexhaustible world of significations." The reality is very different, however. The modern concept of the author "allows a limitation of the cancerous and dangerous proliferation of significations within a world where one is thrifty not only with one's resources and riches, but also with one's discourses and their significations."[9] Luke, battling cancer, succeeded in adapting himself to "our era . . . of individualism and private property" and became "the principle of thrift in the proliferation of meaning"[10] for the scholarly work force. The only meanings now recognized were meanings that Luke himself had made.[11] These meanings guaranteed the paper currency that was the stock-in-trade of scholarly exchange. The vault in which they were kept came to be venerated, scholars approaching Luke's text "as theologians had long approached the book of nature, seeking to find the marks of the divine author's personality."[12] Luke's authority over the work(place) became that of a divine overseer.

6. Barthes, "Death of the Author," 142–43.

7. Foucault, "What Is an Author?" 148. Cf. Foucault, *Archaeology of Knowledge,* 221–22. Rose, "Author as Proprietor," adds flesh to these skeletal accounts, while Walker, "Feminist Literary Criticism," X-rays them for flaws.

8. The role of the redaction critics (e.g., Conzelmann) and their precursors (e.g., Dibelius) has already been noted. Earlier still, in 1927, Henry J. Cadbury argued that, whatever we may say about their raw materials, the Lucan writings in their canonical form should be recognized as the product of Luke's labor. He proposed that this property, the largest in the New Testament, should be unified under a single title—*Luke-Acts* (Cadbury, *The Making of Luke-Acts*).

9. Foucault, "What Is an Author?" 159.

10. Ibid.

11. The following example is indicative. Commenting on patristic and pietistic readings of Luke 2:35b, Brown claims that "much of it is *poor* methodologically, for it seeks to interpret Luke through non-Lucan material" (*Birth of the Messiah,* 462, emphasis added). A richer methodology results, presumably, when one respects Luke's monopoly.

12. Rose, "Author as Proprietor," 75. Cf. Taylor, *Erring,* 81: "That which is created bears the mark of its creator. It is stamped with a ©."

Let us return to Luke's mirror-lined lair. The place of absolute intelligibility in Luke-Acts is occupied by the character God. Within the economy of Lucan studies, the author occupies the corresponding slot. The intelligibility of Luke-Acts is commonly predicated on the conscious intentionality of its Maker. That intentionality is the prelapsarian point of origin to which scholars labor to return. " 'Things are more precious and essential at the moment of birth,' " observes Foucault. "We tend to think that this is the moment of their greatest perfection, when they emerge dazzlingly from the hand of a creator. The origin . . . is associated with the gods, and its story is always sung as a theogony."[13] Biblical scholarship generally is founded on a neo-Gnostic dream of return to the Book at its moment of birth. By contrast, the innumerable books of the scholars are but "opuscules, . . . so many . . . speculations, so many tiny mirrors," so many reflections on, and of, the Book.[14] "The idea of the book is the idea of a totality,"[15] and the Bible is thought to be the total Book. But if its state is total(itarian), its ethos is utilitarian. Within its walls there must be no unemployed elements; everything must work. Above its many entrances signs have been hung that read "Play Prohibited." It is regulated by the Protestant work ethic.

The aim of intention-centered biblical exegesis, like that of the capitalist economies of Western Europe and North America in which it thrives, is the avoidance of waste. It is sustained at times by a belief in omnivorous authorial intentionalities with iron constitutions that are capable of digesting textual matter in toto, leaving nothing to be excreted. Were it ever to complete its enzymatic labors, there would be no waste paper, no recalcitrant words, expressions, sentences, or passages left undigested in the biblical authors' systems. In a canonical body, there can be no posterior opening. Everything must be held inside. Total digestion is the only permissible means of elimination, necessitating absolute anal retention, absolute control.

Should we conclude that biblical scholarship is an iron-cage economic order of the kind analyzed by Max Weber in *The Protestant Ethic and the Spirit of Capitalism*? Such utilitarian economies set themselves up against "the naturally errant . . . impulse to *waste* time (and money)," while "behind and above this austere work ethic hovers the absolutely hidden, inscrutable, and supervisory Calvinist God . . . who with 'His quite incomprehensible decrees has decided the fate of every individual and regulated the tiniest details of the cosmos from

13. Foucault, "Nietzsche, Genealogy, History," 143, citing Nietzsche.
14. Derrida, *Dissemination,* 46; cf. 44.
15. Derrida, *Of Grammatology,* 18. Cf. Blanchot, "Absence of the Book," 151–52.

eternity.' "[16] The fantasy on which so much contemporary biblical scholarship is erected, the fantasy of subordinating even the smaller details of the text to the masterful purpose of a biblical author, seems to be a displaced homage to this stern God with his regulatory function.

The result is a biblical text that bears the sticker "Made in the United State(s)." "Capitalism (from *caput,* head) can be understood as an ontotheological political economy," writes Mark C. Taylor. It is characterized by "fundamentalist belief—belief in the fundaments named identity and unity. This oneness is the principle that founds the united state(s)."[17] What iron hand rattling the dice box of chance has dictated that biblical scholarship in the United States be less tolerant of waste matter—that is to say, be more holistic—than in other countries? Among competing literary approaches to the Gospels, for example, narrative criticism is at present the most successful. It mines general narrative theory in order to exegete the Gospels and Acts. The most holistic form of gospel scholarship to date, its center of production is the United States.[18] Redaction criticism too has recently taken a holistic turn in the United States, more so than in Germany, Great Britain, France, or any of its other traditional strongholds.[19] What *dei*(ty) has determined that the united state should be the goal of so much gospel scholarship, and the United States its locus?

READING WITH UNCOMMON SENSES

Remarkable evidence was given, anon, by an eye, ear, nose and
throat witness.
—James Joyce, *Finnegans Wake*

Strict sexual mores are also ascribed to the penurious, property-conscious authors implicit in so much biblical scholarship. The biblical texts are commonly held to embody their authors' intentions. Thus conceived, they are indeed so many bodies to which the scholar must relate in conformity with strict rules of

16. Spanos, *Repetitions,* 178–79 (internal quotation from Weber). This Calvinist God can count Luke's deity among his forebears. Luke's God "does in fact act within history . . . but behind the way God acts there is no law accessible to human knowledge and therefore at human disposal" (Schweizer, *According to Luke,* 92–93; cf. Tiede, *Prophecy and History,* 84).

17. Taylor, *Altarity,* 256.

18. Arguably, it is the first important methodological innovation in gospel studies to originate in the United States. See Powell, *What Is Narrative Criticism?* and Moore, *Literary Criticism,* 1–68. Frequently in the present book I have been rewriting narrative criticism as fiction.

19. See Moore, *Literary Criticism,* 3–7.

propriety. In playing fast and loose with an author's intentions, then, do we run the unthinkable risk of fondling an author's body?

Victorian scruples regulate our reading habits. We need to rendezvous with the texts in the kitchen garden occasionally, away from the cloying niceties of the drawing room. As Gallop has observed, "once one starts attending to the odd truths revealed in the accidental material of language, one is led into a different kind of reading, no longer a sublimated relation to the spirit of the text, but an intercourse with its body."[20] And such intercourse would not be based upon the (male?) myth "of the book's or the self's or the body's virginal wholeness."[21]

What is at stake is a reorganization of the way we read, for such reading would bring other organs into play besides the sexual organs—the organs of touch, for example. Certain women critics have already begun to feel out the possibilities. "Woman takes pleasure more from touching than from looking," says Irigaray,[22] who has been groping her way toward a tactile epistemology.[23] And Hélène Cixous has confessed that she "caresses" her books.[24] But Barthes also admits: "Language is a skin: I rub my language against the other. It is as if I had words instead of fingers, or fingers at the tip of my words."[25] He writes of what he feels, in other words, or of what touches him. And such writing can be painful. Certain texts have the design of a mousetrap. With bandaged fingers Derrida writes: "There is always a surprise in store for . . . any criticism that might think it had mastered the game, . . . deluding itself, too, in wanting to look at the text without touching it, . . . without risking . . . getting a few fingers caught. . . ."[26] An exegesis of risk, then. The Bible in braille, but for sighted readers: to see, one might need to close one's eyes (compare Mark 4:12; Luke 8:10). The gospel massage, but with more feeling than we are accustomed to. Then the text might say with Jesus: "Someone touched me; for I perceive that power has gone forth from me" (Luke 8:46; compare Mark 5:30).

20. Gallop, *The Daughter's Seduction,* 29. "Language is not immaterial," insists Lacan. "It is a subtle body, but body it is" (*Ecrits,* 87).

21. Gallop, *The Daughter's Seduction,* xiii. "The notions of integrity and closure in a text are like that of virginity in a body" (ibid.).

22. Irigaray, "This Sex," 26.

23. See Irigaray, "This Sex" and "When Our Lips." Susan Graham has argued that the women in Mark have a relationship with Jesus that depends primarily on touch ("Silent Voices").

24. Cixous, "La Venue à l'écriture," 30.

25. Barthes, *A Lover's Discourse,* 73.

26. Derrida, *Dissemination,* 63.

And what of the mouth? "The interpreter lives by eating," mumbles Mark C. Taylor, his mouth full of text; "he sinks his teeth into the text in order to inwardize the outward."[27] Cixous, again, confesses: "I was eating the texts, I was sucking, licking, kissing them."[28] Barthes, too: "The writer of this text employs an unweaned language . . . (those milky phonemes . . .): these are the motions of ungratified sucking."[29] And Geoffrey Hartman exclaims: "I cleave to you, o doublebreasted book."[30] In our kitchen garden there is abundant food for thought.

But what of the nose? "The essence of the rose is its nonessence," notes Derrida (but what of prose?),

> its odor insofar as it evaporates. Whence its effluvial affinity with the fart or the belch: these excrements do not stay, do not even take form. . . . Whence its interest, its lack of interest. How could ontology lay hold of a fart? . . . So the anthropy of a text that makes roses fart must be read. And yet the text does not itself altogether disappear, not altogether as quickly as the farts that blast, prompt, spirit (off) [*soufflent*] the text . . . this suspension of the text . . . could be named effluvium. Effluvium generally designates decomposing organic substances, or rather their product floating in air, that kind of *gas* hanging over marshes for awhile. . . . So the text is a gas . . . between spirit and fermentation. . . . And to read it, the exhalation must be sniffed out.[31]

"The text is a gas." Will my reader be aghast if I then suggest that a Gospel may not only be heard, viewed, approached, and grasped but *inhaled* as well, that its meaning may be sniffed out as if it were a Gas(pel), one from which words are expelled as gas(ps), and in which writing has at last become a (f)art? The nose knows other ways to read.

27. Taylor, "Text as Victim," 65. Cf. Derrida, *Glas,* 119b: "The object of the present work . . . is the *morsel*. Which is always detached . . . by the teeth."

28. Cixous, "La Venue à l'écriture," 19.

29. Barthes, *Pleasure of the Text,* 5.

30. Hartman, *Fate of Reading,* 19. Cf. Ulmer, *Applied Grammatology,* 13: "The book is perhaps the most charged, cathected object in Western civilization, representing, according to Freud's analysis of his own dream of the botanical monograph, the Mother."

31. Derrida, *Glas,* 58b–59b, his emphasis. Cf. Derrida, *Truth in Painting,* 82: "just try to frame a perfume." Patrick Suskind's novel *Perfume* attempts this impossible task, addressing itself to "the fleeting realm of scent," "a domain that leaves no traces in history" (*Perfume,* 3). The essence of the smell is to be unspeakable.

To smell is to draw in air, wind, *pneuma,* Spirit.[32] The Gaspels are in-spired, then, inhaled. Their sense is their essence or fragrance. To devour a book is to digest its meaning, but to sniff out its es-sense is a more intimate act: "Internal penetration (into the lungs) through smell is even more intimate than through the absorptive vessels of mouth or gullet."[33] But intimacy is not always desirable. The church's mission to spread the gaspel has all too often been a harmful emission: "Smell is . . . taste at a distance, and other people are forced to share in the pleasure whether they want to or not."[34]

It seems that Paul was the first to s(m)ell the gospel as a gaspel, to (s)t(h)ink of preaching as olfactory production. Early in 2 Corinthians he exclaims: "But thanks be to God, who in Christ always leads us in triumphal procession, and through us spreads in every place the odor [*osmē*] that comes from knowing him.[35] For we are the aroma [*euōdia*] of Christ to God among those who are being saved and among those who are perishing; to the one an odor [*osmē*] from death to death, to the other an odor [*osmē*] from life to life" (2:14–16; compare Phil 4:18). Later, in Ephesians, there is a further effusion, which may or may not be traceable to Paul: "Christ . . . gave himself up for us, an offering and a sacrifice to God for an odor of sweet fragrance [*eis osmēn euōdias*]" (5:2; compare Matt 26:7, 12; Mark 14:3, 8; Luke 7:37–38, 46; John 12:3, 7). God loves the way his Son smells. Thus, if an apostle is one who is sent,[36] he must also be one who is scent, sprinkled with Jesus' perfume as well as his blood. But Paul was not the first to note that the way to God's heart is through his nostrils: "Then Noah built an altar to the Lord, . . . and offered burnt offerings. . . . And when the Lord smelled [*riah*] the pleasing smell [*reah*], the Lord said in his heart, 'I will never again curse the ground because of humankind' " (8:20–22; compare Exod 29:18, 25, 41; Lev 1:9; Num 15:3; Ezek 20:41).[37] How can theology lay hold of these (nasal) passages without blocking them up?

32. The Greek *pneuma,* like the Hebrew *ruah,* has this range of senses. Hence the pun in John 3:8: "The *pneuma* [wind, (Holy) Spirit] blows where it wills. . . ." Moreover, *pneuō* (cognate of *pneuma*) can mean "to give forth an odor," while *reah* and *riah* (cognates of *ruah*) mean "odor" and "to perceive an odor," respectively (Bauer, *Greek-English Lexicon*; Brown, Driver, and Briggs, *Hebrew and English Lexicon*).

33. Derrida, "Economimesis," 25, citing Kant.

34. Ibid.

35. Aromatic substances such as incense or scented oil were carried in Greco-Roman processions, their fragrance alerting the bystanders to the deity's presence (see Duff, "Transformation of the Spectator," 234, 241, and "Metaphor, Motif, and Meaning," 87–88).

36. *Apostolos* derives from *apostellō,* "I send."

37. God's olfactory pleasure in sacrifice is adduced a total of thirty-five times in Exodus and Numbers alone (Brown, Driver, and Briggs, *Hebrew and English Lexicon,* 926).

A *JOUISSANCE* THAT WRITES

Every stage in the life of Christ is noted and described in the
Gospels as an event of the body. . . . His life cannot be
reduced to speeches given in closed, airless structures, or to
repetitive rituals and disincarnation, . . . or arguing fine
distinctions in which the body is lost to lessons in tact.
—Luce Irigaray, "Equal to Whom?"

A text can have gas, then, but it can also be fluid. It can run through the reader's fingers. This is where solid scholarship comes into (stop the) play. "Solid mechanics and rationality have maintained a relationship of very long standing," notes Irigaray, "one against which fluids have never stopped arguing."[38] What is fluid allows itself to be traversed by other fluids. It passes into them, opens itself up to them, "sometimes dilutes itself in them in an almost homogeneous manner, which makes the distinction between the one and the other problematical."[39] Again we are at the portals of the unconscious, overlooking an underwater abyss. And it is not only Parisian intellectuals who have pearl-dived in its freudful depths. Says Lacan: "You only have to go look at Bernini's statue in Rome to understand right away that she [St. Theresa] is coming [*qu'elle jouit*], there is no doubt about it. And what is the source of this *jouissance*? It is clear that the essential testimony of the mystics is to say that they experience it but know nothing about it."[40] They know nothing about it because id is unmentionable, which is to say, unconscious, and unthinkable, which is to say, unthought. It comes, but not when it is called. Feminine *jouissance* always eludes the grasp of masculine symbolic discourse. (Thus it necessarily gives the slip to Lacanian discourse as well. Irigaray asks incredulously: "In Rome? So far away? To look? At a statue? Of a saint? Sculpted by a man? What pleasure are we talking about? Whose pleasure? For where the pleasure of the Theresa in question is concerned, her own writings are perhaps more telling.")[41] *Jouissance* is a disruption

38. Irigaray, " 'Mechanics' of Fluids," 113. Cf. Irigaray, *Speculum,* 227–40, and Deleuze and Guattari, *Anti-Oedipus,* 5–6.

39. Irigaray, " 'Mechanics' of Fluids," 111. "Words all in one soluble," gurgles the *Wake* (299n3).

40. Lacan, *Le Séminaire, livre XX,* 70–71. *Jouissance*—"ecstasy" with a sexual underlay and a self-dispossessing (death-approximating) edge—is not sexual orgasm per se (any more than the penis is the phallus), although neither is it unrelated to it. And neither are men incapable of it, if Cixous (*Newly Born Woman,* 83–84), Kristeva ("Woman Can Never," 137–38), and Lacan himself (*Le Séminaire, livre XX,* 70) are to be believed. Significantly, Cixous's example of a male writer of *jouissance,* Jean Genet, is also the antihero of *Glas.*

41. Irigaray, "Così Fan Tutti," 91. For Irigaray's own thoughts on feminine mysticism, see her *Speculum,* 191–202.

of the dominant discourse that is always inter-dicted—a debarred di-mention s(l)i(p)tuated between its lines, its words, even its letters. "This knowledge is at work . . . without a master."[42]

Substances that do not flow are called solids. Scholarship can sometimes be too s(t)olid. Heaviness sets in. Gravity takes over. What might *jouissance* have to say to solid biblical scholarship, or to literary biblical criticism in the United State(s)? Imagine a text written on the Gospels with bodily fluids drawn from them—blood ("a woman who had had a flow of blood for twelve years";[43] "this is my blood"), serum ("pierced his side . . . and at once there came out . . . water"), perspiration ("his sweat became like great drops of blood falling down upon the ground"), saliva ("he spat and touched his tongue"; "he spat on his eyes and laid his hands upon him"; "he spat on the ground and made clay of the spittle and anointed the man's eyes with the clay"), tears ("she began to bathe his feet with her tears, and to dry them with the hairs of her head"; "Jesus wept"), milk ("blessed [are] . . . the breasts that you sucked!"). What sorts of sounds would such a text make? Masticatory and digestive sounds, perhaps, as solids are dissolved into fluids ("have you anything here to eat?"). How would it look ("see my hands and my feet")? How would it feel ("handle me and see")? Could it be drunk ("take and drink")? Would it intoxicate? Would it be exe-Jesus? Or even exegesis? Certainly it would be exe-*jouissance*.[44]

Or exe-Joyceance. Again *Finnegans Wake* would provide an esplashially voluable slipping stone. It is immersed in the same horrormeneutical problemishes that we face. It presentiments a Joycean intrepidation of the exejesuistical task. It is a hermetical explosition, in other worryds, with oblivious apperplexicongruity to Muck and Gloop, the Godspools under conslitheration. Clearly, it could provide a mudel for babelical scholarship.

"Are we speachin d'anglas landadge or are you sprakin sea Djoytsch?" asks Joyce.[45] I have speached English for the most part in this book, with occasional lapses into d'an*Glas*. I have attempted to read Mark and Luke, although more often the Mark and the Look, and at times even Muck and Gloop, in the conviction that since we are stuck with them, and stuck in them, we might jest for once readjoyce in them. Like Derrida, I love very much everything that I have deconstricted, with a love that is ambivalent and ambidextrous. You must

---

42. Lacan, "Television," 14 (actually, this aphorism was slipped into Lacan's margin by his scribe, Jacques-Alain Miller). On "inter-diction" and "di-mention" (*inter-dit*), see Lacan, *Ecrits*, 299, and *Le Séminaire, livre XX*, 108.

43. Cf. Cixous, *Prénoms de personne*, 265: "Here, the text, female, menstruates. . . ."

44. Jesus himself is not unacquainted with *Jouissance* as the anagram indicates.

45. Joyce, *Finnegans Wake*, 485.12–13.

be several in order to write, and you must write with several hands. So much the better if you live in a land where odd and unnatural speech acts are perpetrated on the English language every day—Errland, for example.

But this book has been an experiment in "local theology" in more senses (more *jouis*-senses) than one.[46] As I completed the manuscript in Trinity College, Dublin, I would glance up from my work to see the *Book of Kells* looking back at me from its window right across from mine. Eventually I remembered my manners and invited it into my study.

What is more local than the pun? A good pun is a pun that works, and it works to produce an underpriced brand of knowledge. But it will not work just anywhere. It eschews the multinational, the universal. As a rule, it will only work in one language. In my study (or drawing room, although more often in my kitchen garden) signifiers that sound and look alike, as locals generally do, have met, mated, married, and multiplied. And the truths they have borne have all been local truths.

I have tried to scatter semes as Mark's sower scatters seed, in chance configurations that would yield an unpredictable harvest. "The glue of chance makes sense," says the gluer of *Glas*.[47] And to work with that glue is to stick to the letteral sense. Ulmer proffers the following career advice: "If it seems intuitively possible (if not obvious) that puncepts work as well for organizing thought as concepts (. . . similar signifiers rather than similar signifieds), then you are likely to possess a post-modernist sensibility."[48] You are likely to be a local, in other words, content to work in the local post office, conscientiously sorting and resorting the twenty-six letters entrusted to you, along with the evangelists' twenty-four, if you happen to be a New Test-what-is-meant scholar—fifty letters awaiting the post-age stamp. And then there are the many postcards that tumble out of the Gospels when you shake them—all those pictographic images long (mis)shelved by the sorters.

Post-criticism offers other forms of employment, needless to say. But the position of Postmaster is not one of them. The master narratives of modernity—scientific, philosophical, political—have been retired in the current epistemological recession, as Jean-François Lyotard reported in *The Postmodern*

46. "For these chains are not of meaning [*sens*] but of enjoy-meant [*jouis-sens*]" (Lacan, "Television," 10).

47. Derrida, *Glas*, 142b. Lacan too was intrigued by chance, his punning algebra allowing for unanticipated "moments of 'grace' " (Meltzer, "Eat Your *Dasein*," 157).

48. Ulmer, "Puncept in Grammatology," 164. Cf. Kuhn, *Structure of Scientific Revolutions*, 150: "A law that cannot even be demonstrated to one group of scientists may occasionally seem intuitively obvious to another."

Condition, to be replaced by "a pragmatics of language particles," a hetero-geneity of language games.[49] The speculative unity of history and knowledge, long the object of a concerted multinational investment, has lately shown signs of collapse, to be replaced by "local determinism."[50] Many theologians too have come "to the realization that what we call 'the great Christian tradition' consists of a series of 'local theologies.'"[51] And as Latin American, African, and Asian theologies come into their own, European and North American theologies are revealed for the local theologies that they always have been. Both in Europe and in North America an ever more common locale for theology is the post-Christian university, such as the one at which I currently teach. In the office next to mine is a logician who doubles as a Lacanian analyst, next to him another philosopher whose specialty is the history of atheism, while down the hall. . . .

What is more local than the pun—unless it be the body? In an age of *meta*physical recession, our bodies seem more and more "to be the site from which the reality of things is most convincing."[52] As a result, our bookshelves are being repopulated with body books. At first these books modestly made no mention of the body in their titles—*Purity and Danger, The Pleasure of the Text, Glas, Discipline and Punish, The History of Sexuality, Violence and the Sacred . . . .* But more recently the body has been showing (up) everywhere—*Literature and the Body, The Body and Society, Body/Politics, The Tremulous Private Body, Five Bodies, The Body in Pain, The Body in the Mind, Thinking through the Body, The Female Body in Western Culture, The Female Body and the Law, Fragments for a History of the Human Body . . . .*[53] Of course, the pun and the body are not strangers; they regularly meet up in the unconscious, as early Freud never tired of telling us, whether in his dreambook, his jokebook, or his daybook.[54] Recall too Gallop's remark that "attending to the odd truths revealed in the accidental material of language" leads one "into a different kind of reading, no longer a sublimated relation to the

---

49. Lyotard, *The Postmodern Condition,* xxiv. "I define *postmodern* as incredulity toward metanar-ratives [*grands récits*]" (ibid.). Ulmer notes that as epistemology becomes regionalized, claims of mastery are being displaced by the claims of "mystory" ("Mystory," 304).

50. Lyotard, *The Postmodern Condition,* xxiv.

51. Schreiter, *Constructing Local Theologies,* ix (from the foreword by Edward Schillebeeckx).

52. Holquist, "From Body-Talk to Biography," 1.

53. The absent authors/editors are, in turn, Douglas, Barthes, Derrida, Foucault (twice in a row), Girard, Scarry, Turner, Jacobus, Keller and Shuttleworth, Barker, O'Neill, Scarry (again), Johnson, Gallop, Suleiman, Eisenstein, and Feher. In religious studies, body talk is especially associated with the work of Peter Brown (e.g., *Body and Society*).

54. Freud, *Interpretation of Dreams, Jokes and Their Relation to the Unconscious,* and *Psychopathology of Everyday Life.*

spirit of the text, but an intercourse with its body."[55] It is a reading that comes out of the body, that refuses to try and wriggle out of it, and that blurs the boundaries between public and private knowledge, objective and subjective knowledge, and scientific and poetic knowledge.[56]

This book too has been a body book, not to say body bag. I have tried to write a book on the Gospels that would not be bound to the ingested body of a dead Father (Mark or Luke), immeasurably more powerful now than when he was alive,[57] but would be moored more to my own body instead.[58] I have tried to write an incarnate criticism that would say to the (ev)angel(ist), "Be it done unto me according to thy word and not according to thy concept." The scholarship that has resulted, although seldom solid, has nevertheless been objective: it has let the letterary object lead.[59] It has also striven to be sensible in every way; for while it has let itself be taken (in) by the ear and be seduced by visual attraction, it has also followed a paper trail with its nose, its tongue extended for neglected scraps of sense, its fingers busy in the pockets of the page.

As we have seen (heard, smelled, tasted, felt), it is a word-thing (*rhēma*) and not a thought-sound that is the matter on which Luke acts. "You cannot speak 'on' such a text" from above, "you can only speak 'in' it," in its idiom.[60] You can only immerse yourself in its wor(l)d, lose your self in its pages. Covering you with its jacket, gluing you to its spine, it pleads for a critical writing that would be plastic as well as phonetic. It pleads for a rethin(g)king of its sublimated Mat(t)er. The material letter would then cease to oppress, would cease to be something to be unhooked, opened up, cast aside with a sigh of relief. It would no longer be "the exterior body or the corset of meaning."[61] Thus de-constricted, how might Luke's corpus look and act?

An obese androgyn, Look-Acts repels and fascinates. It seeks to arouse us from our Platonic fixation with its ideal, aerated body to have us explore, in graphic detail(s), its sensuous materiality. It favors the missionary position, naturally, but likes to be on top. The largest body of writing in the New

---

55. Gallop, *The Daughter's Seduction,* 29.

56. Cf. Gallop, *Thinking through the Body,* 1–9.

57. "The dead father became stronger than the living one had been" (Freud, *Totem and Taboo,* 143).

58. Moored by a chain of metaphors, puns, and other signifiers, needless to say.

59. Cf. Ulmer, "Object of Post-Criticism," 98.

60. Barthes, *Pleasure of the Text,* 22.

61. Derrida, "Tours de Babel," 204–5.

Testament is luking and acting seductively.[62] It beckons invitingly, but we, prim Victor-ians, bent on (self-)mastery, writ(h)e dryly, shrinking from its touch. Are we so unable to come?

> Jesus himself stood among them. But they were startled and terrified, and supposed that they saw a spirit. And he said to them, "Why are you troubled, and why do questionings arise in your hearts? It is I myself, touch me and see; for a spirit has neither fleshy leaves nor bony binding, as you see that I have." And while they still disbelieved for joy, and wondered, he said to them, "Have you anything here to eat?" They gave him a page of exegesis, and he took it and ate it before them.
>
> —After Luke 24:36–43

---

62. "More body, hence more writing," writes Cixous, apropos of woman's condition, to which Luke-Acts responds, "More writing, hence more body." See Cixous, "Laugh of the Medusa," 257.

Works Cited

Abel, Elizabeth, ed. *Writing and Sexual Difference*. Chicago: University of Chicago Press, 1982.

Abraham, Nicolas, and Maria Torok. "Introjection—Incorporation." In *Psychoanalysis in France,* edited by Serge Lebovici and Daniel Widlocher, 3–16. New York: International Universities Press, 1980.

———. *The Wolf Man's Magic Word: A Cryptonymy*. Translated by Nicholas Rand. Minneapolis: University of Minnesota Press, 1986.

Ahl, Frederick. "Ars Est Caelare Artem (Art in Puns and Anagrams Engraved)." In *On Puns: The Foundation of Letters,* edited by Jonathan Culler, 17–43. Oxford: Basil Blackwell, 1988.

Aichele, George, Jr. *The Limits of Story*. Atlanta: Scholars Press, 1985.

Aland, Kurt. "Der Schluss der Markusevangeliums." In *L'Evangile selon Marc,* edited by M. Sabbe, 435–70. Leuven: Leuven University Press, 1974.

Altizer, Thomas J. J. *History as Apocalypse*. Albany: State University of New York Press, 1985.

Attridge, Derek. "Unpacking the Portmanteau, or Who's Afraid of *Finnegans Wake?*" In *On Puns: The Foundation of Letters,* edited by Jonathan Culler, 140–55. Oxford: Basil Blackwell, 1988.

Balakian, Anna. *Surrealism: The Road to the Absolute*. 3d ed. Chicago: University of Chicago Press, 1986.

Banfield, Ann. *Unspeakable Sentences: Narration and Representation in the Language of Fiction*. Boston: Routledge, 1982.

Barker, Francis. *The Tremulous Private Body: Essays on Subjection*. New York: Methuen, 1984.

Barrett, C. K. *Luke the Historian in Recent Study*. London: Epworth, 1961.

Barthes, Roland. *La Chambre claire: Note sur la photographie*. Paris: Gallimard and Seuil, 1980.

————. "The Death of the Author." In Barthes, *Image—Music—Text*, 142–48.

————. "From Work to Text." In *Textual Strategies: Perspectives in Post-Structuralist Criticism*, edited by Josue V. Harari, 73–81. Ithaca, N.Y.: Cornell University Press, 1979.

————. "The Grain of the Voice." In Barthes, *Image—Music—Text*, 179–89.

————. *Image—Music—Text*. Edited and translated by Stephen Heath. New York: Hill & Wang, 1977.

————. *A Lover's Discourse: Fragments*. Translated by Richard Howard. New York: Hill & Wang, 1978.

————. *The Pleasure of the Text*. Translated by Richard Miller. New York: Hill & Wang, 1975.

————. *The Semiotic Challenge*. Translated by Richard Howard. New York: Hill & Wang, 1988.

————. "The Structural Analysis of Narrative: Apropos of Acts 10–11." In Barthes, *The Semiotic Challenge*, 217–45.

————. *Roland Barthes by Roland Barthes*. Translated by Richard Howard. New York: Noonday Press, 1977.

————. *S/Z*. Translated by Richard Miller. New York: Noonday Press, 1974.

————. "Wrestling with the Angel: Textual Analysis of Genesis 32:23–33." In Barthes, *The Semiotic Challenge*, 246–60.

Bauer, Walter. *A Greek-English Lexicon of the New Testament and Other Early Christian Literature*. Translated and adapted by William F. Arndt and F. Wilbur Gingrich. Revised by F. Wilbur Gingrich and Frederick W. Danker. Chicago: University of Chicago Press, 1979.

Beardslee, William A. "Recent Literary Criticism." In *The New Testament and Its Modern Interpreters*, edited by Eldon Jay Epp and George W. MacRae, 175–98. Philadelphia:. Fortress Press; Atlanta: Scholars Press, 1989.

Beavis, Mary Ann. *Mark's Audience: The Literary and Social Setting of Mark 4.11–12*. Sheffield: JSOT Press, 1989.

Beckett, Samuel. *Murphy*. London: John Calder, 1952.

Berg, Temma F. "*La Carte Postale*: Reading (Derrida) Reading." *Criticism* 28 (1986): 323–40.

————. "Reading in/to Mark." *Semeia* 48 (1989): 187–206.

Black, Max. *Models and Metaphors*. Ithaca, N.Y.: Cornell University Press, 1962.

Blanchot, Maurice. "Absence of the Book." In *The Gaze of Orpheus*, translated by Lydia Davis, 145–60. Barrytown, N.Y.: Station Hill Press, 1981.

Blomberg, Craig L. "Interpreting the Parables of Jesus: Where Are We and Where Do We Go from Here?" *Catholic Biblical Quarterly* 53 (1991): 50–78.

Bloom, Harold. *Agon: Towards a Theory of Revisionism*. Oxford: Oxford University Press, 1982.

————. *Kabbalah and Criticism*. New York: Continuum, 1975.

Bloom, Harold, et al. *Deconstruction and Criticism*. New York: Continuum, 1979.

Boomershine, Thomas E., and Bartholomew, Gilbert L. "Mark 16:8 and the Apostolic Commission." *Journal of Biblical Literature* 100 (1981): 225–39.

————. "The Narrative Technique of Mark 16:8." *Journal of Biblical Literature* 100 (1981): 213–23.

Booth, Wayne C. *The Rhetoric of Fiction.* 2d ed. Chicago: University of Chicago Press, 1983.

Bovon, François. *Luke the Theologian: Thirty-three Years of Research (1950–1983).* Translated by Ken McKinney. Allison Park, Pa.: Pickwick Publications, 1987.

Breech, James. *Jesus and Postmodernism.* Minneapolis: Fortress Press, 1989.

Brown, Francis, S. R. Driver, and Charles A. Briggs. *A Hebrew and English Lexicon of the Old Testament.* Oxford: Oxford University Press, 1975.

Brown, Norman O. *Love's Body.* Berkeley and Los Angeles: University of California Press, 1966.

Brown, Peter. *Body and Society: Men, Women, and Sexual Renunciation in Early Christianity.* New York: Columbia University Press, 1990.

Brown, Peter. *The Book of Kells.* London: Thames and Hudson, 1980.

Brown, Raymond E. *The Birth of the Messiah: A Commentary on the Infancy Narratives in Matthew and Luke.* New York: Doubleday, 1977.

Bultmann, Rudolf. *Glauben und Verstehen: Gesammelte Aufsätze.* 3 vols. Tübingen: Mohr (Siebeck), 1933–59.

————. *Jesus Christ and Mythology.* New York: Scribner, 1958.

————. *History and Eschatology: The Presence of Eternity.* New York: Harper & Row, 1962.

————. *The Theology of the New Testament.* 2 vols. Translated by Kendrick Grobel. New York: Scribner, 1952–55.

Burnett, Fred W. "Postmodern Biblical Exegesis: The Eve of Historical Criticism." *Semeia* 51 (1990): 51–80.

Burnham, Frederic B., ed. *Post-Modern Theology: Christian Faith in a Pluralist World.* San Francisco: Harper & Row, 1989.

Cadbury, Henry J. *The Making of Luke-Acts.* New York: Macmillan, 1927.

Camporesi, Piero. "The Consecrated Host: A Wondrous Excess." In *Fragments for a History of the Human Body,* edited by Michel Feher with Ramona Naddaff and Nadia Tazi, 1:220–37. New York: Zone, 1989.

Caputo, John D. "Derrida and the Study of Religion." *Religious Studies Review* 16 (1990): 21–25.

Castelli, Elizabeth A. *Imitating Paul: A Discourse of Power.* Louisville, Ky.: Westminster/John Knox Press, 1991.

————. "Interpretations of Power in 1 Corinthians." *Semeia* (forthcoming).

Charles, R. H., ed. *The Apocrypha and Pseudepigrapha of the Old Testament in English.* 2 vols. Oxford: Clarendon Press, 1979.

Chatman, Seymour. *Story and Discourse: Narrative Structure in Fiction and Film.* Ithaca, N.Y.: Cornell University Press, 1978.

Cixous, Hélène. *The Exile of James Joyce*. Translated by Sally A. J. Purcell. London: John Calder, 1976.

———. "From the Scene of the Unconscious to the Scene of History." Translated by Deborah W. Carpenter. In *The Future of Literary Theory*, edited by Ralph Cohen, 1–18. New York: Routledge, 1989.

———. "The Laugh of the Medusa." Translated by Keith Cohen and Paula Cohen. In *New French Feminisms: An Anthology*, edited by Elaine Marks and Isabelle de Courtivron, 245–64. New York: Schocken Books, 1980.

———. "Un Morceau de Dieu." *Sorcières* 1 (1976): 14–17.

———. *Prénoms de personne*. Paris: Seuil, 1974.

———. "La Venue à l'écriture." In Hélène Cixous, Annie Leclerc, and Madeleine Gagnon, *La Venue à l'écriture*. Paris: Union Générale d'Editions, Collection 10/18, 1977.

Cixous, Hélène, and Catherine Clément. *The Newly Born Woman*. Translated by Betsy Wing. Minneapolis: University of Minnesota Press, 1986.

Clément, Catherine. *The Lives and Legends of Jacques Lacan*. Translated by Arthur Goldhammer. New York: Columbia University Press, 1983.

Clines, David. "Deconstructing the Book of Job." In *The Bible as Rhetoric: Studies in Biblical Persuasion and Credibility*, edited by Martin Warner, 65–80. New York: Routledge, 1990.

Coggins, R. J., and J. L. Houlden, eds. *A Dictionary of Biblical Interpretation*. Philadelphia: Trinity Press International; London: SCM Press, 1990.

Cohn, Dorrit. *Transparent Minds: Narrative Modes for Presenting Consciousness in Fiction*. Princeton: Princeton University Press, 1978.

Collins, John J. *The Apocalyptic Imagination: An Introduction to the Jewish Matrix of Christianity*. New York: Crossroad, 1984.

Conzelmann, Hans. *The Theology of St. Luke*. Translated by Geoffrey Buswell. New York: Harper & Row, 1960.

———. "Zur Lukas-Analyse." *Zeitschrift für Theologie und Kirche* 49 (1952): 16–33.

Conzelmann, Hans, and Andreas Lindemann. *Interpreting the New Testament: An Introduction to the Principles and Methods of N.T. Exegesis*. Translated by Siegfried S. Schatzmann. Peabody, Mass.: Hendrickson, 1988.

Cosgrove, Charles H. "The Divine *Dei* in Luke-Acts: Investigations into the Lukan Understanding of God's Providence." *Novum Testamentum* 26 (1984): 168–90.

Crossan, John Dominic. *Cliffs of Fall: Paradox and Polyvalence in the Parables of Jesus*. New York: Seabury Press, 1980.

———. "A Form for Absence: The Markan Creation of Gospel." *Semeia* 12 (1978): 41–56.

———. *Four Other Gospels: Shadows on the Contours of Canon*. Minneapolis: Winston, 1985.

———. *In Parables: The Challenge of the Historical Jesus*. New York: Harper & Row, 1973.

Culler, Jonathan. "The Call of the Phoneme." In *On Puns: The Foundation of Letters*, edited by Jonathan Culler, 1–16. Oxford: Basil Blackwell, 1988.

————. *On Deconstruction: Theory and Criticism after Structuralism*. Ithaca, N.Y.: Cornell University Press, 1982.

Cullmann, Oscar. *The Christology of the New Testament*. Translated by S. C. Guthrie and C. A. M. Hall. Philadelphia: Westminster Press, 1959.

Culpepper, R. Alan. *Anatomy of the Fourth Gospel: A Study in Literary Design*. Philadelphia: Fortress Press, 1983.

Davis, Robert Con, ed. *Lacan and Narration: The Psychoanalytic Difference in Narrative Theory*. Baltimore: Johns Hopkins University Press, 1983.

Degenhardt, Hans-Joachim. *Lukas—Evangelist der Armen: Besitz und Besitzversicht in den lukanischen Schriften: Eine traditions- und redaktionsgeschichtliche Untersuchung*. Stuttgart: Katholisches Bibelwerk, 1965.

Deleuze, Gillès. *Foucault*. Translated and edited by Seán Hand. Minneapolis: University of Minnesota Press, 1988.

Deleuze, Gillès, and Félix Guattari. *Anti-Oedipus: Capitalism and Schizophrenia*. Translated by Robert Hurley, Mark Seem, and Helen R. Lane. New York: Viking Press, 1977.

De Man, Paul. *Allegories of Reading: Figural Language in Rousseau, Nietzsche, Rilke, and Proust*. New Haven: Yale University Press, 1979.

————. *Blindness and Insight: Essays in the Rhetoric of Contemporary Criticism*. 2d ed. Minneapolis: University of Minnesota Press, 1983.

————. *Critical Writings, 1953–1978*. Edited by Lindsay Waters. Minneapolis: University of Minnesota Press, 1989.

————. *The Resistance to Theory*. Minneapolis: University of Minnesota Press, 1986.

————. "Shelley Disfigured." In *The Rhetoric of Romanticism*, 93–124. New York: Columbia University Press, 1984.

————. *Wartime Journalism, 1939–43*. Edited by Werner Hamacher, Neil Hertz, and Thomas Keenan. Lincoln: University of Nebraska Press, 1989.

Derrida, Jacques. *The Archeology of the Frivolous: Reading Condillac*. Translated by John P. Leavey, Jr. Lincoln: University of Nebraska Press, 1980.

————. "Choreographies." In Derrida, *The Ear of the Other*, 163–85.

————. *Dissemination*. Translated by Barbara Johnson. Chicago: University of Chicago Press, 1981.

————. *Du droit à la philosophie*. Paris: Galilée, 1990.

————. "Du tout." In Derrida, *The Post Card*, 497–521.

————. *The Ear of the Other: Otobiography, Transference, Translation*. Edited by Christie McDonald. Translated by Peggy Kamuf and Avital Ronell. Lincoln: University of Nebraska Press, 1985.

————. "Economimesis." Translated by Richard Klein. *Diacritics* 11 (1981): 3–25.

————. *Edmund Husserl's Origin of Geometry: An Introduction*. Translated by John P. Leavey, Jr. Stony Brook, N.Y.: Nicholas Hays, 1978.

————. "Envois." In Derrida, *The Post Card*, 1–256.

————. "Le Facteur de la vérité." In Derrida, *The Post Card*, 411–96.

————. "Fors: The Anglish Words of Nicolas Abraham and Maria Torok." Translated by Barbara Johnson. Foreword to Nicolas Abraham and Maria Torok, *The Wolf Man's*

Magic Word, translated by Nicholas Rand, xi–xlviii. Minneapolis: University of Minnesota Press, 1986.

———. "Freud and the Scene of Writing." In Derrida, *Writing and Difference,* 196–231.

———. "Géopsychanalyse 'and the rest of the world.' " In *Psyché: Inventions de l'autre,* 327–52. Paris: Galileé, 1987.

———. *Glas.* Translated by John P. Leavey, Jr., and Richard Rand. Lincoln: University of Nebraska Press, 1986.

———. "Hear Say Yes in Joyce." Translated by Tina Kendall and Shari Benstock. In *James Joyce: The Augmented Ninth. Proceedings of the Ninth International James Joyce Symposium,* edited by Bernard Benstock, 27–75. Syracuse, N.Y.: Syracuse University Press, 1988.

———. "How to Avoid Speaking: Denials." Translated by Ken Frieden. In *Languages of the Unsayable: The Play of Negativity in Literature and Literary Theory,* edited by Sanford Budick and Wolfgang Iser, 3–70. New York: Columbia University Press, 1989.

———. "Ja, ou le faux bond." *Digraphe* 11 (1977): 84–121.

———. "The Law of Genre." Translated by Avita Ronell. *Glyph* 7 (1980): 202–29.

———. "Let Us Not Forget—Psychoanalysis." Translated by Geoffrey Bennington and Rachel Bowlby. *Oxford Literary Review* 12 (1990): 3–7.

———. "Like the Sound of the Sea Deep Within a Shell: Paul de Man's War." Translated by Peggy Kamuf. In *Responses: On Paul de Man's Wartime Journalism,* edited by Werner Hamacher, Neil Hertz, and Thomas Keenan, 127–64. Lincoln: University of Nebraska Press, 1989.

———. *Limited Inc.* Edited by Gerald Graff. Translated by Samuel Weber and Jeffrey Mehlman. Evanston, Ill.: Northwestern University Press, 1988.

———. "Living On: Border Lines." Translated by James Hulbert. In Bloom et al., *Deconstruction and Criticism,* 75–176.

———. *Margins of Philosophy.* Translated by Alan Bass. Chicago: University of Chicago Press, 1982.

———. "Me—Psychoanalysis." Translated by Richard Klein. *Diacritics* 9 (1979): 4–12.

———. "My Chances/*Mes Chances*: A Rendezvous with Some Epicurean Stereophonies." Translated by Irene Harvey and Avital Ronell. In *Taking Chances: Derrida, Psychoanalysis, and Literature,* edited by Joseph H. Smith and William Kerrigan, 1–32. Baltimore: Johns Hopkins University Press, 1984.

———. "No Apocalypse, Not Now (full speed ahead, seven missiles, seven missives)." Translated by Catherine Porter and Philip Lewis. *Diacritics* 14 (1984): 20–31.

———. "Of an Apocalyptic Tone Recently Adopted in Philosophy." Translated by John P. Leavey, Jr. *Semeia* 23 (1982): 63–97.

———. *Of Grammatology.* Translated by Gayatri Chakravorty Spivak. Baltimore: Johns Hopkins University Press, 1976.

———. *Of Spirit: Heidegger and the Question.* Translated by Geoffrey Bennington and Rachel Bowlby. Chicago: University of Chicago Press, 1989.

————. *Positions*. Translated by Alan Bass. Chicago: University of Chicago Press, 1981.

————. *The Post Card: From Socrates to Freud and Beyond*. Translated by Alan Bass. Chicago: University of Chicago Press, 1987.

————. "Proverb: 'He That Would Pun . . .' " In *Glassary,* edited by John P. Leavy, Jr., 17–21. Lincoln: University of Nebraska Press, 1986.

————. "Psyche: Inventions of the Other." Translated by Catherine Porter. In *Reading de Man Reading,* edited by Lindsay Waters and Wlad Godzich, 25–65. Minneapolis: University of Minnesota Press, 1989.

————. "Scribble (pouvoir/écrire)." Introduction to William Warburton, *Essai sur les hiéroglyphes des égyptiens,* translated by Léonard des Malpeines, 5–43. Paris: Aubier Flammarion, 1977.

————. "Shibboleth." Translated by Joshua Wilner. In *Midrash and Literature,* edited by Geoffrey H. Hartman and Sanford Budick, 307–47. New Haven: Yale University Press, 1986.

————. *Signéponge/Signsponge*. Translated by Richard Rand. New York: Columbia University Press, 1984.

————. *Speech and Phenomena and Other Essays on Husserl's Theory of Signs*. Translated by David B. Allison. Evanston, Ill.: Northwestern University Press, 1973.

————. *Spurs: Nietzsche's Styles/Eperons: Les Styles de Nietzsche*. Translated by Barbara Harlow. Chicago: University of Chicago Press, 1979.

————. "Structure, Sign, and Play in the Discourse of the Human Sciences." In *The Structuralist Controversy: The Languages of Criticism and the Sciences of Man,* edited by Richard Macksey and Eugenio Donato, 247–72. Baltimore: Johns Hopkins University Press, 1970.

————. "Telepathy." Translated by Nicholas Royle. *The Oxford Literary Review* 10 (1988): 3–41.

————. "The Time of a Thesis: Punctuations." In *Philosophy in France,* edited by Alan Montefiori, 34–50. Cambridge: Cambridge University Press, 1982.

————. "To Speculate—on 'Freud.' " In Derrida, *The Post Card,* 257–409.

————. "Des Tours de Babel." In *Difference in Translation,* edited by Joseph F. Graham, 165–207. Ithaca, N.Y.: Cornell University Press, 1986.

————. *The Truth in Painting*. Translated by Geoff Bennington and Ian McLeod. Chicago: University of Chicago Press, 1987.

————. "Two Words for Joyce." Translated by Geoff Bennington. In *Post-Structuralist Joyce: Essays from the French,* edited by Derek Attridge and Daniel Ferrer, 145–59. Cambridge: Cambridge University Press, 1984.

————. "Tympan." In Derrida, *Margins of Philosophy,* ix–xxix.

————. *Ulysse Gramophone: Deux Mots pour Joyce*. Paris: Galilée, 1987.

————. "Women in the Beehive: A Seminar with Jacques Derrida." In *Men in Feminism,* edited by Alice Jardine and Paul Smith, 189–203. New York: Methuen, 1987.

————. *Writing and Difference*. Translated by Alan Bass. Chicago: University of Chicago Press, 1978.

Descombes, Vincent. *Modern French Philosophy*. Translated by L. Scott-Fox and J. M. Harding. Cambridge: Cambridge University Press, 1980.

Detweiler, Robert, ed. "Derrida and Biblical Studies." *Semeia* 23 (1982).

Dewey, Joanna. "Recent Studies on Mark." *Religious Studies Review* 17 (1991): 12–16.

Dibelius, Martin. *Studies in the Acts of the Apostles*. Edited by H. Greeven. Translated by M. Ling. London: SCM Press, 1956.

Dillard, Annie. *The Writing Life*. New York: Harper & Row, 1989.

Dillon, Richard J. *From Eye-Witnesses to Ministers of the Word: Tradition and Composition in Luke 24*. Rome: Biblical Institute Press, 1978.

———. "Previewing Luke's Project from His Prologue (Luke 1:1–4)." *Catholic Biblical Quarterly* 43 (1981): 205–27.

———. "The Prophecy of Christ and His Witness according to the Discourses of Acts." *New Testament Studies* 32 (1986): 544–56.

Donahue, John R. *The Gospel in Parable: Metaphor, Narrative, and Theology in the Synoptic Gospels*. Philadelphia: Fortress Press, 1988.

Douglas, Mary. *Purity and Danger: An Analysis of the Concepts of Pollution and Taboo*. London: Routledge & Kegan Paul, 1966.

Duff, Paul B. "Metaphor, Motif, and Meaning: The Rhetorical Strategy behind the Image 'Led in Triumph' in 2 Corinthians 2:14." *Catholic Biblical Quarterly* 53 (1991): 79–92.

———. "The Transformation of the Spectator: Power, Perception, and the Day of Salvation." In *Society of Biblical Literature 1987 Seminar Papers,* edited by Kent Harold Richards, 233–43. Atlanta: Scholars Press, 1987.

Eco, Umberto. *The Middle Ages of James Joyce: The Aesthetics of Chaosmos*. Translated by Ellen Esrock. London: Hutchinson Radius, 1989.

Ehrman, B. D., and M. A. Plunkett. "The Angel and the Agony: The Textual Problem of Luke 22:43–44." *Catholic Biblical Quarterly* 45 (1983): 401–16.

Eisenstein, Zillah R. *The Female Body and the Law*. Berkeley and Los Angeles: University of California Press, 1988.

Ellman, Richard. *James Joyce*. 2d ed. Oxford: Oxford University Press, 1982.

Epp, Eldon Jay, and George W. MacRae, eds. *The New Testament and Its Modern Interpreters*. Philadelphia: Fortress Press; Atlanta: Scholars Press, 1989.

Ernst, Josef. *Das Evangelium nach Lukas*. Regensburg: Pustet, 1977.

Esler, Philip F. *Community and Gospel in Luke-Acts: The Social and Political Motivations of Lucan Theology*. Cambridge: Cambridge University Press, 1987.

Farmer, William R. *The Last Twelve Verses of Mark*. Cambridge: Cambridge University Press, 1974.

Faur, José. *Golden Doves with Silver Dots: Semiotics and Textuality in Rabbinic Tradition*. Bloomington: Indiana University Press, 1986.

Feher, Michel, with Ramona Naddaff and Nadia Tazi, eds. *Fragments for a History of the Human Body*. 3 vols. New York: Zone, 1989.

Felman, Shoshana. *Jacques Lacan and the Adventure of Insight: Psychoanalysis in Contemporary Culture*. Cambridge, Mass.: Harvard University Press, 1987.

————. *The Literary Speech Act: Don Juan with J. L. Austin, or Seduction in Two Languages*. Translated by Catherine Porter. Ithaca, N.Y.: Cornell University Press, 1983.

————. "Turning the Screw of Interpretation." In *Literature and Psychoanalysis. The Question of Reading: Otherwise,* edited by Shoshana Felman, 94–207. Baltimore: Johns Hopkins University Press, 1982.

Felperin, Howard. *Beyond Deconstruction: The Uses and Abuses of Literary Theory*. Oxford: Oxford University Press, 1985.

Fiorenza, Elisabeth Schüssler. *In Memory of Her: A Feminist Theological Reconstruction of Christian Origins*. New York: Crossroad, 1983.

Fish, Stanley E. *Doing What Comes Naturally: Change, Rhetoric, and the Practice of Theory in Literary and Legal Studies*. Durham, N.C.: Duke University Press, 1989.

————. *Is There a Text in This Class? The Authority of Interpretive Communities*. Cambridge, Mass.: Harvard University Press, 1980.

Fitzmyer, Joseph A. *The Gospel according to Luke I–IX*. Garden City, N.Y.: Doubleday, 1981.

————. *The Gospel according to Luke X–XXIV*. Garden City, N.Y.: Doubleday, 1985.

Flender, Helmut. *Heil und Geschichte in der Theologie des Lukas*. Munich: Kaiser Verlag, 1965.

Foucault, Michel. *The Archaeology of Knowledge*. Translated by A. M. Sheridan Smith. New York: Pantheon Books, 1972.

————. "Behind the Fable." Translated by Pierre A. Walker. *Critical Texts* 5 (1988): 1–5.

————. *The Birth of the Clinic: An Archaeology of Medical Perception*. Translated by Alan Sheridan. New York: Pantheon Books, 1973.

————. "Clarifications on the Question of Power." In *Foucault Live (Interviews, 1966–84),* edited by Sylvere Lotringer and translated by John Johnson, 179–92. New York: Semiotext(e), 1989.

————. *Discipline and Punish: The Birth of the Prison*. Translated by Alan Sheridan. New York: Vintage Books, 1977.

————. "The Eye of Power." In *Power/Knowledge: Selected Interviews and Other Writings, 1972–1977,* edited by Colin Gordon and translated by Colin Gordon et al., 146–65. New York: Pantheon Books, 1980.

————. *The History of Sexuality. Volume I: An Introduction*. Translated by Robert Hurley. New York: Pantheon Books, 1978.

————. "Nietzsche, Genealogy, History." In *Language, Counter Memory, Practice: Selected Essays and Interviews,* edited by Donald F. Bouchard and translated by Donald F. Bouchard and Sherry Simon, 139–64. Ithaca, N.Y.: Cornell University Press, 1977.

————. *The Order of Things: An Archaeology of the Human Sciences*. New York: Vintage Books, 1970.

————. "The Subject and Power." Afterword to Hubert L. Dreyfus and Paul Rabinow, *Michel Foucault: Beyond Structuralism and Hermeneutics,* 208–226. 2d ed. Chicago: University of Chicago Press, 1983.

————. "What Is an Author?" Translated by Josué V. Harari. In *Textual Strategies:*

Perspectives in Post-Structuralist Criticism, edited by Josué V. Harari, 141–60. Ithaca, N.Y.: Cornell University Press, 1979.

Fowler, Robert M. *Let the Reader Understand: Reader-Response Criticism and the Gospel of Mark.* Minneapolis: Fortress Press, 1991.

———. "Postmodern Biblical Criticism." *Forum* 5 (1989): 3–30.

———. "Reading Matthew Reading Mark: Observing the First Steps toward Meaning-as-Reference in the Synoptic Gospels." In *Society of Biblical Literature 1986 Seminar Papers,* edited by Kent Harold Richards, 1–16. Atlanta: Scholars Press, 1986.

Freud, Sigmund. *Beyond the Pleasure Principle. The Standard Edition of the Complete Psychological Works of Sigmund Freud,* 18:1–64. Edited and translated by James Strachey. London: Hogarth Press, 1953–74.

———. *Civilization and Its Discontents. Standard Edition,* 21:64–145.

———. "Instincts and Their Vicissitudes." *Standard Edition,* 14:109–40.

———. *The Interpretation of Dreams. Standard Edition,* vols. 4 and 5.

———. *Jokes and Their Relation to the Unconscious. Standard Edition,* 8:1–238.

———. *Leonardo da Vinci and a Memory of His Childhood. Standard Edition,* 11:59–137.

———. *New Introductory Lectures on Psycho-Analysis. Standard Edition,* 22:1–182.

———. *The Origins of Psychoanalysis: Letters to William Fliess. Drafts and Notes, 1887–1902.* Edited and translated by Eric Mosbacher and James Strachey. New York: Basic Books, 1954.

———. *The Psychopathology of Everyday Life. Standard Edition,* vol. 6.

———. *Three Essays on the Theory of Sexuality. Standard Edition,* 7:125–245.

———. *Totem and Taboo. Standard Edition,* 13:1–161.

Funk, Robert W. *Parables and Presence.* Philadelphia: Fortress Press, 1982.

Gallop, Jane. *The Daughter's Seduction: Feminism and Psychoanalysis.* Ithaca, N.Y.: Cornell University Press, 1982.

———. *Reading Lacan.* Ithaca, N.Y.: Cornell University Press, 1985.

———. *Thinking through the Body.* New York: Columbia University Press, 1988.

Garrett, Susan R. *The Demise of the Devil: Magic and the Demonic in Luke's Writings.* Minneapolis: Fortress Press, 1989.

———. "'Lest the Light in You Be Darkness': Luke 11:33–36 and the Question of Commitment." *Journal of Biblical Literature* 110 (1991): 93–105.

Gasché, Rodolphe. *The Tain of the Mirror: Derrida and the Philosophy of Reflection.* Cambridge, Mass.: Harvard University Press, 1986.

Gasque, Ward. *A History of the Criticism of the Acts of the Apostles.* Grand Rapids, Mich.: Eerdmans, 1975.

Gay, Peter. *Freud: A Life for Our Time.* New York: Norton, 1988.

Genet, Jean. *Our Lady of the Flowers.* Translated by Bernard Frechtman. Boston: Faber and Faber, 1973.

Girard, René. *Violence and the Sacred.* Translated by Patrick Gregory. Baltimore: Johns Hopkins University Press, 1977.

Glück, J. J. "Paronomasia in Biblical Literature." *Semitics* 1 (1970): 50–78.

Gnilka, Joachim. *Das Evangelium nach Markus.* 2 vols. Zurich, Einsiedeln, and Cologne: Benziger Verlag; Neukirchen-Vluyn: Neukirchener Verlag, 1979.

Goux, Jean-Joseph. *Symbolic Economies: After Marx and Freud.* Translated by Jennifer Curtiss Gage. Ithaca, N.Y.: Cornell University Press, 1990.

Graham, Susan. "Silent Voices: Women in the Gospel of Mark." *Semeia* (forthcoming).

Gray, Bennison. *The Phenomenon of Literature.* The Hague and Paris: Mouton, 1975.

Green, William Scott. "Romancing the Tome: Rabbinic Hermeneutics and the Theory of Literature." *Semeia* 40 (1987): 147–68.

Griffin, David Ray, William A. Beardslee, and Joe Holland, eds. *Varieties of Postmodern Theology.* Albany: State University of New York Press, 1989.

Grosz, Elizabeth. *Jacques Lacan: A Feminist Introduction.* New York: Routledge, 1990.

Grundmann, Walter. *Das Evangelium nach Lukas.* Berlin: Evangelische Verlagsanstalt, 1961.

Guelich, Robert A. *Word Biblical Commentary, Volume 34a: Mark 1–8:26.* Dallas: Word Books, 1989.

Güttgemanns, Erhardt. *Fragmenta Semiotico-Hermeneutica: Eine Texthermeneutik für den Umgang mit der Hl. Schrift.* Bonn: Linguistica Biblica, 1983.

———. "'Gêmatriyya' und Lechëshbôn: Zur Semiotik des 'Gramma' und der Zahl im Judentum." *Linguistica Biblica* 64 (1990): 23–52.

———. "Die Semiotik des Traums in apokalyptischen Texten am Beispiel von Apokalypse Johannis 1." *Linguistica Biblica* 59 (1987): 7–54.

Haenchen, Ernst. *The Acts of the Apostles: A Commentary.* Translated by B. Noble and G. Shinn. Philadelphia: Westminster Press, 1971.

Hamacher, Werner. "The Reader's Supper: A Piece of Hegel." Translated by Timothy Bahti. *Diacritics* 11 (1981): 52–67.

Hamacher, Werner, Neil Hertz, and Thomas Keenan, eds. *Responses: On Paul de Man's Wartime Journalism.* Lincoln: University of Nebraska Press, 1989.

Hamburger, Käte. *The Logic of Literature.* Translated by Marilynn Rose. Bloomington: Indiana University Press, 1973.

Hamm, Dennis. "Sight to the Blind: Vision as Metaphor in Luke." *Biblica* 67 (1986): 457–77.

Handelman, Susan. *The Slayers of Moses: The Emergence of Rabbinic Interpretation in Modern Literary Theory.* Albany: State University of New York Press, 1982.

Harland, Richard. *Superstructuralism: The Philosophy of Structuralism and Post-Structuralism.* New York: Methuen, 1987.

Hartman, Geoffrey H. *The Fate of Reading and Other Essays.* Chicago: University of Chicago Press, 1975.

———. *Saving the Text: Literature/Derrida/Philosophy.* Baltimore: Johns Hopkins University Press, 1981.

———. "The State of the Art of Criticism." In *The Future of Literary Theory,* edited by Ralph Cohen, 86–101. New York: Routledge, 1989.

Hartman, Geoffrey H., and Sanford Budick, eds. *Midrash and Literature*. New Haven: Yale University Press, 1986.

Heath, Stephen. "Ambiviolences: Notes for Reading Joyce." Translated by Isabelle Mahieu. In *Post-Structuralist Joyce: Essays from the French,* edited by Derek Attridge and Daniel Ferrer, 31–68. Cambridge: Cambridge University Press, 1984.

Hegel, G. W. F. *Lectures on Aesthetics*. Translated by T. M. Knox. Oxford: Oxford University Press, 1975.

Heidegger, Martin. *The Question Concerning Technology and Other Essays*. Translated by William Lovitt. New York: Harper & Row, 1977.

———. *The Question of Being*. Translated by William Kluback and Jean T. Wilde. New Haven: Yale University Press, 1958.

Henke, Suzette A. *James Joyce and the Politics of Desire*. New York: Routledge, 1990.

Henry, Françoise. *The Book of Kells*. London: Thames and Hudson, 1974.

Hogan, Patrick Colm, and Lalita Pandit, eds. *Criticism and Lacan: Essays and Dialogue in Language, Structure, and the Unconscious*. Athens: University of Georgia Press, 1990.

Holquist, Michael. "From Body-Talk to Biography: The Chronobiological Bases of Narrative." *Yale Journal of Criticism* 3 (1989): 1–35.

Horst, P. W. van der. "Can a Book End with *gar*? A Note on Mark 16:8." *Journal of Theological Studies* 23 (1972): 121–24.

Hug, Joseph. *La Finale de l'évangile de Marc (Marc 16:9–20)*. Paris: Gabalda, 1978.

Hughes, Kirk T. "Framing Judas." *Semeia* (forthcoming).

Hull, John M. *Hellenistic Magic and the Synoptic Tradition*. London: SCM Press, 1974.

Huyssen, Andreas. *After the Great Divide: Modernism, Mass Culture, Postmodernism*. Bloomington: Indiana University Press, 1986.

Irigaray, Luce. "Così Fan Tutti." In *This Sex Which Is Not One,* translated by Catherine Porter with Carolyn Burke, 86–105. Ithaca, N.Y.: Cornell University Press, 1985.

———. "Equal to Whom?" Translated by Robert L. Mazzola. *differences* 1 (1989): 59–76.

———. "Femmes divines." *Critique* 41 (1985): 294–308.

———. "Les Femmes, le sacré, l'argent." *Critique* 42 (1986): 372–83.

———. *Marine Lover of Friedrich Nietzsche*. Translated by Gillian C. Gill. New York: Columbia University Press, 1991.

———. "The 'Mechanics' of Fluids." In Irigaray, *This Sex,* 106–18.

———. *Speculum of the Other Woman*. Translated by Gillian C. Gill. Ithaca, N.Y.: Cornell University Press, 1985.

———. "This Sex Which Is Not One." In Irigaray, *This Sex,* 23–33.

———. "When Our Lips Speak Together." In Irigaray, *This Sex,* 205–18.

Jabès, Edmond. *The Book of Questions*. Translated by Rosmarie Waldrop. Middletown, Conn.: Wesleyan University Press, 1972.

Jacobus, Mary, Evelyn Fox Keller, and Sally Shuttleworth, eds. *Body/Politics: Women and the Discourses of Science*. New York: Routledge, 1989.

Jardine, Alice A. *Gynesis: Configurations of Woman and Modernity*. Ithaca, N.Y.: Cornell University Press, 1985.

Jobling, David. "Writing the Wrongs of the World: The Deconstruction of the Biblical Text in the Context of Liberation Theologies." *Semeia* 51 (1990): 81–118.

Jobling, David, and Stephen D. Moore, eds. "Poststructuralism as Exegesis." *Semeia* (forthcoming).

Jay, Martin. "In the Empire of the Gaze: Foucault and the Denigration of Vision in Twentieth-Century French Thought." In *Foucault: A Critical Reader,* edited by David Couzens Hoy, 175–204. Oxford: Basil Blackwell, 1986.

Johnson, Barbara. *The Critical Difference: Essays in the Contemporary Rhetoric of Reading*. Baltimore: Johns Hopkins University Press, 1980.

————. *A World of Difference*. Baltimore: Johns Hopkins University Press, 1987.

Johnson, Mark. *The Body in the Mind: The Bodily Basis of Meaning*. Chicago: University of Chicago Press, 1987.

Joyce, James. *Finnegans Wake*. London: Faber and Faber, 1975.

————. *Letters of James Joyce*. Edited by Stuart Gilbert. 3 vols. New York: Viking Press, 1966.

Kafka, Franz. "In the Penal Colony." In *The Penal Colony: Stories and Short Pieces,* 191–230. Translated by Willa Muir and Edwin Muir. New York: Schocken Books, 1948.

Kamuf, Peggy, ed. *A Derrida Reader: Between the Blinds*. New York: Columbia University Press, 1991.

Karris, Robert J. *Luke: Artist and Theologian. Luke's Passion Account as Literature*. Mahwah, N.J.: Paulist Press, 1985.

Käsemann, Ernst. "The Problem of the Historical Jesus." In *Essays on New Testament Themes,* translated by W. J. Montague, 15–47. London: SCM Press, 1964.

Kealy, Seán P. *Mark's Gospel: A History of Its Interpretation*. Ramsey, N.J.: Paulist Press, 1982.

Keegan, Terence. *Interpreting the Bible: A Popular Introduction to Biblical Hermeneutics*. Mahwah, N.J.: Paulist Press, 1985.

Kelber, Werner H. "Narrative and Disclosure: Mechanisms of Concealing, Revealing, and Reveiling." *Semeia* 43 (1988): 1–20.

————. *The Oral and the Written Gospel: The Hermeneutics of Speaking and Writing in the Synoptic Tradition, Mark, Paul, and Q*. Philadelphia: Fortress Press, 1983.

Kermode, Frank. "Anteriority, Authority, and Secrecy: A General Comment." *Semeia* 43 (1988): 155–67.

————. *The Genesis of Secrecy: On the Interpretation of Narrative*. Cambridge, Mass.: Harvard University Press, 1979.

Knight, Douglas A., and Gene M. Tucker, eds. *The Hebrew Bible and Its Modern Interpreters*. Philadelphia: Fortress Press; Atlanta: Scholars Press, 1985.

Koester, Helmut. "History and Development of Mark's Gospel (From Mark to *Secret Mark* and 'Canonical' Mark)." In *Colloquy on New Testament Studies: A Time for Reap-*

praisal and Fresh Approaches, edited by Bruce Corley, 35–57. Macon, Ga.: Mercer University Press, 1983.

Kofman, Sarah. "Un philosophe 'unheimlich.'" In Lucette Finas et al., *Ecarts: Quatres essais à propos de Jacques Derrida,* 107–204. Paris: Fayard, 1973.

Krauss, Rosalind. "Poststructuralism and the 'Paraliterary.'" *October* (1980): 36–40.

Kristeva, Julia. "A propos du 'discours biblique.'" In *La Traversée des signes,* edited by Julia Kristeva et al., 223–27. Paris: Seuil, 1975.

———. "Holbein's Dead Christ." In *Fragments for a History of the Human Body,* edited by Michel Feher with Ramona Naddoff and Nadia Tazi, 1:238–69. New York: Zone, 1989.

———. *Language: The Unknown. An Initiation into Linguistics.* Translated by Anne M. Menke. New York: Columbia University Press, 1989.

———. "Lire la Bible." *Esprit* 69 (1982): 143–52.

———. *Powers of Horror: An Essay on Abjection.* Translated by Leon S. Roudiez. New York: Columbia University Press, 1982.

———. *Tales of Love.* Translated by Leon S. Roudiez. New York: Columbia University Press, 1987.

———. "Within the Microcosm of 'The Talking Cure.'" Translated by Thomas Gora and Margaret Waller. In *Interpreting Lacan,* edited by Joseph H. Smith and William Kerrigan, 33–48. New Haven: Yale University Press, 1983.

———. "Woman Can Never Be Defined." Translated by Marilyn A. August. In *New French Feminisms: An Anthology,* edited by Elaine Marks and Isabelle de Courtivron, 137–41. New York: Schocken Books, 1980.

Krupnik, Mark, ed. *Displacement: Derrida and After.* Bloomington: Indiana University Press, 1983.

Kuhn, Thomas S. *The Structure of Scientific Revolutions.* 2d ed. Chicago: University of Chicago Press, 1970.

Kümmel, Werner Georg. "Current Theological Accusations against Luke." *Andover Newton Quarterly* 16 (1975): 131–45.

———. *Promise and Fulfillment: The Eschatological Message of Jesus.* Translated by Dorothea M. Barton. London: SCM Press, 1957.

Lacan, Jacques. "Desire and the Interpretation of Desire in *Hamlet.*" Edited by Jacques-Alain Miller. Translated by James Hulbert. In *Literature and Psychoanalysis. The Question of Reading: Otherwise,* edited by Shoshana Felman, 11–52. Baltimore: Johns Hopkins University Press, 1982.

———. *Ecrits: A Selection.* Translated by Alan Sheridan. New York: Norton, 1977.

———. *Feminine Sexuality: Jacques Lacan and the école freudienne.* Edited by Juliet Mitchell and Jacqueline Rose. Translated by Jacqueline Rose. New York: Norton, 1982.

———. *The Four Fundamental Concepts of Psycho-Analysis.* Edited by Jacques-Alain Miller. Translated by Alan Sheridan. New York: Norton, 1978.

————. "Introduction to the Names-of-the-Father Seminar." Edited by Jacques-Alain Miller. In Lacan, *Television*, 81–95.

————. "Of Structure as an Inmixing of an Otherness Prerequisite to Any Subject Whatever." In *The Structuralist Controversy: The Languages of Criticism and the Sciences of Man,* edited by Richard Macksey and Eugenio Donato, 186–200. Baltimore: Johns Hopkins University Press, 1970.

————. Preface to Anika Lemaire, *Jacques Lacan,* vii–xv. Translated by David Macey. New York: Routledge & Kegan Paul, 1977.

————. *Le Séminaire, livre III: Les Psychoses.* Edited by Jacques-Alain Miller. Paris: Seuil, 1981.

————. *Le Séminaire, livre VII: L'Ethique de la psychanalyse.* Edited by Jacques-Alain Miller. Paris: Seuil, 1986.

————. *Le Séminaire, livre XI: Les Quatres Concepts fondamentaux de la psychanalyse.* Edited by Jacques-Alain Miller. Paris: Seuil, 1973.

————. *Le Séminaire, livre XX: Encore.* Edited by Jacques-Alain Miller. Paris: Seuil, 1975.

————. *The Seminar of Jacques Lacan, Book I: Freud's Papers on Technique, 1953–1954.* Edited by Jacques-Alain Miller. Translated by John Forrester. New York: Norton, 1988.

————. *The Seminar of Jacques Lacan, Book II: The Ego in Freud's Theory and in the Technique of Psychoanalysis, 1954–1955.* Edited by Jacques-Alain Miller. Translated by Sylvana Tomaselli. New York: Norton, 1988.

————. "Seminar on 'The Purloined Letter.'" Translated by Jeffrey Mehlman. In *The Purloined Poe: Lacan, Derrida, and Psychoanalytic Reading,* edited by John P. Muller and William J. Richardson, 28–54. Baltimore: Johns Hopkins University Press, 1988.

————. *Television: A Challenge to the Psychoanalytic Establishment.* Edited by Joan Copjec. Translated by Denis Hollier et al. New York: Norton, 1990.

————. "Television." Edited by Jacques-Alain Miller. In Lacan, *Television,* 1–46.

Lacan, Jacques, et al. *Joyce avec Lacan.* Edited by Jacques Aubert. Paris: Navarin, 1987.

Lagrange, Marie-Joseph. *Evangile selon Saint Marc.* Paris: Gabalda, 1929.

Lambrecht, Jan. *Once More Astonished: The Parables of Jesus.* New York: Crossroad, 1981.

Laplanche, Jean, and J.-B. Pontalis. *The Language of Psychoanalysis.* Translated by Donald Nicholson-Smith. London: Hogarth Press, 1973.

Lawrence, Joy. "Response to Stephen Moore's 'The Gospel of the Look.'" Paper presented at the New England Regional Meeting of the Society of Biblical Literature. Hartford, Conn., 25 March 1991.

Leavey, John P., Jr., ed. *Glassary.* Nebraska: University of Nebraska Press, 1986.

Leitch, Vincent B. *Deconstructive Criticism: An Advanced Introduction.* New York: Columbia University Press, 1983.

Lemaire, Anika. *Jacques Lacan.* Translated by David Macey. New York: Routledge & Kegan Paul, 1977.

Lernout, Geert. *The French Joyce.* Ann Arbor: University of Michigan Press, 1990.

Levin, David Michael. *The Opening of Vision: Nihilism and the Postmodern Situation*. New York: Routledge, 1988.

Lincoln, Andrew T. "The Promise and the Failure: Mark 16:7, 8." *Journal of Biblical Literature* 108 (1989): 283–300.

Litz, A. Walton. *The Art of James Joyce: Method and Design in* Ulysses *and* Finnegans Wake. Oxford: Oxford University Press, 1961.

Lodge, David. *Nice Work*. New York: Viking Penguin, 1989.

Lohfink, Gerhard. *Die Himmelfahrt Jesu: Untersuchungen zu den Himmelfahrts- und Erhö-hungstexten bei Lukas*. Munich: Kösel-Verlag, 1971.

Luther, Martin. *First Lectures on the Psalms, I: Psalms 1–75. Luther's Works,* vol. 10. Edited by Hilton C. Oswald. Translated by Herbert J. A. Bouman. St. Louis: Concordia Publishing House, 1974.

Lyotard, Jean-François. *The Postmodern Condition: A Report on Knowledge*. Translated by Geoff Bennington and Brian Massumi. Minneapolis: University of Minnesota Press, 1984.

MacCannell, Juliet Flower. *Figuring Lacan: Criticism and the Cultural Unconscious*. Lincoln: University of Nebraska Press, 1986.

Mack, Burton. *A Myth of Innocence: Mark and Christian Origins*. Philadelphia: Fortress Press, 1988.

Magness, J. Lee. *Sense and Absence: Structure and Suspension in the Ending of Mark's Gospel*. Atlanta: Scholars Press, 1986.

Malbon, Elizabeth Struthers. "Fallible Followers: Women and Men in the Gospel of Mark." *Semeia* 28 (1983): 29–48.

———. *Narrative Space and Mythic Meaning in Mark*. San Francisco: Harper & Row, 1986.

Malmede, Hans H. *Die Lichtsymbolik im Neuen Testament*. Wiesbaden: Harrassowitz, 1986.

Mann, C. S. *Mark: A New Translation with Introduction and Commentary*. Garden City, N.Y.: Doubleday, 1986.

Marcus, Joel. *The Mystery of the Kingdom of God*. Atlanta: Scholars Press, 1986.

Marshall, I. Howard. *The Gospel of Luke: A Commentary on the Greek Text*. Grand Rapids, Mich.: Eerdmans, 1978.

Marxsen, Willi. *Mark the Evangelist: Studies in the Redaction History of the Gospel*. Translated by James Boyce et al. Nashville: Abingdon Press, 1959.

McIndoe, J. H. "The Young Man at the Tomb." *Expository Times* 80 (1968–69): 125.

McKnight, Edgar V. *Postmodern Use of the Bible: The Emergence of Reader-Oriented Criticism*. Nashville: Abingdon Press, 1988.

Megill, Allan. *Prophets of Extremity: Nietzsche, Heidegger, Foucault, Derrida*. Berkeley and Los Angeles: University of California Press, 1985.

Meltzer, Françoise. "Eat Your *Dasein*: Lacan's Self-Consuming Puns." In *On Puns: The Foundation of Letters,* edited by Jonathan Culler, 156–63. Oxford: Basil Blackwell, 1988.

Metzger, Bruce M. *A Textual Commentary on the Greek New Testament*. New York: United Bible Societies, 1971.

Meyer, Marvin W. "The Youth in the *Secret Gospel of Mark*." *Semeia* 49 (1990): 129–53.

Miller, J. Hillis. "Ariadne's Thread: Repetition and the Narrative Line." In *Interpretation of Narrative,* edited by Mario J. Valdes and Owen J. Miller, 148–66. Toronto: University of Toronto Press, 1978.

————. "The Critic as Host." In Bloom et al., *Deconstruction and Criticism,* 217–53.

————. *The Ethics of Reading: Kant, de Man, Eliot, Trollope, James, and Benjamin.* New York: Columbia University Press, 1987.

————. "*Heart of Darkness* Revisited." In *Heart of Darkness by Joseph Conrad: A Case Study in Contemporary Criticism,* edited by Ross C. Murfin, 209–24. Boston: St. Martin's Press, 1989.

————. *Tropes, Parables, Performatives: Essays on Twentieth-Century Literature.* Durham, N.C.: Duke University Press, 1991.

Minear, Paul S. *To Heal and to Reveal: The Prophetic Vocation according to Luke.* New York: Seabury Press, 1976.

Miscall, Peter D. *1 Samuel: A Literary Reading.* Bloomington: Indiana University Press, 1986.

Moi, Toril. *Sexual/Textual Politics: Feminist Literary Theory.* New York: Routledge, 1985.

Moore, Stephen D. *Literary Criticism and the Gospels: The Theoretical Challenge.* New Haven: Yale University Press, 1989.

————. "The 'Post-' Age Stamp: Does It Stick? Biblical Studies and the Postmodernism Debate." *Journal of the American Academy of Religion* 57 (1989): 543–59.

Morgan, Robert, with John Barton. *Biblical Interpretation.* Oxford: Oxford University Press, 1988.

Muller, John P., and William J. Richardson, eds. *The Purloined Poe: Lacan, Derrida, and Psychoanalytic Reading.* Baltimore: Johns Hopkins University Press, 1988.

Myers, Ched. *Binding the Strong Man: A Political Reading of Mark's Story of Jesus.* Maryknoll, N.Y.: Orbis Books, 1988.

Neill, Stephen, and Tom Wright. *The Interpretation of the New Testament, 1861–1986.* 2d ed. Oxford: Oxford University Press, 1988.

Nietzsche, Friedrich. "On Truth and Falsity in an Extra-Moral Sense." In *Early Greek Philosophy and Other Essays.* Translated by M. A. Mugge. *The Complete Works of Nietzsche,* vol. 2. Edited by Oscar Levy. New York: Russell & Russell, 1964.

Nolland, John. *Word Biblical Commentary, Volume 35a: Luke 1–9:20.* Dallas: Word Books, 1989.

Norris, Christopher. *Deconstruction: Theory and Practice.* New York: Methuen, 1982.

————. *Derrida.* Cambridge, Mass.: Harvard University Press, 1987.

Norris, Margot. *The Decentered Universe of* Finnegans Wake: *A Structuralist Analysis.* Baltimore: Johns Hopkins University Press, 1976.

Nuttall, Geoffrey F. *The Moment of Recognition: Luke as Story-Teller.* London: Athlone Press, 1978.

O'Neill, John. *Five Bodies: The Human Shape of Modern Society.* Ithaca, N.Y.: Cornell University Press, 1985.

Ong, Walter J. *The Presence of the Word: Some Prolegomena for Cultural and Religious History.* Minneapolis: University of Minnesota Press, 1981.

Owens, Craig. "The Discourse of Others: Feminists and Postmodernism." In *The Anti-Aesthetic: Essays on Postmodern Culture,* edited by Hal Foster, 57–82. Port Townsend, Wash.: Bay Press, 1983.

Perrin, Norman. *What Is Redaction Criticism?* Philadelphia: Fortress Press, 1969.

Pesch, Rudolf. *Die Apostelgeschichte.* 2 vols. Zurich, Einsiedeln, and Cologne: Benziger Verlag; Neukirchen-Vluyn: Neukirchener Verlag, 1986.

————. *Das Markusevangelium.* 2 vols. Freiburg, Basel, and Vienna: Herder, 1976–1977.

Petersen, Norman R. "When Is the End Not the End? Literary Reflections on the Ending of Mark's Narrative." *Interpretation* 34 (1980): 151–66.

Pfister, Oskar. "Die Entwicklung des Apostels Paulus: Eine religionsgeschichtliche und psychologische Skizze." *Imago* 6 (1920): 243–90.

Phillips, Gary A. "Exegesis as Critical Praxis: Reclaiming History and Text from a Postmodern Perspective." *Semeia* 51 (1990): 7–50.

Phillips, Gary A., ed. "Poststructural Criticism and the Bible: Text/History/Discourse." *Semeia* 51 (1990).

Phillips, Gary A., and Stephen D. Moore, eds. *The Bible, Literary Theory, and Cultural Criticism.* New Haven: Yale University Press, forthcoming.

Plato. *Phaedrus.* In *The Collected Dialogues of Plato.* Edited by Edith Hamilton and Huntington Cairns. Translated by R. Hackforth. Princeton: Princeton University Press, 1961.

Plummer, Alfred. *A Critical and Exegetical Commentary on the Gospel according to St. Luke.* 5th ed. New York: Scribner, 1922.

Ponge, Francis. *Le Savon.* Paris: Gallimard, 1976.

Powell, Mark Allan. *What Is Narrative Criticism?* Minneapolis: Fortress Press, 1990.

Quesnell, Quentin. *The Mind of Mark: Interpretation and Method through Exegesis of Mk 6:52.* Rome: Biblical Institute Press, 1969.

Radl, Walter. *Paulus und Jesus im lukanischen Doppelwerk: Untersuchungen zu Parallelmotiven im Lukasevangelium und in der Apostelgeschichte.* Bern: Herbert Lang; Frankfurt: Peter Lang, 1975.

Ragland-Sullivan, Ellie. *Jacques Lacan and the Philosophy of Psychoanalysis.* Urbana and Chicago: University of Illinois Press, 1986.

Räisänen, Heikki. *Die Parabeltheorie im Markusevangelium.* Helsinki: Finnish Exegetical Society; Leiden: E. J. Brill, 1973.

Rajchman, John. "Foucault's Art of Seeing." *October* 44 (1988): 89–117.

Redfern, Walter. *Puns.* Oxford: Basil Blackwell, 1984.

Rengstorf, Karl Heinrich. "*Sēmeion, sēmainō, sēmeioō, asēmos, episēmos, eusēmos, sussēmon.*" In *Theological Dictionary of the New Testament,* edited by Gerhard Friedrich and translated by Geoffrey W. Bromiley, 7:200–69. Grand Rapids, Mich.: Eerdmans, 1971.

Ricoeur, Paul. "Biblical Hermeneutics." *Semeia* 4 (1975): 29–148.

Ronell, Avital. *The Telephone Book: Technology—Schizophrenia—Electric Speech*. Lincoln: University of Nebraska Press, 1989.

Rorty, Richard. *Contingency, Irony, and Solidarity*. Cambridge: Cambridge University Press, 1989.

———. "Deconstruction and Circumvention." *Critical Inquiry* 11 (1984): 1–23.

Rose, Jacqueline. *Sexuality in the Field of Vision*. London: Verso, 1986.

Rose, Mark. "The Author as Proprietor: *Donaldson v. Becket* and the Genealogy of Modern Authorship." *Representations* 23 (1988): 51–85.

Roudinesco, Elisabeth. *Jacques Lacan & Co.: A History of Psychoanalysis in France, 1925–1985*. Translated by Jeffrey Mehlman. Chicago: University of Chicago Press, 1990.

Ryan, Michael. *Marxism and Deconstruction: A Critical Articulation*. Baltimore: Johns Hopkins University Press, 1982.

Sanders, E. P., and Margaret Davies. *Studying the Synoptic Gospels*. Philadelphia: Trinity Press International, 1989.

Sarup, Madan. *An Introductory Guide to Post-Structuralism and Postmodernism*. Athens: Georgia State University Press, 1989.

Saussure, Ferdinand de. *Course in General Linguistics*. Edited by Charles Bally and Albert Sechehaye, with Albert Riedlinger. Translated by Wade Baskin. New York: Philosophical Library, 1959.

Scarry, Elaine. *The Body in Pain: The Making and Unmaking of the World*. Oxford: Oxford University Press, 1985.

Scarry, Elaine, ed. *Literature and the Body: Essays on Populations and Persons*. Baltimore: Johns Hopkins University Press, 1990.

Schneiderman, Stuart. *Jacques Lacan: The Death of an Intellectual Hero*. Cambridge, Mass.: Harvard University Press, 1983.

Schreiter, Robert J. *Constructing Local Theologies*. London: SCM Press, 1985.

Schubert, Paul. "The Structure and Significance of Luke 24." In *Neutestamentliche Studien für Rudolf Bultmann, zu seinem siebzigsten Geburtstag,* edited by Walther Eltester, 165–86. Berlin: Verlag Alfred Töpelmann, 1954.

Schürmann, Heinz. *Das Lukasevangelium. I. Teil: Kommentar zu 1,1–9,50*. Freiburg, Basel, and Vienna: Herder, 1969.

Schweizer, Eduard. *The Good News according to Luke*. Translated by David E. Green. Atlanta: John Knox Press, 1984.

Scott, Bernard Brandon. *Hear Then the Parable: A Commentary on the Parables of Jesus*. Minneapolis: Fortress Press, 1989.

Serres, Michel. *Le Parasite*. Paris: Grasset, 1980.

Simms, George Otto. *Exploring the Book of Kells*. Dublin: O'Brien Press, 1988.

Simpson, David. "Going on about the War without Mentioning the War: The Other Histories of the 'Paul de Man Affair.'" *Yale Journal of Criticism* 3 (1989): 163–73.

Skeat, W. W. *An Etymological Dictionary of the English Language*. Oxford: Oxford University Press, 1910.

Smith, Morton. *The Secret Gospel: The Discovery and Interpretation of the Secret Gospel according to Mark*. New York: Harper & Row, 1973.

Smith, Richard. "Afterword: The Modern Relevance of Gnosticism." In *The Nag Hammadi Library in English*, edited by James M. Robinson, 532–549. 3d ed. San Francisco: Harper & Row, 1988.

Sontag, Susan. *On Photography*. New York: Penguin Books, 1973.

Spanos, William V. *Repetitions: The Postmodern Occasion in Literature and Culture*. Baton Rouge: Louisiana State University Press, 1987.

Spivak, Gayatri Chakravorty. *In Other Worlds: Essays in Cultural Politics*. New York: Routledge, 1988.

Sternberg, Meir. *Expositional Modes and Temporal Ordering in Fiction*. Baltimore: Johns Hopkins University Press, 1978.

Stewart, Garrett. *Reading Voices: Literature and the Phonotext*. Berkeley and Los Angeles: University of California Press, 1990.

Sturrock, John, ed. *Structuralism and Since: From Lévi-Strauss to Derrida*. Oxford: Oxford University Press, 1979.

Strack, Hermann L., and Paul Billerbeck. *Kommentar zum Neuen Testament aus Talmud und Midrasch*. 6 vols. Munich: Beck, 1922–1961.

Suleiman, Susan R., ed. *The Female Body in Western Culture: Contemporary Views*. Cambridge, Mass.: Harvard University Press, 1988.

Sullivan, Edward. *The Book of Kells*. London: Studio, 1920.

Suskind, Patrick. *Perfume: The Story of a Murderer*. Translated by John E. Woods. New York: Penguin Books, 1986.

Swete, Henry Barclay. *Commentary on Mark: The Greek Text with Introduction, Notes and Indexes*. 3d ed. Grand Rapids, Mich.: Kregel Publications, 1977.

Talbert, C. H. "Shifting Sands: The Recent Study of the Gospel of Luke." *Interpretation* 30 (1976): 381–95.

Taylor, Mark C. *Altarity*. Chicago: University of Chicago Press, 1987.

————. *Erring: A Postmodern A/theology*. Chicago: University of Chicago Press, 1984.

————. "Foiling Reflection." In Taylor, *Tears*, 87–103.

————. "p.s. fin again." In Taylor, *Tears*, 55–72.

————. *Tears*. Albany: State University of New York Press, 1990.

————. "Text as Victim." In Thomas J. J. Altizer et al., *Deconstruction and Theology*. New York: Crossroad, 1980.

Taylor, Vincent. *The Gospel according to St. Mark: The Greek Text with Introduction, Notes, and Indexes*. 2d ed. London: Macmillan, 1966.

Theissen, Gerd. *Psychological Aspects of Pauline Theology*. Translated by John P. Galvin. Philadelphia: Fortress Press, 1987.

Tiede, David L. *Prophecy and History in Luke-Acts*. Philadelphia: Fortress Press, 1980.

Tindall, William York. *A Reader's Guide to James Joyce*. London: Thames and Hudson, 1959.

Todorov, Tzvetan. *Introduction to Poetics*. Translated by Richard Howard. Minneapolis: University of Minnesota Press, 1981.

Tolbert, Mary Ann. *Perspectives on the Parables: An Approach to Multiple Interpretations*. Philadelphia: Fortress Press, 1979.

————. *Sowing the Gospel: Mark's World in Literary-Historical Perspective*. Minneapolis: Fortress Press, 1989.

Turner, Bryan S. *The Body and Society*. Oxford: Basil Blackwell, 1984.

Ulansey, David. "The Heavenly Veil Torn: Mark's Cosmic *Inclusio*." *Journal of Biblical Literature* 110 (1991): 123–25.

Ulmer, Gregory. *Applied Grammatology: Post(e)-Pedagogy from Jacques Derrida to Joseph Beuys*. Baltimore: Johns Hopkins University Press, 1985.

————. "Mystory: The Law of Idiom in Applied Grammatology." In *The Future of Literary Theory*, edited by Ralph Cohen, 304–23. New York: Routledge, 1989.

————. "The Object of Post-Criticism." In *The Anti-Aesthetic: Essays on Postmodern Culture*, edited by Hal Foster, 83–110. Port Townsend, Wash.: Bay Press, 1983.

————. "The Puncept in Grammatology." In *On Puns: The Foundation of Letters*, edited by Jonathan Culler, 164–89. Oxford: Basil Blackwell, 1988.

————. *Teletheory: Grammatology in an Age of Video*. New York: Routledge, 1990.

Unnik, W. C. van. "Luke-Acts, a Storm Center in Contemporary Scholarship." In *Studies in Luke-Acts: Essays Presented in Honor of Paul Schubert*, edited by Leander E. Keck and J. Louis Martyn, 15–32. Nashville: Abingdon Press, 1966.

Veeser, H. Aram. "Introduction." In *The New Historicism*, edited by H. Aram Veeser, ix–xvi. New York: Routledge, 1989.

Via, Dan O. "Irony as Hope in Mark's Gospel: A Reply to Werner Kelber." *Semeia* 43 (1988): 21–28.

Via, E. Jane. "Women in the Gospel of Luke." In *Women in the World's Religions: Past and Present*, edited by Ursula King, 38–55. New York: Paragon House, 1987.

Vielhauer, Phillipp. "On the 'Paulinism' of Acts." Translated by William C. Robinson, Jr., and Victor P. Furnish. In *Studies in Luke-Acts: Essays Presented in Honor of Paul Schubert*, edited by Leander E. Keck and J. Louis Martyn, 33–50. Nashville: Abingdon Press, 1966.

Walker, Cheryl. "Feminist Literary Criticism and the Author." *Critical Inquiry* 16 (1990): 551–71.

Watson, Wilfred G. E. *Classical Hebrew Poetry: A Guide to Its Techniques*. 2d ed. Sheffield: JSOT Press, 1986.

Weber, Max. *The Protestant Ethic and the Spirit of Capitalism*. Translated by Talcott Parsons. New York: Scribner, 1958.

Weeden, Theodore J. *Mark: Traditions in Conflict*. Philadelphia: Fortress Press, 1971.

White, Hayden. *The Tropics of Discourse: Essays in Cultural Criticism*. Baltimore: Johns Hopkins University Press, 1978.

White, S. G. "Inside CNN: What Do They Put in Chicken Noodle News?" *New Haven Advocate,* 7 March 1991, 8–9.

Williams, James G. *Gospel against Parable: Mark's Language of Mystery.* Sheffield: Almond Press, 1985.

Wittels, Fritz. *Sigmund Freud: His Personality, His Teaching, and His School.* Translated by Eden Paul and Cedar Paul. New York: Dodd & Mead, 1924.

Woycik, Jan. *The Road to Emmaus: Reading Luke's Gospel.* West Lafayette, Ind.: Purdue University Press, 1989.

Wrede, William. *Das Messiasgeheimnis in den Evangelien.* Göttingen: Vandenhoeck & Ruprecht, 1901.

Wyschogrod, Edith, David Crownfield, and Carl A. Raschke, eds. *Lacan and Theological Discourse.* Albany: State University of New York Press, 1989.

Zahn, Theodor von. *Introduction to the New Testament.* 3 vols. Translated by John Moore Trout et al. New York: Scribner, 1909.

The following acknowledgments are gratefully made. Figures: Reproduced from the *Book of Kells*, by permission of the Board of Trinity College Dublin. Quotations: Reprinted from the New Revised Standard Version Bible, copyright 1989 by the Division of Christian Education of the National Council of the Churches of Christ in the U.S.A. Used by permission. Reprinted from the Greek New Testament, 3d ed. (corrected). Copyright © 1966, 1968, 1975, 1983, by the United Bible Societies. Used by permission. Reprinted from *Television, A Challenge to the Psychoanalytic Establishment,* by Jacques Lacan, translated by Denis Hollier, Rosalind Krauss, Annette Michelson, and Jeffrey Mehlman, edited by Joan Copjec, by permission of W. W. Norton and Company, Inc. Copyright © 1990 by J. A. Miller. Reprinted from *Language, Counter-Memory, Practice: Selected Essays and Interviews,* by Michel Foucault, translated from the French by Donald F. Bouchard and Sherry Simon, edited by Donald F. Bouchard. Copyright © 1977 by Cornell University. Used by permission of the publisher, Cornell University Press. Reprinted from *This Sex Which Is Not One,* by Luce Irigaray, translated by Catherine Porter. Copyright © 1985 by Cornell University. Used by permission of the publisher, Cornell University Press. Reprinted from *The Post Card: From Socrates to Freud and Beyond,* by Jacques Derrida, translated by Alan Bass. Copyright © 1987 by the University of Chicago Press. Reprinted from *The Birth of the Clinic: An Archaeology of Medical Perception,* by Michel Foucault, translated by Alan Sheridan. Copyright © 1973 by Random House, Inc. Reprinted from *The Nag Hammadi Library in English,* rev. ed. by James M. Robinson. Copyright © 1988 by E. J. Brill, Leiden, The Netherlands. By permission of HarperCollins Publishers, Inc. Reprinted from *The Book of Questions,* by Edmond Jabès, vol. 1, translated by Rosmarie Waldrop. Copyright © 1976 by Rosmarie Waldrop. Wesleyan University Press. By permission of University Press of New England. Reprinted from *Interpreting the New Testament: An Introduction to the Principles and Methods of New Testament Exegesis,* by Hans Conzelmann and Andreas Lindemann, translated by Siegfried S. Schatzmann. Copyright © 1989 by Hendrickson Publishers, Peabody, Mass. Used by permission. Reprinted from *differences* 1.1, by permission of Indiana University Press. Reprinted from *Beyond the Pleasure Principle,* by Sigmund Freud, translated and edited by James Strachey, by permission of W. W. Norton and Company, Inc. Copyright © 1961 by James Strachey. Copyright renewed 1989. Reprinted from *Ecrits, A Selection,* by Jacques Lacan, translated from the French by Alan Sheridan, by permission of W. W. Norton and Company, Inc. Copyright © 1977 by Tavistock Publications Limited. Reprinted from *The Pleasure of the Text,* by Roland Barthes. Translation copyright © 1975 by Farrar, Straus and Giroux, Inc. By permission of Hill and Wang, a division of Farrar, Straus and Giroux, Inc. Reprinted from *Letters of James Joyce,* vol. 3, by Richard Ellmann. Copyright © 1966 by F. Lionel Munro, as Administrator of the Estate of James Joyce. Introduction and editorial material copyright © 1966 by Richard Ellmann. Used by permission of Viking Penguin, a division of Penguin Books U.S.A., Inc. Reprinted from *Finnegans Wake,* by James Joyce. Copyright © 1939 by James Joyce. Copyright renewed © 1967 by George Joyce and Lucia Joyce. Used by permission of Viking Penguin, a division of Penguin Books U.S.A., Inc. Reprinted from *New Testament Apocrypha,* edited by Edgar Hennecke and Wilhelm Schneemelcher. Copyright © 1963 by Westminster Press. Used by permission of Westminster / John Knox Press.

Index of Biblical and Ancient Sources

Page numbers in italic designate an explicit interpretation of a verse or verses.

General Index

Acts of the Apostles: ecclesiology of, 94–95; soteriology of, 94. *See also* Luke-Acts
Anagrams, 33, 57, 68, 83, 154n44
Authorial intentions. *See* Derrida, Jacques; Luke-Acts

Barrett, C. K., 88
Barthes, Roland, 23, 32, 68; on the Bible, xv; on birth of author, 146–47; on death of author, xvii, 78; on eroticism, 34; on grain of voice, 110; on language as skin, 150; on text as braid, 29–30; on text as tissue, 33; on text vs. work, 40; on unweaned language, 151
Bentham, Jeremy, 131, 135
Berg, Temma F., 17, 69
Biblical scholarship: as babelical scholarship, 154; as capitalist system, 147, 148–49; and deconstruction, xiii, xiv–xv; as neo-Gnostic enterprise, 148; as objective scholarship, 157; and poststructuralism, xiv–xv; as sensible scholarship, 157; as solid enterprise, 148, 153, 154; as sound enterprise, 102–3; structured like Luke-Acts, 145–46; and Victorian scruples, 149–50, 158. *See also* Redaction criticism
Body books, 156–57
Book of Kells: chi page in, 76; and local theology, 155; Mark's initial page in, 78–80; *Tunc* page in, 77–78; as visual commentary, 74–75. See also *Finnegans Wake*
Book of Revelation, 107
Booth, Wayne C., 138

Bovon, François, 87
Brown, Norman O., 137
Bultmann, Rudolf, 87, 88, 110. *See also* Conzelmann, Hans; Dillon, Richard J.

Cadbury, Henry J., 147
Camporesi, Piero, 104
Caputo, John D., 9, 109
Cixous, Hélène, 150, 151. See also *Ecriture feminine*
Coggins, R. J., xiv
Cohn, Dorrit, 139
Concrete criticism, xviii, 74–76, 78, 82–83, 129, 155. *See also* Incarnate criticism
Conzelmann, Hans, 147: Bultmannian approach of, 87, 88, 90; and Heidegger, 90; logocentrism of, 89. *See also* Dillon, Richard J.

Davies, Margaret, xiv
Deconstruction: and biblical studies, xiv–xv; birth of, 88; and death of God, 109; negative connotations of, 3; in the *1990s*, xiii n1; and puns, 67, 68; range of, xiii; and redaction criticism, 88; and visual arts, xvii, 73, 82n87. *See also* De Man, Paul; Derrida, Jacques; Poststructuralism
De Man, Paul, xiii, xv, 20, 146; on Derrida, 9n24; on disfiguration, 30n10; and Freud, 7–8; on ideology, 118; on text as machine, 8; wartime journalism of, xvi n11. *See also* Deconstruction
De Montesquiou, Robert, 134